CHINUA ACHEBE
THE MAN AND HIS WORKS

By

ROSE URE MEZU

Dedication

To

Professor Christie Achebe
who has so selflessly stood by a husband
in sore need of support and love
from those he loves.

Table of Contents

Preface

The several novels of Chinua Achebe can stand alone and can be read, appreciated and studied in isolation. They also can form an integrated corpus some progressing either spatially, historically and genealogically from one to the other. The chapters that form *Chinua Achebe: The Man and His Works* by Rose Ure Mezu can be viewed and read in much the same way as Achebe's novels. Each chapter while forming part of a whole can stand in isolation and on its own.

The work is not a novel to be read from the beginning to the end but should be seen as rooms with separate and connecting doors in a house each designed with a specific purpose in mind, sufficient unto itself yet forming part of the whole. These rooms or chapters may naturally share common walls and ideas which Dr. Rose Ure Mezu purposefully uses to reinforce the unit rather than repeat or duplicate parts of the whole. The reader of *Chinua Achebe: The Man and His Works* can therefore end with the beginning or begin with the end chapter or simply move into the central chapter or living room and from there explore the house that Chinua Achebe built, or better still try to climb the iroko tree that Achebe planted with its foundations rooted in pre-colonial Africa and its branches extending to the diaspora.

Dr. Rose Ure Mezu, in this work, inaugurates a new tradition, juxtaposing Achebe's thoughts and concepts and those of diasporan literary and cultural groundbreakers such as Olaudah Equiano (*The Interesting Narrative of the Life of Olaudah Equiano or Gustavus Vassa, the African, Written by Himself*, 1789) and Zora Neale Hurston (*Their Eyes Are Watching God*, 1937). Equiano's work has lately become the focus of some controversies by some people who are neither Igbos nor inhabitants of Essaka. These people question, out of ignorance, the authenticity of Equiano's place of birth. Without setting out to do so, Mezu in *Chinua Achebe: The Man and His Works* has presented veritably a defense of the truth about Igbo / African culture and Equiano's recollection of it. As pointed out in this work and as established by

Cheikh Anta Diop and other scholars, Africa was not and is not culturally, socially and technologically a *tabula rasa*.

Literature brings the world together, interlocks human experience and brings out the universal in the individual experience. Chinua Achebe in extolling the individual succeeded in celebrating humanity with his works and now Dr. Rose Ure Mezu has celebrated in this work the humanity of Chinua Achebe. It reads almost like a novel and certainly one would hope there will be a sequel to this volume.

Dr. S. Okechukwu Mezu

Introduction

C*hinua Achebe: The Man and His Works* is not a biography (even though it contains some biographical materials), but a critical analysis of Chinua Achebe's novels and other writings, evaluating them for themes, and their relevance to the problems besieging Africa and African peoples in the global community. Achebe confesses that he did not set out to validate African civilization in any conscious way, but the circumstances of his birth, family upbringing and training at the University College of Ibadan impelled him towards the eventual defense and reconstructive validation of Africa's pristine civilization. Born on November 16, 1930 at Ogidi to parents who were evangelical Protestants, he received his religious formation from his father, a teacher in a missionary school, while his mother, sister and maternal great-grandparents inculcated in him a love of the traditional culture.

His essay, "Named for Victoria, Queen of England" published in his 1975 *Morning Yet on Creation Day* (*MYOCD*), contains autobiographical information necessary to understand the novelist's familial and cultural background. Receiving education of the best kind that colonial society had to offer, Achebe was well-equipped to do a critical reevaluation of the role of colonialism in Africa and this with Europe's own critical tools. Most of the essays in *Morning Yet on Creation Day*: "Colonialist Criticism," "Africa and Her Writers," "The Novelist as a Teacher," "The African Writer and the English Language" expound on the writer's multiple functions, while also explaining the urgent necessity for the new kind of language employed in *Things Fall Apart* which inaugurated a new tradition of Cultural Nationalism, Black aesthetics and Colonialist criticism. His later novels, short stories, poetry, and essays speak for themselves and explain his present enormous stature as one of the world's greatest writers, with a towering, but reasoned intellect and versatility.

His pace-setting first book, *Things Fall Apart* is a great and important resource book used to teach across disciplines. For its multi-faceted utility, teachers of Political Science, African Economic System,

African and Diasporan History, Agricultural Science, Religion, Literary Studies, Linguistics, and Fine Arts, to name but a few, find the book an indispensable quarry. It is required reading not just in Africa but also in the United States, especially in Historically Black Colleges and Universities (HBCUs), and some Ivy League Colleges, with Cornell University recently adopting it as required text. The book is read all over the world and translated into many different languages of the world.

Teaching Achebe's novels in class is always a rewarding venture and involves challenging strategies. Students largely empathize with Okonkwo as a cultural nationalist who fiercely defends and dies for the authentic values of his community. Because some students appear shocked at Okonkwo's misogyny, this becomes a fertile ground for a discussion of gender politics, at the end of which some come to see that Okonkwo, removed from his specific cultural context and transported to their era and environment, looks like many of their fathers, uncles and other people they have known.

I have had groups of students dramatize modern adaptations of selected incidents in *Things Fall Apart* in which the rebellious Ojiugo, for instance, ends up profiting from current principles of gender equality to tame her macho husband into a more accommodationist Okonkwo – which is quite a feat. A particularly imaginative adaptation had provided a Joanna [Johnny] Cochran who debates with the District Commissioner in a court of law as to the merits / evils of both the native Umuofia culture and the supplanting alien colonial administration, even though historical accuracy dictates that Okonkwo dies, anyway. A comparison with Toni Morrison's Nobel Prize winning novel, *Beloved* has one of my classes imagining Ezinma, intrepid and freedom-loving just like her father Okonkwo, being transplanted to the shores of America as Sethe's grandmother. Faithful to her culture, she totally rejects all children born of her white captors to preserve and nurture only the child she conceived freely with a black man. The book *Things Fall Apart* is thus easily the most-taught novel in schools, for between it and *Arrow of God*, Achebe's hope that his tradition-based novels could also serve peoples of African descent finds fruition as he earnestly wanted:

> to help my society regain belief in itself and put away the complexes of the years of denigration and self-abasement [...] [f]or no thinking

African [Black] can escape the wound on his soul. [...] I would be quite satisfied if my novels (especially the ones I set in the past) did no more than teach my readers that their past--with all its imperfections--was not one long night of savagery from which the first European acting on God's behalf delivered us ("The Novelist as a Teacher" in *MYOCD* 45).

In my Elementary and Secondary School in Port Harcourt in Nigeria, a semi-cloistered convent environment where books on European literature and history were the norm as it was when the young Achebe received his education, we were taught by Irish Catholic missionary sisters of the Holy Rosary Congregation and it was inconceivable that books like *Things Fall Apart* could be used as a teaching text:

> And it never once occurred to me to question my complete socialization into a Euro-cultural universe not my own, nor to wonder why my missionary teachers never introduced me to such great African novels as *Things Fall Apart* and *No Longer at Ease*, by Chinua Achebe, or *Cry the Beloved Country* by the white Alan Paton, or *Mine Boy* by Peter Abrahams, or the prison *Letters to Martha* of Dennis Brutus and the writings of Esk'ia Mphalele - all of which would have exposed to me South Africa's Apartheid policies. I had no way of questioning the texts we did in literature. [...] Because I did not know, I never asked why no representative works by Africana men and women were ever considered worthy texts for Nigerian schools (Rose Mezu, "Africana Women: Their Historic Past and Future Activism," <http://www.nathanielturner.com/africana women2.htm>).

As later happened to me, Achebe discovered that he and members of his generation (Wole Soyinka, Elechi Amadi, John Pepper Clark, Kole Omotoso and others) at the University College of Ibadan were actually those denigrated, stereotypical "primitives" being devalued in Joseph Conrad's *Heart of Darkness* (1902*).* This and Joyce Carey's *African Witch* (1936) and *Mr. Johnson* (1939) impelled Achebe to use his personal story to attempt a revalorization of Africa's history and culture. Thus, the fictional Umuofia provides the cosmological prism through which Achebe tells his own story as counterfoil to the prevalent image of peoples of African origin and as an indigenous African, he was better qualified to tell his and Africa's story.

Whoever encounters this man knows that part of Achebe's great gifts as a story-teller is his ability to accommodate other viewpoints because for him, "[w]herever Something stands, Something Else will stand beside it. Nothing is absolute" (*MYOCD* 94). Speaking with Chinua Achebe in 1996, and finally meeting him in July 1999 increased my appreciation of the writer's great intellectual gifts. Achebe as a man is gentle and soft-spoken, with a keen listening ear, rollicking humor, great wit suffused with sensibility and, yes, humility. And yet, one is left in no doubt that Achebe is tough-minded, principled, very resilient and a survivor which reminds his readers of what he thinks of intemperate, single-minded characters like Okonkwo, Ezeulu, or even the hot-headed Obika, the latter's son. Cynical critics have wondered why many people who have encountered Achebe seem not to think that Achebe has faults like everyone else. I am sure he has, but it is difficult to have a bad word for the man, precisely because you know from reading his works that even though he is a great artist, indeed an awesome one, he also has great dignity and a self-assurance that is tinged with humility. These are the attributes of a great genius. On meeting him, one feels as if one had known him all along, at least all of one's adult reading life. This is because through his fictional characters, you heard in his voice the wisdom of traditional African Antiquity, the wit of the storyteller, the pragmatism of the politician, and the idealism of his fictional intellectual heroes. I have often thought as aptly suited to Chinua Achebe what Weinberg said about W.E.B. Du Bois, quoting the Cuban poet / patriot José Martí (1853-1895): "Mountains culminate in peaks, and nations in men" (cited in *Africa and the Diaspora: the Black Scholar and Society* 10).

Achebe's desire to help his "people" regain their pride of Self and Nation to enable them enjoy God's gift of freedom again reminds one of Martí's challenge to those who would live free:

> "Let those who desire a secure homeland conquer it. Let those who do not conquer it live under the whip and in exile, watched over like wild animals, cast from one country to another, concealing the death of their souls with a beggar's smile from the scorn of free men" (<http://en.thinkexist.com/quotes/top/nationality/cuban/>).

Achebe's literary thoughts have given to all Africans, descendants of enslaved Africans, and all marginalized peoples, the weapon of freedom to defend the historico-cultural values of their homeland.

Achebe has embodied in his writings every theme – race and racism, democracy, socialism and capitalism, imperialism, colonialism, neo - and post-colonialism, revolution, war and peace, cultural nationalism, and even more. As I remark in Chapter Ten: "The Mezus Visit with the Achebes," this writer "has given back to all Blacks in the Diaspora that **something** which slavery had taken away."

Chinua Achebe: the Man and his Works has ten chapters. His novels receive full critical discussion and comparative treatment with the works of other writers. Chapters Nine and Ten, being interviews with the writer are self-explanatory. In them, Achebe reiterates and expatiates on many of the themes which inform his writings. I make use of these ideas in the chapter discussions of his novels and essays. At the core of all of his novels, whether tradition-based or urban fiction, is to be found as central preoccupation, the problem and dynamics of proper governance and the place of the human beings within this centrality. Equally, I believe, his stories have yielded good results when dealt comparatively with seminal, groundbreaking texts such as Zora Neale Hurston's *Their Eyes Were Watching God* (1939) and Olaudah Equiano's masterpiece, *The Interesting Narrative of the Life of Olaudah Equiano or Gustavus Vassa the African, Written by Himself* (1789).

Achebe himself encourages writers not to sit on the sidelines of urgent national issues, but to be very committed as a *guide* of the people should. As they say in Igbo, "*Ana ekwu ekwu, ana eme eme*" or in United States of America political *lingo* –"*You talk the talk and walk the walk.*" This Achebe did himself in 1983, during Nigeria's Second Republic when he joined the People's Redemption Party (PRP) founded by the late crusader, Mallam Aminu Kano. Chinua Achebe was elected deputy national president of the party. Thus, he tried also to put into practice his commitment to change. As Director of Heinemann Educational Books in Nigeria, he helped encourage the publication of the works of dozens of African writers. In 1971, he became founding editor of *Okike*, a journal of Nigerian writings and in 1984, he founded the bilingual magazine, *Uwa ndi Igbo*, a valuable source for Igbo studies Presently, Chinua Achebe is the Charles P. Stevenson Professor of Literature at Bard College in Upstate New York

Works Cited

Achebe, Chinua. *Things Fall Apart.* New York: Doubleday, 1994.

--- *Arrow of God.* New York: Random House, 1969.

--- *Morning Yet On Creation Day: Essays.* London: Heinemann Educational Books, 1975.

Marti, José. <http://en.thinkexist.com/quotes/top/nationality/cuban/>

Mezu, Rose Ure. <http://www.nathanielturner.com/africanawomen 2.htm>

Morrison, Toni. *Beloved.* New York: Penguin, 1987.

Weinberg, Meyer. Ed. "Introduction." In *W. E. B. Du Bois: A Reader.* New York: Harper & Row, 1970.

1

Chinua Achebe's *Things Fall Apart*: Implications for Black Cultural Nationalism and Revisionism

For, as my forefathers said; the firewood which a people have is
adequate for the kind of cooking they do.
(Achebe, Morning Yet On Creation Day 16)

The writer cannot expect to be excused from the task of re-education
and regeneration that must be done. In fact, he should march right in front
[as] the sensitive point of his community.
(MYOCD 45)

A chebe's *Things Fall Apart* (1958) is a slim but power-packed, multi-faceted work of literary revision that seeks to correct misconceptions, challenge the misrepresentations of the political history and culture of African peoples, and rearrange other established notions on who the African is. No perspective on Africa can afford to neglect this novel because it has modified in a unique way the traditions of fiction. From this work can be gleaned several aspects of African traditional life. It is sociological because it imaginatively recreates an organized African community that possesses both social hierarchy, traditions, mores and taboos, none of which can be infringed upon with impunity. Umuofia becomes a prototype of traditional Africa before the advent of the Europeans. It reveals an organized juridical system - composed of elders and masquerades - that imposes respect and awe. The book reveals the existence of an organized religion with beliefs in the logical ordering of both the physical world and the world beyond. It exposes an organized agricultural system based on crop rotation. Its cultural world further exposes a social system well-known for its unbridled republicanism, a democratic and hierarchical order of elders and achievers that makes no distinction between persons, but rather rewards the bold, the courageous, the valiant and the "fortunate," no matter how disadvantaged the beginning. Umuofia may, at times, even seem patriarchally oppressive, but there is still room for a rebellious individualist ethos. Ekwefi, for instance, runs away from a forced marriage to Okonkwo whom she loves. Elsewhere, an ordinary woman like Chielo, because of her power of divination, is transformed into an awe-inspiring mystical figure that compels the submission of even the intrepid Okonkwo. The book reveals a universe redolent of poetry, folklore and legends, made memorable through its wisdom accumulated across the ages, condensed in the form of proverbs, folktales, *et cetera*, designed to instruct and to entertain.

Achebe's Umuofia is indeed the prototype of an ordered society that is non-aggressive, yet self-assured, knowing when to embark on swift retaliatory martial expeditions that keep her sage neighbors well-cautioned and conciliatory. *Things Fall Apart* finally is a historical reconstruction of a lost civilization which, despite inherent flaws that will eventually be the nuclei of its destabilization, was friendly and welcoming to strangers - qualities that worked ultimately to its disadvantage. The fictive world of *Things Fall Apart* is ultimately a holistic and moral world bound by laws, mores and beliefs indicative of a pristine civilization. This fact in itself is *la raison d'être* that compelled Achebe to write the masterpiece.

Sited in an Igbo society at the very heart of the continent from which life began, the story speaks of values, moral issues, truth, wisdom and an appreciation of human respect and dignity. The issues treated below arising from its rereading could constitute some possible areas of focus in considering the writings of Achebe and other creative Black writers. Above all, the novel opens doors for black writers in and outside Africa. And because the book helps to restore that vital "essence" taken away by slavery, its revisionist stance directly impacts Black Cultural Nationalism. The ideological considerations below drawn from *Things Fall Apart* are vital issues that have relevance to black and other writers.

Correction of Misconceptions

Chinua Achebe states that his reason for writing the book is

[...] to help my society regain belief in itself and put away the complexes of the years of denigration and self-abasement [...] [f]or no thinking African [Black] can escape the wound on his soul. [...] I would be quite satisfied if my novels (especially the ones I set in the past) did no more than teach my readers that their past--with all its imperfections--was not one long night of savagery from which the first European acting on God's behalf delivered us ("The Novelist as a Teacher" in *MYOCD* 45).

Thus did Achebe inaugurate the tradition of novels of cultural nationalism which promotes consciousness of what is great in African culture, imaginatively recreated, spiced with local proverbs, myths and legends while celebrating festivals, rituals, folklore. He rehabilitates the dignity of the black world so badly bruised by colonial subjugation as depicted in such novels as Joyce Carey's *Mr. Johnson,* and *The African Witch* and in the infamous Tarzan movies. By so doing, he fathered a progeny of "sons and daughters of Achebe": Elechi Amadi (*The Concubine*, 1966), Ngugi wa 'Thiong'o (*Weep Not Child*, 1964), Onuora Nzekwu (*Highlife for Lizards*, 1965), Flora Nwapa (*Efuru*, 1966), *et cetera*.

Equally, Camara Laye (*Dark Child*, 1953) pitches his tent alongside Achebe's when he restates his own reason for writing as stemming from a desire to show the beauty of his culture so that "people who had not been aware of Africa [may] grasp the significance of our past and civilization" (Camara Laye 22). Recreating the beauty of his civilization not only to enlighten Africa's detractors but also to educate peoples of African origin seemed to Achebe a revolution worthy of espousal. Therefore, Achebe insists, the writer must not expect to be excused from the task of re-education and regeneration that must be done: "In fact he should march right in front. For he is after all – as Ezekiel Mphahlele says in his *African Image* - the sensitive point of his community (*Morning Yet On Creation Day* 45). This commitment to the restoration of the dignity of his civilization informs all Achebe's novels, essays, plays and poetry. This conviction of the responsibilities of the writer naturally leads to a consideration of the writer and his art.

The Writer and his Art

In the controversy over the nature of writing - whether it should be abstract - "art for art's sake" - or committed, Achebe takes an unmistakable stand that reveals a personal world view that commits him to write from experience about what one knows, and from where one stands: "Every literature must seek the things that belong unto its peace (*sic*) - must, in other words, speak of a particular place, evolve out of the necessities of its history, past and current, and the aspirations and destiny of its people" ("Colonialist Criticism" 7).

Art, Achebe maintains, had always been used in the service of humanity:

Our ancestors created their myths and legends and told their stories for a human purpose (including, no doubt, the excitation of wonder and pure delight); they made their sculptures in wood and terra cotta, stone and bronze to serve the needs of their times. The artists lived and moved and had their being in society, and created their works for the good of that society (*MYCOD* 19).

Since traditional artists used their art to shape and to serve their environment, Achebe therefore believes that modern writers guided by their peoples' needs must employ their art to better their environment. Thus, he makes a cogent case against abstract art, arguing instead for committed art. In "The Novelist as a Teacher," Achebe puts it thus: "I hold, however, and have held from the very moment I began to write that earnestness is appropriate to my situation. Why? Because I have a deep-seated need to alter things within that situation, to find for myself a little more room than has been allowed me in the world" (14). From Achebe's perspective, change is imperative and because the West runs the world, things turned upside down must be rectified. Therefore, the writer must intend to change things through the earnestness of his art.

And should individuals or groups be satisfied with the amount of room apportioned to them in the world? It is evidently a case of the individual or the Race wanting to grow, to come out from under the shadow of economic overlords - first, colonial, next, subtly in the form of neo-colonial manipulation of black rulers, followed by fellow blacks turning into military tyrants. In an interview with Angela Jackson, Achebe states with felt urgency:

There is so much to do. I mean you look to the right and there's work waiting to do, left, front, behind and really it's very, very difficult

> [...] because this is what makes our lives different from the life of poets and artists in cultures where poetry and story-telling are no longer taken seriously. [...] Art is still very important and this is why people can be thrown into prison or worse for writing a poem, for writing a novel and this is our situation; it is a very, very important and real situation because we are dealing with real issues, with things that touch society deeply [...] (*Black Books Bulletin* 53-8).

And so in *Things Fall Apart*, we see a committed writer bent on refuting the Western idea (started actually with Kant's *Critique of Judgment* - 1790) that true aesthetic pleasure should always be "disinterested," and divorced from practical considerations of everyday life and politics. In the late nineteenth century, this search for aesthetic pleasure led the French, German and Russian symbolist poets to propound the theory of *"l'art pour l'art* - art for art's sake, or that art should be accountable to no one, and needs no one to justify itself.

Achebe disagrees and, rather counsels that just as the Owerri *Mbari* artists traditionally would withdraw into seclusion to employ their art in service of *Ala* - that powerful deity of the Igbo pantheon - African and other Black writers must pause occasionally and consider what aspects of their traditional aesthetics can be used for the benefit of their contemporary condition. This Achebean belief would thereafter shape the direction of post-colonial African critical theories including those of African American and Caribbean artists who realize that their art must be both functional and aesthetic if they are to be relevant to their people.

For these groups, the principal thrust of this controversy is a rejection of "universalism" which Achebe considers part of the "narrow, self-serving parochialism of Europe" (Achebe, MYCOD 9). This is what Molefi Kete Asante means when he interprets "Eurocentrism as an ethnocentric view posing as a universal view" ("What is Afrocentrism" 15). In fact, Achebe recommends placing a "ban" on the word "universalism" until the West extends its "horizon to include all the world" (Achebe, *MYCOD* 9). Thus inspired by Chinua Achebe, post-colonialist criticism produced a new African intellectual elite, European-educated, effectively attacking Europe's presence and influence in Africa with Europe's own intellectual weapons. The result is a tradition of writings which focused on particular experiences, on collective national / continental identity and on the fate of the individual unique subject within the collective, with that individual (such as Okonkwo) serving as the collective's consciousness.

Consequently, *Things Fall Apart* is art used in the service of the community. It is for its lack of environmental relevance that Achebe mercilessly critiques the "alien" symbolism of Ayi Kwei Armah's *The Beauyful Ones Are Not Yet Born* (1969). Ayi Kwei Armah, like any other African writer seeking to become a universalist writer, is the alienated native because in Achebe's view, "a man is never more defeated than when he is running away from himself [...] . And if writers should opt for such escapism, who is to meet the challenge?" (Achebe, *MYCOD* 25-7). Rather than mere negative criticism, writings about Africa by Africans need to explore in depth the truth about Africa's human condition and values, and bring out an instructive message. And if an African is reminded that the place to send messages is Western Union, Achebe quips tongue-in-cheek, the reply should be, "Perhaps.[...] But the plain fact is that we are not Americans. Americans have their vision; we have ours. We do not claim that ours is superior; we only ask to keep it. For, as my forefathers said; the firewood which a people have is adequate for the kind of cooking they do" (16). In the political treatise, *The Trouble with Nigeria* (1983), Achebe identifies with clarity the locus of his own space:

Nigeria is where God in his infinite wisdom chose to plant me. Therefore I don't consider that I have any right to seek out a more comfortable corner of the world which someone else's intelligence and labor have tidied up. I know enough history to realize that civilization does not fall from the sky; it has always been the result of people's toil and sweat, the fruit of their long search for order and justice under brave and enlightened leadership (10).

Achebe's intention and commitment to help ameliorate that space, to own his own "corner of the world" from where he speaks to the world constantly, provide fuel and inspiration to his writings. The problems arising from the struggle, Achebe believes, help to create good and important literature whereas the easy, comfortable circumstances of Western societies render their writers nonchalant and self-preoccupied with the result that, "they create literature that is easy going, personal and frivolous (quoted in Ezenwa-Ohaeto's *Chinua Achebe* 263). All of these considerations logically raise the question of the kind of language to be used in transmitting the Black person's vision of the world.

The Black Writer and the English Language

Chinua Achebe is concerned with the proper use of the colonial masters' languages vis-à-vis the colonized and their situation. He is ever conscious of the "integrity" of language, the pains of its crafting be it by Ezra Pound, T.S. Eliot, or, Jean Toomer (*Cane* 1923). In "Four Quartets," for instance, he notices that T.S.Eliot verbally paints the agony and the ecstasy involved in creating the "word":

> Trying to learn to use words, and every attempt
> Is a whole new start and a different kind of failure
> Because one has only learnt to get the better of words
> For the things one no longer has to say, or the way in which
> One is no longer disposed to say it. [...]
> And every phrase
> And sentence that is right (every word is at home,
> Taking its place to support the others,
> The word neither diffident nor ostentatious,
> An easy commerce of the old and the new,
> The common word exact without vulgarity,
> The formal word precise but not pedantic
> The complete consort dancing together)
> Every phrase and every sentence is an end and a beginning
> every poem an epitaph
>
> (Four Quartets in Bergonzi 33).

Therefore, one can argue, if the owners of the English language such as T. S. Eliot can agonize so greatly over its proper fashioning and application, consider the native African or the American / Caribbean African writer whose experiences are radically different, yet, who is forced to resort to the colonial master's language to translate a cultural worldview. Thus, in the ongoing debate amongst African writers concerning this issue, Achebe weighs the situation and grants everyone the right to deal with such a complex problem in one's own way. He nevertheless proclaims his own right to use the English Language to translate the complexities of his indigenous, plus colonial heritage. That the colonizer's language also belongs to the colonized and should be submitted to various advantageous uses is the price a world language should pay for it dominating others. Achebe insists, "let no one be fooled by the fact that we may write in English, for we intend to do unheard of things with it" (*MYCOD* 7). And in doing this, it is not necessary to use this new language like a native speaker; rather, "the African writer should aim to use English in a way that brings out its message best without altering the language to the extent that its value as a medium of international exchange will be lost. He should aim at fashioning out an English language which is at once universal and still able to carry his peculiar experience [...]" (*MYCOD* 61). Achebe goes on to quote from an interview given to the *London Observer* in which Baldwin states:

> My quarrel with English Language has been that the language reflected none of my experience. But now I begin to see the matter another way [...]Perhaps, the language was not my own because I had never attempted to use it, and only learned to imitate it. If this were so, it might be made to bear the burden of my experience if I could find the stamina to challenge it, and me, to such a test.

Baldwin did find the artistic talents or stamina to keep on prodding the conscience of society; he did challenge all kinds of discrimination, and did bear witness to truth and by his inspiring use of language did elevate the struggle for human freedom. Achebe himself successfully learned how to make the English language carry the weight of his African experience. Through the medium of *Things Fall Apart*, Achebe fashioned, like Baldwin, "a new English, still in full communion with its ancestral home but altered to suit its new African surroundings" (*MYCOD* 61-2). Readers familiar with the works of both writers will readily testify to the simultaneity of their struggle to elevate black literature to the status of world literature; that, in fact, Chinua Achebe like James Baldwin did find the "stamina" to successfully challenge both the English language and himself to this test, thus inaugurating a new African literary tradition.

The English language he hones and polishes is at once strong and supple, poetic and nimble, deceptively simple yet profound enough to convincingly try to translate the proverbs, idioms and even the poetry of his environment without losing their native flavor. Evidently, Achebe is satisfied that he and his generation have made the best use of their talents as shown by his response during a *Daily Times* interview:

> I think what we did was literally to create African Literature. [...] We were at the crossroads; we just happened to be there. [...] There may be different opinions about the quality of particular texts but nobody anywhere who lays any claims to being knowledgeable can ignore African literature now. (*Daily Times*. November 18, 1989, 12).

Achebe has always described himself as a "conscious artist" as opposed to the Yoruba folklorist Amos Tutuola, whom he thinks of as a "natural artist." Writing in 1975, Achebe declared he had no choice but to use the English language. In my first interview with Achebe in 1996, he insisted that since 1975, he had been writing in his native Igbo tongue and that some of his best poems are written in Igbo. I had this exchange with him:

Mezu: Can you see a day when an indigenous language can effectively replace the language of the erstwhile colonial masters as the official reading / writing language?

Achebe: One can not say that it is impossible to write in native languages. Whatever arguments we make, we make today. Situations change. What if tomorrow there is an Igbo nation and the government wants to use Igbo as the official language? Theoretically, anything is possible. For now, however, I believe it is impossible to dispense with the English language. But those who have the ability to write in indigenous languages should do so. I do (April 1996).

The Gender Question - Women in the Structure of the Nation-State

One can not read or study Achebe's writings without being heavily conscious of the issues of gender. Achebe has been critiqued over the years as a sexist writer. His first two novels presented a traditionalist view of how things were; the men were warriors, prosperous farmers and patriarchs, upholding clan and communal prestige [while the] wives and children (sons mainly) work the farms and build up unrivaled yam barns (Mezu, *Women in Chains* 91). It was an unapologetic view of a polygamous society where women were items of property and could be chastised at will for failing to serve the man. Feminists would ever after pick issues with Achebe for his female portraiture and he would thereafter strive to modernize his view of the role and place of women.

In my article, "Women in Achebe's World"(*The Womanist*, 1995), the omniscient narrator was described as taking over the narrative voice of women in *Things Fall Apart* since their "voice" appeared too timid to be heard. This not withstanding, in *Things Fall Apart*, the female viewpoint does exist, albeit muted and subdued. The women's "voices" lack the resonant vigor and authority of those of Achebe's men. When Okonkwo's restless anger at the community-enforced inactivity occasioned by the New Yam Festival finds an outlet in a supposedly mutilated banana tree, Okonkwo beats heavily his second wife - the alleged culprit. Her only daughter Ezinma weeps in a tearful "voice" and the other wives dare not interfere "beyond an occasional and tentative: 'it's enough Okonkwo' pleaded from a reasonable distance" (38).

Their "voice" is timid, for the narrator confesses that the wife, Ekwefi, who was nearly shot, did not do much that was wrong. Their voice, though timid is often heard in subtle rebellious manifestations such as when Ojiugo, Okonkwo's third wife, deliberately neglects to prepare his mid-day meal, choosing instead to go hair-plaiting. She knew she would get a beating and one that resulted in Okonkwo breaking the sacredness of the Week of Peace: "it was unheard of to beat anybody during the sacred week" (30). That drew a strong reprimand from the male priest of the Earth goddess *Ani*, Ezeani:

> Your wife was at fault but even if you came to your obi and found her lover on top of her, you would still have committed a great evil to beat her. [...] The evil you have done can ruin a whole clan. The earth goddess whom you have insulted may refuse to give us her increase and we shall all perish (*Things Fall Apart* 30).

Obviously, violence against Ojiugo translates to a violation of Ani's law. Thus, mortal woman, and a formidable, implacable female divinity bond together symbolically in a mute but telling silence of condemnation. Together, their "voice" is invincible. And for reparation, Okonkwo is made to pay a stiff penalty of gifts to the shrine of *Ani*. Ojiugo must have been fed up with the eternal tedium of the daily grind of female life; perhaps also, Ojiugo wanted to exploit the in-built protective and restraining principle of the sacred week to prove a point: that as an autonomous being, she also has needs and has the right to employ her leisure time as she likes and not, in the evocative words of Nigerian critic, Juliet Okonkwo, spend it all in drudgery,

> coming and going with mounds of foofoo, pots of water, market baskets, fetching kola, being scolded and beaten before. [...] disappear[ing] behind the huts of their compound ("The Talented Woman in African Literature" 36).

Women's voices even when vocally silent can yet make powerful statements through silent "action." Achebe records unprecedented incidents in *Things Fall Apart*. When, after four instances of twin babies thrown away, Nneka, the wife of Amadi joined the Christians, she was acting out her condemnation and defiance of that cruel aspect of her traditional religion. Ekwefi, as a girl, was Okonkwo's love but he was too poor then to marry and so, she was married off to Anene. After two years, the mature Ekwefi ran away from her husband to Okonkwo. Thus, she chooses a husband for herself, contrary to traditional ethos. But Ekwefi, nonetheless, had demonstrated a "voice" in choosing Okonkwo as a husband; a voice nonetheless, even if muted and timid. But, some of the other women had no voice. To an innocent question from his first wife, he, Okonkwo **thunders**, "Do what you are told woman, when did you become one of the *Ndichie* of Umuofia!" (*Things Fall Apart* 18), after which his first wife subsided into silent invisibility.

The "voices" of the male *Eqwugwu* - masquerade, ancestral spirits and judges - come "guttural and awesome" (84). Most ceremonies were for men while the women, the narrator says, "looked on from the fringe like outsiders" (83). Obviously, the only female "voices" really capable of matching the men's in vigor and resonant authority are those of ordinary females when they assume the mystical mantle of divinity like *Ani*, or are the priestesses of divinity like Chielo. It is worthy of note that the awesome and inescapable *Ani* (*Ala* in other parts of Igboland), the earth goddess, who determines fertility - biological and agricultural, who disdains the burial on her soil of people who have died ignominiously like Unoka or Okonkwo - has Ezeani, a man no less, to serve her as priest. And the men of Umuofia live in mortal awe of her retributive powers and are quick to pacify her, which Okonkwo readily does by "bringing gifts of she-goat, one hen, a length of cloth and a hundred cowries" (32). When he even brings an additional pot of palmwine, he over-compensates.

Female Bonding

A remarkable feature of the female world in Umuofia is found in their sisterhood whether as guardians of communal wealth by chasing stray goats that destroy agricultural products, or as cooks and functionaries during wedding ceremonies or even as protectors of one another under a heavy-handed husband such as Okonkwo. In answer to Okonkwo's deceptively calm question concerning the absence of one of his wives, Nwoye's mother, his first wife who is the big mother to the children, covers for her co-spouse:

"Did she ask you to feed them [Ojiugo's children] before she went?"

'Yes' lied Nwoye's mother, trying to minimize Ojiugo's thoughtlessness (21).

The final verdict however is that it is not the whole of male Umuofia, but a specific aberrant attitude (like that of Okonkwo) that is responsible for the silencing of some women's voices in Umuofia. Women would eventually prove, as shown earlier, that a restive and independent mind resides behind the "silent voice" when mothers and daughters of *osus* - outcasts - as well as mothers of killed twins show their bottled-up resentment against tribal inequities by going off and joining the Christian church that acknowledges them as human beings with feelings.

However, Chinua Achebe is a pragmatic ideologue who knows in which direction the winds of change are blowing. The secret of his revisionist feminist stance can be deduced from the central theme of his two tradition-based novels - *Things Fall Apart* and *Arrow of God* – namely: that in a world of sweeping change, whoever is not flexible and adaptable will be swept aside. Okonkwo fails in his single-minded quest for greatness because he lacks effective balance, having determinedly expunged from his consciousness the female principle present in his father Unoka and in his son, the gentle Nwoye. In Okonkwo's cosmic view, "to show affection was a sign of weakness; the only thing worth demonstrating was strength" (30). So, Achebe the novelist, in contrast to his tragically stubborn epic heroes, Okonkwo and the inflexible Ezeulu (*Arrow of God*), profits from their mistakes and bows to the winds of change. An example illustrates this: in *Anthills of the Savannah*, he acknowledges that the malaise the African polity is experiencing is as a result of not including women in the scheme of things.

Through his persona, Ikem, Achebe accepts that his former attitude towards women had been too respectful, too idealistic. Attempting to upgrade the image of the woman, his heroine, Beatrice, is portrayed as articulate, independent, self-realized and able to hold her own. But the onus for this re-valuation falls on the woman's shoulder. Ikem therefore tells Beatrice: "I can't tell you what the new role for Woman will be. I don't know. I should never presume to know. You have to tell us" (98), a prescription which accords with the principles of feminism that women must be the agents of their own emancipation.

In *Anthills*, Beatrice also gets to tell her own version of events; in the process she participates both in the creation of the story, and in wrapping it up. Thus, it can be seen how Nkolika, a name given to female children and meaning – "Recalling-Is-Greatest" - becomes a concept that re-establishes the role of traditional woman as shaper and nurturer of humankind.

In *Things Fall Apart*, Ekwefi transmits to Ezinma the myths and legends of the quarrel between Earth and Sky; Nwoye's mother regales her son with tales of peace and love, thereby shaping him into a gentle, peace-loving boy, albeit a disappointment to the androcentric Okonkwo. Yes, the women of Umuofia do have a decisive role / voice – that of preserving culture.

The critic, Ojinmah confesses that "Achebe also uses Beatrice (*Anthills*) to synthesize both Ikem's and Chris's dialectics and views about the nature of society" (104). When I confronted the novelist with the observation that Beatrice still functions as the comforter / sounding board that helps the male characters clarify their different ideological positions, that holds things together, Achebe quipped back,

> And who is to blame? You see, many people do not read fiction the way it should be read - as representing what is. They think it should show what "ought to be." Fiction is not a political argument. The book showed what there is. I am telling a story that illustrates that society had a huge flaw. [...] You see, Beatrice has been coming in stages through all my work. In *A Man of the People*, she is called Eunice. All along, my vision of a woman's role has been developing,

28

growing in intensity as the role of the Igbo woman has been growing in the Igbo society.[2]

Chinua Achebe, in turn, asks me a question:

Achebe: Tell me, how do you think I viewed women in *Things Fall Apart*?

Mezu: You viewed the concept of the mother idealistically. Women were treated sympathetically. In fact, Okonkwo received indictment for being violent with his wives.

Achebe: But Okonkwo was always violent with everyone. Both he and his society had weaknesses which included the female species, and the adoration of power. They paid terrible prices for these. Okonkwo paid a terrible price by being banished for ever in the evil forest, and so did the Igbo society by suffering defeat at the hands of an alien civilization.

Perhaps, Chinua Achebe, who more than any other, has fostered the growth of African literature, should be taken at his word - that his vision of the role of women is a progressive one. In that case, readers will expect women characters of future works to achieve the level of emancipation commensurate with women's real-life status and achievements in modern Nigeria / Africa.

The Writer as a Teacher / Visionary

When Structuralist scholar Sunday Anozie subtly critiqued Achebe and the late poet, Okigbo thus, "No doubt the thrill of actualized prophecy can sometimes lead poets [...] to confuse their roles with that of seers, and novelists to see themselves as teachers [...]" (*Christopher Okigbo* 17), Achebe promptly challenged this critique of the role of a writer. Should the writer attempt to change things? Achebe says a categorical "yes," because both the missionary and the builders of the British Empire also came to Africa's primeval forest to change things ("Colonialist Criticism" 14). The only person, he believes, who has the proper enlightenment tools needed to rectify matters is the educated writer. What then does it means to be a creative writer in a society? The artist, as conceptualized by Chinua Achebe, is the repository and teller of stories, the griot - *Nkolika* – "Recalling-Is-Greatest".

Wading into the Platonian-Aristotelian controversy of who the writer is - inspired poet/teacher/healer? Or, a mad scandal to the youth? Achebe comes out firmly on the side of Aristotle. While Plato believes writers are under the influence of *Madness* and should be chased out of his ideal Republic, because it is not safe to entrust them with the education of the youth - the guardians of the commonwealth, Aristotle believes that a writer should be kept in the Republic because the poet tells what is possible and may happen.

Achebe believes the artist to be under the control of *Agwu* - the god of the healers, *Agwu* being brother to Madness. If the poet were mad, he would be incoherent. But in Achebe's opinion, the poet is not mad. He is merely inspired; and under inspiration, he perfects human actions in drama so that one may imitate that which is imitable. Achebe, like Aristotle, believes that:

> though born from the same womb he [the poet] and Madness were not created by the same *chi*. Agwu is the right hand a man extends to his fellows; Madness, the forbidden hand. Madness unleashes and rides his man roughly into the wild savannah. Agwu possesses his own just as securely but has him corralled to serve the compound. Agwu picks his disciple, rings his eye with white chalk and dips his tongue, willing or not, in the brew of prophecy and right away the man will speak and put head and tail back to the severed trunk of our tale (*Anthills* 125).

Therefore, Achebe, like Aristotle, makes a distinction between the writer possessed by correct inspiration - *Agwu* - and the individual possessed by Madness, which Plato *mistakenly* believes, rides the writer. Artists whether writers, critics, dancers, painters, sculptors, are all *griots*, who Niane describes as "vessels of speech [...] the repositories which harbor secrets many centuries old [...] [for whom] the art of eloquence has no secrets [...] they are the memory of mankind" (*Sundiata: the Epic of Mali* 1).

The writer is also the visionary, who the African Nobel writer, Nadine Gordimer believes, can "without stirring from his stool [...] tell you how commodities are selling in a distant market place. His chalked eye will see every blow in a battle he never fought" (26). And Senghor, the writer / artist proudly proclaims of himself, "*Je suis le Dyali*" [I am the griot]. W. E. B. Du Bois equally thinks of the artist as the "bard, healer, interpreter of the unknown [...] the supernatural avenger of wrong and the one who expresse[s] the longing, the disappointment and resentment of a stolen and oppressed people (*Du Bois: A Reader* 207).

Using the metaphor of *Nkolika*, (*Anthills*) Achebe henceforth sums up in creative writing the primacy of content over form, commitment (functional art) over abstraction (art-for-art sake), although the two concepts can co-habit harmoniously:

> The sounding of the battle-drum is important; the fierce waging of the war itself is important; and the telling of the story afterwards - each is important in its own way. I tell you, there is not one of them we could do without. But if you ask me which of them takes the eagle-feather, I will say boldly: the story.

As the creator of the story, the artist / visionary becomes also the readers' guide. As Achebe conceptualizes it, the story - *Nkolika* - owns and directs; in the best formalist manner, it has a rich, complete and independent life of its own:

> Recalling-Is-Greatest. Why? Because it is only the story that can continue beyond the war and the warrior. It is the story that outlives the sound of war-drums and the exploits of brave fighters. It is the story, not the others, that saves our progeny from blundering like blind beggars into the spikes of the cactus fence. The story is our escort; without it, we are blind [...] the story is everlasting (123-4).

Excerpts of the interview with the writer on March 7, 1996 confirm his view of the functionalism of creative writing:

Mezu: Writing and its relevance! What do you consider as the core message in your works?

Achebe: To make people think. Just as a good story keeps revealing itself in different ways, in different connotations. The meaning is not finished. To make you see yourself in a different light.

Mezu: That is the meaning of the word you used in the *Anthills* - Nkolika - the Story is Greatest?

Achebe: Yes!

For Achebe, therefore, the craft of writing is a grave responsibility since the writer is both the observer and recorder of societal mores as well as critic and teacher. Speaking to Yusuf Hassan, Achebe explains that:

> [...] the real value of a work of art, and indeed of a good teacher, is
> that they start something in the mind of everybody, not just the elite,
> not just the writer. Not just the one person. But you engage the
> whole people in evaluating their condition [...] because ultimately the
> fundamental values are clear enough. Humane-ness, decency,
> fairplay, and so on. (*African Events* 51-5)

The Harlem Renaissance author of *Cane* (1923), Nathan Eugene
Toomer, equally believed that the primary purpose of literature is to
teach and to teach well (Turner, xxiv). Thus is underlined once again
the functionality of writing. The artist is also the conscience of his
people; therefore, the writer, like the gadfly, should sting people into
an introspective self-knowledge. However, any meaningful and
progressive social change must emanate, not from the masses, but
from the leadership, which re-interpreted, equates with W.E.B.Du Bois'
ideology of the "Talented Tenth." Consequently, for the writer, the
obligation to guide and direct becomes doubly necessary. In Achebe's
world view, for Africans throughout the Diaspora, and indeed for all
groups under siege by a plethora of problems (ranging from foreign
manipulation to endemic internal ills like hunger, drugs, violence,
AIDS, or other forms of deprivation), the theory of "art for art's sake"
becomes an unaffordable luxury.

Writer after writer reiterates Achebe's view that in particular
situations the artist cannot afford to be on the fringe of, or hostile to
society as normally happens in the West; but s/he must be there at the
forefront as "the sensitive point of [the] community" (Achebe, *MYCOD*
45). Achebe explains that a necessary part of this re-examination
involves a revision, the primary task of looking back "to try and find
out where we went wrong, where the rain began to beat us" (44); it
involves a proper understanding of the meaning of the word
"education"; it involves re-educating races of people not to accept the
label of inferiority, but rather to sufficiently appreciate their cultures to
make even their weather, landscape, *et cetera*, worthy subjects of poetry
for literature remains literature whether handed down by word of
mouth, or, read in print. It is for these reasons that Achebe sets the
examples with his own writings.

Ralph Ellison, with his finely textured writing and skillful
characterization, shows a similar understanding of fiction's potential
for influencing change, when he observes:

a novel could be fashioned as a raft of hope, perception and entertainment that might help keep us afloat as we tried to negotiate the snags and whirlpools that mark our nation's vacillating course towards and away from the democratic ideal (Ellison, *Invisible Man* xx-xxii).

The lessons of literature through the lives of characters living in fictional societies prevent us from repeating their mistakes and teach us proper human values or in the words of Achebe himself, enable us:

> [...] to encounter in the safe manageable dimensions of make-believe the very same threats to integrity that may assail the psyche in real life; and at the same time provide through the self-discovery which it imparts, a veritable weapon for coping with these threats whether they are found within our problematic and incoherent selves or in the world around us (What has literature got to do with it? 117).

Thus, while making content functional, Achebe, for one, has successfully by his works (especially *Things Fall Apart* and *Anthills of the Savannah*) shown fidelity to the art of writing, with African peoples as his primary audience. This is achieved through his fervent belief that the artist is visionary, should be a revisionist, a prophet and a guide of his / her society. John Edgar Wideman's literary judgment on *Things Fall Apart* speaks for other diasporan Africans, it's as if the great antiquity, wisdom, poise and dignity of traditional Africa begins to speak to me through the eloquent voices of a traditional elder (quoted in Ezenwa-Ohaeto's *Chinua Achebe* 283). There is no better assessment of the relevance and immortality of Chinua Achebe's art than his own words published in the *Daily Times* of November 18, 1989 when he defined great literature as:

> Literature which alters the situation in the world. A great and important book does that and nothing can be done without reference to it. It has made a statement which changes the relationships and perceptions of the world (cited in *Chinua Achebe* 272).

Things Fall Apart has done just that. It is a great and important book which Somalian novelist Nuruddin Farah believes to be the most singular contribution the continent of Africa has made to world literature. During a discussion with this writer, Okechukwu, my husband, and Christie, Achebe's wife, the veteran novelist said with satisfaction, "One of the things that give me joy is that with *Things Fall Apart* I have placed the Igbo culture on the world map.[3]" Indeed, he has been a most eloquent interpreter of both African and human experiences captured in writing that is at once moving, full of irony and great wit, a life-altering brand of writing that teaches both truth and wisdom about human life, thus enriching all humanity. Similar to the eclectic German writer Johann Wolfgang von Goethe's concept of World Literature, Achebe has realized for Africans the dream of bringing Africa's rich and distinctive gifts and placing them alongside others in the great festival of cultural harvests of the world which Léopold Sédar Senghor calls *"la civilization de l'universel"*(Mezu, S. Okechukwu, *Léopold Sédar Senghor,* 1969).

The foregoing are some of the issues that can be gleaned from *Things Fall Apart* and selected writings of Chinua Achebe. These issues are equally pertinent to the situation of diasporan Black peoples. *Things Fall Apart*, Achebe insists, has traveled to more places than he himself has done.[4] Other people from the developing nations of the world are able to perceive in his works issues analogous to their own socio-historical situations. It is envisaged that scholars across disciplines, other notable achievers in various areas of black creativity, university students and diverse linguistic communities can through dialogue and increased interaction, achieve a clearer vision of who black people are, their present and future progress in history, and hereafter work to promote better understanding among themselves and with other races for the sake of wholeness and harmony in this World.

Notes

[1] *Morning Yet on Creation Day* will hereinafter be known as *MYOCD.*

[2] Telephone Interview I held with Chinua Achebe on March 11, 1996.

[3] June 15, 1999 family discussion with Chinua Achebe and his wife, Christie, my husband Okechukwu and myself.

[4] *Ibid.*

Works Cited

Achebe, Chinua. *Anthills of the Savannah*. Ibadan, Nigeria: Heinemann Educational Books, 1988.

--- *Morning Yet On Creation Day: Essays*. Nigeria: Heinemann, 1977.

--- Colonialist Criticism in *Morning Yet On Creation Day*. London: Heinemann, 1975.

--- *Things Fall Apart*. London: Heinemann, 1958

Achebe, Chinua. *Anthills of the Savannah*. Ibadan, Nigeria: Heinemann Educational Books, 1988.

--- *Morning Yet On Creation Day*: Essays. Nigeria: Heinemann,

--- What has literature got to do with it? In *Hopes and Impediments*. London: Heinemann Educational Books, 1988.

Anozie, Sunday. *Christopher Okigbo*. London: Evans Brothers, 1972.

Asante, Molefi, K. "What is Afrocentrism" in *Left, Right and Center: Voices from Across the Political Spectrum*. Ed. Robert Atwan & Jon Roberts. Boston: St. Martins Press, 1996.

Bergonzi, Bernard. Ed. T. S. Eliot, *Four Quartets: A Case Book*. London: MacMillan, 1969.

Darah, G. G. and Afam, Ake. "Achebe at 59." In *Daily Times*, 18 November 1989.

Ellison, Ralph. *Invisible Man*. New York: Random House, 1952.

Ezenwa-Ohaeto. *Chinua Achebe: A Biography*. Indianapolis: Indiana University Press, 1997.

Gordimer, Nadine. "Tyranny of Clowns" in *The New York Times Book Review* (Feb. 21), 1988.

Hassan, Yusuf. "More Fiction than Real" in *African Events*, 3, 11 (1987), 51-5.

Jackson, Angela. *Black Books Bulletin*, 8 (1991) pp. 53-8

Laye, Camara. Interview by J. Steven Rubin in *Africa Report*. Washington, D.C.. May 1972.

Mezu, Rose Ure. *Women in Chains: Abandonment in Love Relationship in the Fiction of Selected West African Writers*. Randallstown, MD: Black Academy Press, 1994.

--- "Women in Achebe's World" in *The Womanist.* Georgia: University of Georgia Press, (Spring) 1995.

Mezu, S. Okechukwu, *Léopold Sédar Senghor et la défense et illustration de la civilisation noire.* Paris. Editions Marcel Didier, 1968

Niane, D. T. *Sundiata: an epic of Mali.* Transl. G.D. Pickett. London: Heinemann, 1993.

Ojinmah, Umelo. *Chinua Achebe: New Perspectives*. Nigeria: Spectrum Books Ltd., 1991.

Okonkwo, Juliet. "The Talented Woman in African Literature." In *African Quarterly*, 15. 1& 2, 1975.

Okoye, Emmanuel Meziemadu. *The Traditional Religion and its Encounter with Christianity in Achebe's Novels*. New York: Peter Lang, 1987.

Peterson, Kirsten Holst and Anna Rutherford, eds. *Chinua Achebe: A Celebration*. Oxford: Heinemann, 1990.

Turner, Darwin T. *"Introduction" to Cane*. N.Y.: W. W. Norton, 1975.

2

Achebe's *Arrow of God*: Ezeulu and the Limits of Power

It now remains for us to consider what ought to be the conduct and bearing of a Prince in relation to his subjects and friends [...] It is essential, therefore, for a Prince who would maintain his position, to have learned how to be other than good, and to use or not to use his position as necessity requires. (The Prince[1] Chapter xv)

And herein comes the question, whether it is better to be loved rather than feared, or feared rather than loved. It might be answered that we should wish to be both; but since love and fear can hardly exist together, if we must choose between them, it is far safer to be feared than loved. For of men, it may generally be affirmed that they are thankless, fickle, false. [...] The Prince, therefore, who without otherwise securing himself and builds wholly on their professions, is undone (The Prince, Chapter xvii, 1711).

One of the central theses of Chinua Achebe's third novel, *Arrow of God* focuses on what constitutes a proper governing authority – an exploration of the limits of power as exercised by a ruler. And the questions abound: To what extent can individuals or citizens be given freedom and still ensure that a strong central authority retains its preeminence? Is it enough for a leader to be a good man? Should the leader even bother to seek popularity at the expense of expedient utilization of power for the good of the governed?

Cast in the light of the above questions, *Arrow of God* spawns a story of the exercise of power, the exploration of the nature of power and its limits which generate fractious conflicts. It is also a story of war and peace amidst these pervasive cultural, economic and religious upheavals. All these issues generate several intricately interwoven conflicts which form important sub-themes: European-run civic versus indigenous authority, religious and cosmic order versus communal freedom and individual humanism. At the end, the eventual outcome hinges on the proper interpretation of the Italian word *virtù*.

In Niccolò Machiavelli's *The Prince* (1513), *virtù* is defined not as "virtue" but as the ability of a human being to measure oneself. This then begs the speculation as to the degree one in authority can impose his/her particular regime or interpretation of the law on the governed? This quality of *virtù* will always help the ruler - be it Machiavelli's eponymous Prince, Sundiata, Emperor of Mali, or Sophocles' Creon (*Antigone*) or Ezeulu - a priest-king, or Winterbottom or Tony Clarke, his assistant - to understand the character of the particular people being governed, and thus know the limits to which one can go in the exercise of civic / religious authority.

The ability to measure oneself should also include taking into account the whims and caprices of fortune. This essay therefore examines Ezeulu's exploration of the extent and limits of his power as the venerable, old Chief Priest of Ulu. It analyzes aspects of his character that hurtle him forward towards this quest for unlimited power, and the character and cultural composition of the people of Umuaro, as well as the caprices of fortune (in the form of his encounters with Winterbottom / Clarke and their colonial administration, Oduche's adventures with the sacred python, and the tragically cruel death of his favored son Obika) that set limits to the realization of Ezeulu's ambition for total, unlimited power.

Virtù as Metaphor for Power Unparalleled

In Ezeulu resides an innate desire to control. An early intimation of this trait is seen in the quality of handshake he gives to young people to show them that he is as good as they, or even better for "whenever they shook hands with him he tensed his arm and put all his power into the grip, and being unprepared for it, they winced and recoiled from pain" (*Arrow of God* 2). Ezeulu is a priest of the god, Ulu, the central deity of Umuaro. His job demands that each year he watches for the appearance of the new moon that will herald the Festival of the Pumpkin Leaves, a signal for the commencement of the planting season, and the New Yam Feast.

In an agriculture-based society, personal and communal wealth and well-being of society hinge on an early planting season rightly-timed, and on an abundant yield of yam crops. Heavy symbolism therefore surrounds the twelve sacred yams that Ezeulu, as priest, must eat before he can declare open the planting season. Understandably, the priest of Ulu wields an immense power that is primarily religious yet is of a simultaneous secular - economic, cultural and political - urgency. Consequently, Winterbottom can be said to be right when he describes Ezeulu as a priest-king.

Being the Chief Priest of Ulu, Ezeulu is strongly tempted to conflate his personal ambitions with his interpretation of the proper duties of the people to their god, Ulu. In fact, he constantly pushes and stretches the exercise of his power, testing its limits to gauge how far he can apply it, as seen in the narrator's commentary: "Whenever Ezeulu considered the immensity of his power over the year and the crops and, therefore, over the people he wondered if it was real" (3). Rather than envision his job as that of a watchman or a superintendent, Ezeulu in his ambition wants more: "No! The Chief Priest of Ulu was more than that. If he should refuse to name the day there would be no festival--no planting and no reaping. But could he refuse? No Chief Priest had ever refused" (3). So, it can not be done; he would not dare his cautionary Self argues to his Super Ego.

In Ezeulu's mind, even this acknowledgment implies a sneaking limitation to his power which in turn sparks off an unconscious resistance from which the germ of an idea – "to *dare*" – is sown in his mind. Hence, his barked reply to his dual Self, "take away that word *dare*. Yes, I say take it away. No man in all Umuaro can stand up and say that I dare not. The woman who will bear the man who will say it has not been born yet" (4). Clearly, Ezeulu's hubris is rebelling internally against this perceived limitation; but without humility and compassion, excessive power will degenerate to tyranny, and this is the point of contest with Ezeulu's enemies.

As Machiavelli's *Prince* suggests, a ruler must comprehend the particular nature of his own people. Ezeulu realizes that he faces a people who cling tenaciously to tradition, are opposed to change, yet pragmatic enough to desire change when their individual / communal wellbeing is threatened, a transformative capacity embodied in the essence of the dancing mask which becomes an ongoing metaphor throughout the drama.

When *Arrow of God* opens, all is not well in Umuaro. And Ezeulu, as our opening guidepost, is clearly bitter that his enemies seek "to lay on his head" the blame for the disunity that exist within the six villages of Umuaro because "he had spoken the truth before the white man[...]Wintabota" (6). Umuaro blames the white man's law for increased conflicts, and by extension, Ezeulu whom Winterbottom has called "the only witness of truth." Clearly, Colonial government as an external element becomes involved in the internal drama with the potential to act as catalyst unleashing a chain of tragic events.

Ezeulu's own character comes into full play in his relationship with his family and with the people of Umuaro. His is a proud personality, plainspoken but uncompromising in his convictions, indeed autocratic, brooking no opposition. Like the mask, he is a figure of duality – Akuebue says to him "one half of you is man and the other half spirit" (132), and duplicity – desiring one thing but saying another. Ezeulu has a temper, which is always threatening to erupt into violence. But his eventual undoing will not be through eruption but because of the superhuman restraint he strives to show as a controlled front at all times, which sometimes allows a crack through which escapes a kind of laughter that sends a chill into his listeners, prefiguring his final insanity. In fact, the story is replete with numerous references to "madness" in the narrative, foreshadowing the eventual madness of Ezeulu. His words to his wives are devoid of tenderness, consisting of scolding and ultimatums. To his head wife Matefi, whose food is late, he warns: "What I am saying is that if you want that madness of yours to be cured, bring my supper at this time another day [...] " (9); "The madness which they say you have must now begin to know its bounds" (47), *et cetera*. His handling of his family breeds animosity amongst both wives and children. Matefi, his senior wife, feels that he always favors the junior, more attractive, younger Ugoye and she says so unmistakably.

His grown children resent him because he treats them like children; and they resent one another because he has favorites. Edogo believes Ezeulu's favorite sons are Obika and Nwafo, and that by sending Oduche to the Christian school to be his father's "eye there," the father sacrificed this young son on the altar of his ambitions, and at the same time disqualified Oduche from the priesthood of Ulu. Accordingly, Oduche himself behaves like a sacrificial lamb with nobody ever remembering if ever Ezeulu showed much affection to Oduche, who in the end, colludes with the Christians, withholding vital information from his father when it mattered most.

Obika is the son after his father's heart, a mirror image of the Priest's longing for paternal authority, and secular domination whereas according to Simon Gikandi, the "moral and transcendental side to Ezeulu is reflected in the elder son, Edogo, the carver of the mask and the interpreter of its social semiotics" (*Reading Chinua Achebe* 55). But Edogo's quiet gentleness and tentativeness, Ezeulu rejects as "cold ash", preferring the fervor and bravado of Obika. Except for a degenerate penchant (denoting excess) he has for keeping bad company (Ofoedu), getting drunk and sleeping late, Obika who looks like his father is "one of the handsomest young men in Umuaro and all the surrounding district, his face finely cut and his nose *gem*[...] his skin like his father's, the colour of terracotta" (*Arrow of God* 10), and acts like him – hotheaded, intrepid and outspoken.

But even with Obika, Edogo complains to Akuebue that Ezeulu lacks the trust and patience to give this favored son the benefit of the doubt in his fight with the roadbuilder Wright; blaming his drinking, Ezeulu rashly prophesies to Obika "this is only the beginning of what palm wine will bring to you. The death that will kill a man begins as an appetite" (89).

It is Edogo's contention that the older his children grew the more Ezeulu disliked them (91). For this preferential treatment, Nwafo receives a rough, unloving treatment from Edogo in their father's absence. As Edogo, surprised at the depth of his ill-will towards his father, points out to Akuebue, "A man should hold his compound together, not plant dissension among his children" (127). Edogo remembers his dead mother, remarking that "Ezeulu's only fault was that he expected everyone—his wives, his kinsmen, his children, his friends, and even his enemies—to think and act like himself. Anyone who dared to say no to him was an enemy" (93).

Clearly, Ezeulu's good leadership ability to dispense justice without fear or favor is called into question and thus, the internal wrangling amongst his wives and children, a constant source of irritation to him, weakened the structure of Ezeulu's family rule, and contributed to his internal disequilibrium.

To be Loved or to be Feared? - That is the Question

Evidently, this ambivalent desire to be loved, respected and feared at the same time characterizes Ezeulu's entire relationship with his people and with his sons. And so he shares with Machiavelli's Prince a thorny dilemma of desires: "whether it is better to be loved rather than feared, or feared rather than loved." The Prince's crisp answer suffices: "we should wish to be both; but since love and fear can hardly exist together, if we must choose between them, it is far safer to be feared than loved" (Chapter XVII). Ezeulu indeed desires the love and approbation of his people, of his family (its lack is the reason for his great hurt and "smoldering anger") but he would not do, or fails to even recognize, what is expedient to secure that approval or respect. Inflexible by nature, he is unable to do anything other than what he considers right.

By evoking the authority of Ulu, "the deity that kills a man when life is sweetest to him," by taking sides against the people of Umuaro, ceding the disputed land to Okperi, and vowing that Ulu the god of Umuaro will not fight in blame, he believes he is speaking only the universal truth, and protecting the integrity of his god in an age of chaos, flux and disorder, for "how could a man who held the holy staff of Ulu know that a thing was a lie and speak it?" (*Arrow of God* 6). Yet, by so doing, he alienates forever the affection of the very people he serves, Umuaro people, who would not forget that a foreigner, a white man, praised him for giving victory to Okperi through his testimony. If Ezeulu wished to be feared, respected, even if not loved, he like Machiavelli's Prince should have based his policies on the platform of political rather than moral expediency.

As the Igbo saying goes, no one man can win a case against his people. Ever since its founding, the martial invincibility of Umuaro people lay in their unity. To protect themselves from the terrorizing Abam warriors, Umuaro came together and installed a protective deity, Ulu, with Ezeulu's forebears as Chief Priests. As long as Umuaro's cause is just, the god gives them military victory, and they in turn obey and respect his priest. But times change and when Umuaro, led by Nwaka, decide to take their fate into their own hands, they expect Ulu and Ezeulu to go along with them.

In the person of Nwaka, Ezeulu confronts his single most formidable, implacable and intractable opponent. Nwaka - rich, powerful, one of three people to have taken the fourth and highest title in the six villages of Umuaro – is from Umunneora, the first and strongest village of Umuaro. He is protected by Ezidemili, the priest of Idemili, Ogwugwu, Eru and Udo, who resents the supremacy of Ezeulu, correctly discerning the lofty ambitions of Ezeulu to transcend the limits of his authority as priest of Ulu and become at once "king, priest, diviner, all" (27). But Ezeulu and even some of his opponents correctly discern the true motive behind Ezidemili's support of Nwaka – to overthrow the priest of Ulu and replace Ulu with Idemili, the god of Umunneora.

Thus, emerges a fierce struggle on many levels between the two priests. Ezidemili would in time pounce on the opportunity provided by the unforeseen chance adventure of Oduche with the sacred python (owned by Idemili) to throw a challenge to Ezeulu to purify his land of the abomination committed by his son – a challenge that further angers Ezeulu who says to the messenger, "Go back and tell Ezidemili to eat shit" (53). Ezidemili further furnishes Nwaka with all the background knowledge of things religious and political the eloquent speaker needs to verbally devastate Ezeulu's authority.

Nwaka has the arrogance of the fearless, the ambitious and the talented. As a skilled orator, Nwaka is able to stir many hearts who call him "owner of words" (144); he knows how to turn Ezeulu's words against him. Slyly, he arrogates to himself the authority of tradition and communal mythology, appealing to the people's nationalism and thus insinuates that Ezeulu has a compromised motive for siding with Okperi – the hometown of Ezeulu's mother.

Eloquently persuasive, Nwaka's sly but political astuteness surpasses the plainspoken, honest rhetoric of Ezeulu who, like the Trojan princess Cassandra, speaks the plain truth which no one wants to hear. On the other hand, the people revere grand oratory and bravado, and the fact that Nwaka, having bullied and belittled Ulu the god, still escapes unharmed is instrumental in the gradual but sure demythification of Ulu, "for his [Nwaka's] head did not ache, nor his belly; and he did not groan in the middle of the night" (40). Indeed, Nwaka survived his rash insults to both Ezeulu and Ulu to even don the Mask called Ogalanya or Man of Riches, and brag about his continued good health:

> I returned from my sojourn. Afo passed, Nkwo passed, Eke passed,
> Oye passed. Afo came round again. I listened, but my head did not
> ache, my belly did not ache; I did not feel dizzy. Tell me folk
> assembled, a man who did this, is his arm strong or not?

And the narrator affirms that the crowd, the flute and drums all joined in replying, "his arm is indeed very strong" (*Arrow of God* 40). Had Ezeulu known or read Machiavelli's *The Prince*, he would have agreed with its assessment of the governed:

> For of men, it may generally be affirmed that they are thankless,
> fickle, false, studious to avoid danger, greedy of gain, devoted to you
> while you confer benefits upon them [...] but when it [danger] comes
> near, they turn against you. The Prince, therefore, who without
> otherwise securing himself and builds wholly on their professions, is
> undone[...] . Nevertheless a Prince should inspire fear in suchwise
> that if he do not win love, he may escape hate. For a man may very
> well be feared and not hated. [...] (Chapter XVII).

But Ezeulu, lacking the necessary people's skills, does not secure his vulnerabilities, nor obtain the loyalty of even family and friends. And so, through obstinacy, he refuses the white administrator's summons and eventual offer of kingship – a position which could assure Ezeulu enough personal power as to break the constraints put on his exercise of his priestly authority and thus effect the kind of change in Umuaro that necessitated his sending his son Oduche to the colonial school; for Ezeulu had correctly guessed that "the world is changing [...] My spirit tells me that those who do not befriend the white man today will be saying *had we known* tomorrow" (46).

Had Ezeulu collaborated with Winterbottom, his power, as Machiavelli's *The Prince* states, would be such as to "*inspire fear in suchwise that if he do[es] not win love, he may escape hate,* " because having before them the example of the obliteration of their rebellious neighboring town Abame[2] the people would not have dared work against Ezeulu since Winterbottom – "breaker-of-guns"- is a "man as inflexible" as the Priest and who will not brook rebelliousness. But Ezeulu, irritated by the convergence of events of Oduche's python and his family's wrangling, unwisely (if viewed from a pragmatic and selfish point of view) sent away Winterbottom's messengers.

Preferring to preserve the integrity of tradition, rather than seek to be feared and respected, he opts to seek his people's approbation / love by calling an assembly of his peers – one that turns out disastrously, for his arch enemy Nwaka, with his verbal dexterity, makes mincemeat of him.

Ruler, Know Thy People!

In determining what constitutes proper governance, the character of the people of Umuaro must be considered. Fiercely egalitarian, they boast that Igbo people do not know kings but rather must through disputation, peer consultation and debates make decisions concerning the general polity. It is precisely to avoid autocracy or tyranny that their ancestors reputedly gave the priesthood of Ulu to the weakest of the six villages of Umuaro. Challenging Ezeulu's insistence that Ulu would never support a war of blame, Nwaka states that though a god, Ulu can remain so only if the people says it is, reminding Umuaro: "And we have all heard how the people of Aninta dealt with their deity when he failed them. Did they not carry him to the boundary between them and their neighbors and set fire to him" (27).

Thus, in Igbo religious cosmology, the very close and frequent intercourse between deity and people leaves no illusions as to the existence of a quid-pro-quo, a dialectic that is strictly pragmatic. This appeal to Umuaro's prideful individuation persuades one half of Umuaro to remember the ultimate utilitarian and humanistic goal in the worship of their, or any, deity - the good of their community.

And so, Umuaro allows itself to be persuaded by Nwaka's eloquence and embarks on a war with its neighbor. But, a god that wreaks hardship on his people must be overthrown. In many respects, the Igbo traditional gods appear to resemble the Greek gods as wish fulfillment - images erected to stand for superior men and women in strength, beauty and immortality. If people's wellbeing is threatened, an abstract, unseen god who can no longer offer adequate safeguard, ceases to hold sway over the fate of the living mainly because this god is unable to serve their immediate human and material needs. Then, it is time to discard him and move on to another, more functional deity. This supports the view that in Igbo traditional religion, there are no religious absolutes in the mentality of a people ready to bestow allegiance on the condition of the deity's proven functionality.

Perhaps, this provides a clue to why African traditional religion, unlike the absolutist Christian and Islamic theology, never engaged in proselytizing or saving souls from damnation. And as Rev. Ezewudo points out, in both Christianity and Islam, the belief in One God and in a unique and exclusive Revelation, makes tolerance of other creeds look like an abdication of one's belief in the one Way, the one Truth, and the one Life (in *Religion and Society* 56).

Consequently, when Nwaka in his preamble states that "wisdom is like a goatskin bag; every man caries his own, Ezeulu has told us what his father told him about the olden days [...] My father told me a different story," he is restating the absolutism or tyranny of relativism, the premise that truth may be many-sided and subject to individual interpretation; that if Ezeulu's authority becomes indisputable, then he becomes a king over them whereas the reason for giving the god over to Umuachala, the smallest and weakest of the six villages and to the Ezeulus as priests was precisely to prevent the tyranny of the strongest. Nwaka's argument is the ultimate in pragmatism.

But if truth be said, Ezeulu himself has earlier expressed this ideology of relativism when he, custodian of the people's tradition / rituals of the past and guarantor of continuity, evokes the figure of the mask as reason for sending his son Oduche to study the foreign religion: *The world is like a Mask dancing. If you want to see it well, you will not stand in one place* (*Arrow of God* 46). This unconscious expression of doubt about the survival of Umuaro culture in the face of colonial cultural onslaught disguised as a desire for cultural transformation accords with the paradigmatic nature of the mask as trope of ambiguity, that is – saying one thing but meaning another.

Nevertheless, to the prideful, uncompromising Ezeulu, Nwaka's challenge to limit his power is galling. The narrator describes Ezeulu's riled, embittered ego. When he speaks to the people, "his salute is like that of an enraged bull" (18). And so the rivalry between these two men with similar ambitions for leadership sets the tone for the central conflict that spawns yet others in *Arrow of God*. It also seeks to distinguish the universal from the historical as Ezeulu defines a universal dogma of truth by insisting that the disputed land belongs to Okperi: "It was Okperi who gave us their piece of land to live in. They also gave us their deities[...] If you choose to fight a man for a piece of a farmland that belongs to him, I shall have no hand in it." He further sets up a historic parameter for measuring the justness of any cause: "If in truth the farmland is ours, Ulu will fight on our side. But if it is not we shall know soon enough [...] our fathers did not fight a war of blame" (15).

But Nwaka representing Umuaro desires that the Chief Priest support the aspirations and needs of Umuaro. The rabble-rousing Nwaka wins the debate and Umuaro sends the intemperate emissary, Akukalia, whose actions (22-24) help to unleash a war that Umuaro does not win.

To Ezeulu's warning about a strong man challenging his *chi*, Nwaka, posing as the champion of the people counters with an appeal to the people's sense of self-determinism and pride that seeks not to unduly empower any *chi*:, "Let us not listen to anyone trying to frighten us with the name of Ulu. If a man says yes his *chi* also says yes" (26). The "big, savage war" (50) that ensues will be arbitrated by Captain Winterbottom, nicknamed "Otiji-Egbe - Breaker of guns", with Umuaro losing the land on the testimony of Ezeulu. And Umuaro will not forget that its Chief Priest has witnessed against the people.

If Ezeulu had a correct insight into the true nature of his people, if he knew how to be pragmatic, he would have seen in Captain T.K.Winterbottom a politically expedient tool to achieve civic power to complement his spiritual authority and become in fact and in truth the Priest-King that Winterbottom supposed him to be. The administrator insightfully has told Clarke, " [...] the man's title is Eze Ulu. The prefix *eze* in Ibo means king. So the man is a kind of priest-king" (107). In fact, there is immediate empathy between Ezeulu and Winterbottom who can be said to be kindred souls. Both are hot-tempered, stubborn and decisive. Both are straight-dealing but inflexible – a fact that has cost Winterbottom promotions, being passed over for less competent newcomers.

That Ezeulu and Winterbottom come into conflict in the matter of the chieftaincy should be ascribed to poor timing, tragic convergence of internal circumstances (the issue of the python that Oduche desecrated had exacerbated both familial and communal feelings), and the inept attitude of the two self-serving colonial government intermediaries whose insolence and corrupt tendencies irritate and rub Ezeulu the wrong way, coupled with the uncontrolled outbursts of the hot-tempered Obika.

Ezeulu had surprisingly shown some pragmatism by sending his son Oduche to the Mission school to be "his eyes" – a decision which later in the eyes of Umuaro undermines his opposition to the white man. But meanwhile, Winterbottom has admiration for "that impressive-looking fetish-priest" Ezeulu, who while other witnesses perjured themselves, was the man who spoke the truth (59). With the white man, Ezeulu's physical handsomeness further works in his favor - "a priest-king in Umuaro who witnessed against his people [...] A most impressive figure of a man. He was very light in complexion, almost red" (36).

Even Akuebue would describe his friend as being "tall as the iroko tree and his skin white like the sun. In his youth he was called Nwa-anyanwu – [son of the sun]" (153). By Winterbottom's reckoning, Ezeulu's physical and moral attributes make him truly heroic, kinglike. And so when Winterbottom begins to implement the British system of Indirect Rule, using natives as Warrant Chiefs, Ezeulu is the logical choice. And so he reiterates to Clarke, "As far as Umuaro is concerned, I have found their Chief" (108). But Ezeulu does not heed well the Prince's cardinal principle:

> what ought to be the conduct and bearing of a Prince in relation to his subjects and friends [...] [of how] it is essential for a Prince who would maintain his position, therefore, to have learned how to be other than good, and to use or not to use his position as necessity requires (The Prince, Chapter XV).

Not having learned how to be other than good or how to profitably use his position as the situation warrants, Ezeulu is unable to bend, and reap when opportunity comes calling. Unfortunately, he cares greatly what the people think of him even though Nwaka and his friends believe Ezeulu's ultimate ambition is to be king and that Winterbottom as his friend will make Ezeulu king. To disprove their suspicion, Ezeulu disdains to answer the administrator's summons and when offered the honor of kingship, rejects it, thereby incurring the wrath of his erstwhile admirer, Winterbottom. To the offer of Chieftaincy, and enraged at what he perceives as insults implied in Clarke's mode of questioning, Ezeulu answers unflinchingly: "Tell the white man that Ezeulu will not be anybody's chief, except Ulu."

"What! Is the fellow mad?" exclaimed the astounded Clarke. "I tink so say," said the Interpreter. "In that case he goes back to prison." And thus, the new assistant Tony Clarke subjects Ezeulu to the indignity of a long imprisonment, a punishment that the enraged

Winterbottom had sanctioned before a projected journey, "As soon as he comes, you are to lock him up in the guardroom. I do not wish to see him until after my return to Enugu. By that time, he should have learnt good manners. I won't have my natives thinking they can treat the administration with contempt" (151). Unfortunately, Winterbottom fell sick: When Clarke consults with the sick man, the crisp command is - "Leave him inside until he learns to co-operate with the Administration" (177). And the consequences would be disastrous for Ezeulu and his people.

Umuaro as Paradigm of a Pristine African Culture Versus an Encroaching Alien Ideal

On a deeper level, the conflict between Okperi and Umuaro translates to a struggle between Western modernity and African traditionalism. It has been argued that what makes *Arrow of God* so attractive is its unsentimental evocation of a rich, vital way of life that really satisfies those lucky enough to be born in it. Certainly, by using his novels to reveal pristine, hitherto unknown spiritual and geographical territories, Achebe aims to inform, and to expand his readers' humanistic horizons. Okperi is more developed because quite early it welcomed missionaries and colonial administration with its court system.

For Winterbottom, Umuaro in its backwardness has nothing to offer and so, Ezeulu's witnessing in Okperi's favor fits into the colonial objectives. Nwodika, the white man's steward, has reason to lament that the rat that does not run fast enough must make room for the tortoise. In his narrative to Akuebue and Ezeulu, he laments the lack of infrastructural facilities and non-progress of Umuaro since people from smaller town like Elumelu, Aninta, Umuofia and Mbaino are all prospering from the white man's administration whereas there is no "Umuaro man among the wealthy people here. Not one. Sometimes I feel shame when others ask me where I come from. We [Umuaro] have no share in the market; we have no share in the white man's office. We have no share anywhere" (*Arrow of God* 170).

And so, this patriotic son of Umuaro, who even though he comes from the enemy village of Umunneora feels joy that Winterbottom has summoned Ezeulu, the wise man of all Umuaro, for a privileged consultation. As Nwodika's friend Ekemezie reminds readers, "a man of sense does not go on hunting little bush rodents when his age mates are after big game" (169).

There is also the conflict between the peaceful, communal life and the supercilious paternalism and racist perception of Africans as the *Other* by the Western aliens who make fun of, and insult, the Africans. "One thing you must remember in dealing with natives is that like children they are great liars" (37). "Shut up, you black monkeys and get down to work!" Wright shouts at Obika's age-grade being used *gratis* as road workers (83). On native customs, Winterbottom "would wonder what unspeakable rites went on in the forest at night, or was it the heart-beat of the African darkness" (*Arrow of God* 30). Palmwine is called "that dreadful stuff" (37). The foreigner is seen as being "depressed about the climate and food." Sleep is almost impossible in this "dear old land of waking nightmares" (30). These however did not stop the invader from exploiting the Continent's wealth of human and other resources to build up the conqueror to Empire status.

The typical colonial administrator plays at being God's agent sent to deliver the natives from what Achebe styles their long night of savagery. And so, mistaking the Government's intention for paternalism, Ezeulu misses the opportunity to solidify his hold over his people and bring them into a period of prosperity and Western enlightenment, and continues to chase "rodents." Therefore, the internal conflicts between the two villages of Umuaro intensify to a point of *"kill and take the head,"* with incidents of poisoning spreading until unity is broken and Umuaro divides into Ezeulu and Nwaka camps. This facilitates the eventual supplanting of the traditional society by the foreign colonial / missionary administration – a process that rhymes with and validates actual historical facts of alien take-over in Igboland.

Essentially, *Arrow of God* is a dark drama, whose epic hero's fall from grace is comparable to Okonkwo's. Whereas *Things Fall Apart* has flashes of a light, rich, sunny ambience, and playful communal ceremonies, the atmosphere in *Arrow of God* is marked with dark, morbid humor, shown even in the reply to greetings: "Nobody has died;" "Did they not say you died two markets come next afo?" "Life alone is not enough[...] For there is a kind of slow and weary life which is worse than death" (94-5) are the supposed humorous answers to ordinary greetings. In fact, the dramas are suffused with references to death and insanity. Equally, the ceremonies in *Arrow of God* are innately marked by conflicts. The tale of the jealousy of two wives as told by Ugoye parallels the Pandora myth of how disease came into the world. It warns children against envy but has far-reaching implications, capturing the layers and types of conflicts in the book, which can be broken down as follows:

a. There are major and minor rivalries between various persons and gods in Umuaro whose relentless struggles generate unrest throughout the novel. This internal unrest that culminates in fragmentation of the entire society are between Edogo, Ezeulu's oldest son and Nwafo, the youngest son; between Matefi and Ugoye; between Ezeulu and Ugoye over Oduche, the son he sent to school who is used as a sacrificial lamb; between Ezeulu and Okeke Omenyi, his elder brother over the sacerdotal mantle.

b. Intense rivalry exists between Umuaro and Okperi, the seat of government administration.

c. There is also the rivalry between Ezeulu, the high priest of Umuaro and Nwaka of Umunneora, his truculent opponent; and the fatal rivalry between Ezeulu, the high priest of Ulu and Ezidemili, the Priest-guardian of the royal python bring matters to a head;

d. And among the Christians, there exists a tense conflict between Mr. Goodcountry, the missionary and Moses Unachukwu, the new convert over Christian attitude towards the royal python;

e. Then, there is the ideological conflict over the system of indirect rule/appointment of paramount Chiefs between Mr. Winterbottom, the colonialist, knowledgeable in the ways of the natives and his superiors who however always overrule his decisions.

Above all, the belligerent shadow of Nwaka's personality, that of his mentor, and the brooding bitterness of Ezeulu stalk the entire drama suffusing it with dark, melancholy overtones. While Okonkwo's tragic demise is brought about by a kind of unwitting and unthinking impulsiveness, a lack of reflection before acting, the decisions that trigger Ezeulu's downfall are personally calculated and deliberate. Ezeulu has the entire span of the drama to brood and plan to hurt his own people.

Priest-King, Know Thyself!

The character of Ezeulu is of immense significance in this poignantly tragic drama of political and religious intrigues. As has been mentioned earlier, the priest of Ulu who already has been seen to be intractable, inflexible, controlling is becoming increasingly more vengeful, uncommunicative and unpredictable. Ultimately, he fails to relate well to people – "even his sons do not know him" (131). And Akubue, who had shown him the kind of true friendship that Obierika showed to *Things Fall Apart's* Okonkwo, at last, fails to fathom the "unkowningness" in which Ezeulu himself exults. Refusing to heed his friend's advice, Ezeulu insists:

> I have my own way and I shall follow it. I can see things where other men are blind. That is why I am **known** and at the same time **unknowable**. You are my friend and you know whether I am a thief or a murderer or an honest man. But you cannot know the **thing** which beats the drum to which Ezeulu dances. **I can see tomorrow** [...] (132; my emphases).

"Known" yet **"Unknowable"** – the contradictions implicit in this paradoxical personality form a rich quarry from a psychoanalytical perspective. Uncommunicative and repressed, hot tempered, yet always struggling to be in control while pretending not to care: "For once he had taken a stand on any matter, he did not want to appear eager for other's support; *it was not his concern but theirs*" (170; my emphasis). In *Anti-Oedipus: Capitalism and Schizophrenia*, Deleuze and Guatarri posit that schizophrenia is a disconnection from painful reality, but that it need not be a malady since it is a process, not an illness. It can only become an illness if there is constrained arrest or forcible stopping of the process or its continuation in the void because there is no worthwhile venture for instance to replace the void; in such a situation [...] the schizo is neuroticized, and it is this neuroticization which constitutes his actual illness (363).

Four concepts of psychoanalysis are at work simultaneously in Ezeulu: there is **repression** of huge emotions of anger and bitterness - bitterness as he struggles to appear unconcerned and in control of situations within Umuaro and his family which are clearly out of control; there is also **isolation** as he rejects the friendly overtures of friends, family and even Winterbottom; there is **intellectualization** as he rationalizes all the causes of conflicts with Nwaka and Ezidemili, and within his family. But there is also **neurosis** for these negative issues are not well-repressed into the subconscious. In the end, he ends up not really knowing himself; too restrained, too uptight, he has no means of recreation or outside medium of releasing tension. Internalizing everything, Ezeulu becomes like a boiling volcano waiting to erupt. Madness is a huge leitmotif in *Arrow of God*. There are profuse references to "madness" or death in the narrative tying in with the eventual actual madness of Ezeulu. Obika's death would constitute the clincher and the final transition to insanity.

Unactualized Prophecy - A Fight to the Finish

Clearly, Ezeulu was wrong when he arrogantly prophesied, "I can see tomorrow." He fails to see the havoc that tomorrow will bring. And so he piles on the mistakes of judgment. He calls Umuaro to unite with him "in seeing and hearing what I have seen and heard, for when a man sees a snake all by himself he may wonder whether it is an ordinary snake or the untouchable" (143).

To his chagrin, his mortal enemy Nwaka of Umunneora, manipulates his words, twisting the meaning out of context. Nwaka wonders out loud, "The *white man* is Ezeulu's friend and has sent for him. What is strange about that [...] Or does Ezeulu think their friendship should stop short of entering each other's houses? Do not our elders tell us that as soon as we shake hands with a *leper* he will want an embrace? It seems to me that Ezeulu has shaken hands with a man of *white body*" (144).

Thus Nwaka cleverly links the words "*white man*" with the dreaded words "*white body*" – meaning leprosy, and the people laughed at his finesse, murmuring in admiration of the "owner of words." Nwaka reminds the people that even though a priest, Ezeulu had gone **alone** to Okperi before, and so whoever tied the knot should know how to untie it. He ends his speech by laying the burden of dealing with the white man on Ezeulu alone, "You passed the shit that is smelling; you should carry it away[...] Who was the white man's witness that year we fought for our land—and lost?" (144). Thus Akuebue's counsel to his friend was vindicated for he had warned his friend earlier about the non-wisdom of some of his actions – sending Oduche to the Christian school:

> [...] but you forget one thing: that no man however great can win judgment against a clan. You may think you did in that land dispute but you are wrong. Umuaro will always say that you betrayed them before the white man. And they will say that you are betraying them again by sending your son to join in desecrating the land (131).

Ezeulu's lapses in judgment are occasioned by the unbridled bitterness, stubborn pride and impatience that make him treat friends and foes alike, for when Nwokeke Nnabenyi, Akuebue, and his own brother Okeke Onenyi offer to travel to Okperi with him, Ezeulu arrogantly and unwisely refuses. And when therefore, the convergence of circumstances and misunderstanding causes him to be imprisoned at Okperi, he takes umbrage at the fact that Umuaro people do not stage a public demonstration of support on his behalf. He tells Nwodika, Clarke's steward from Umunneora, who is cooking and looking after the priest, "They call me the friend of the white man. They say Ezeulu brought the white man to Umuaro[...] They say I betrayed them to the white man" (179). And thereafter, he starts to plan on how to pay back Umuaro for abandoning him.

Dreams, especially, nightmares are powerful indicators of a troubled mind. Ezeulu, even in dreams, struggles with the intricacies of governing a headstrong people, a dynamic body of people who had made their own god for their protection and who will abide with that god so long as it ensures their well-being. Ezeulu's prison dream foreshadows coming events as his people revolt against him, even his powerful grandfather, spitting upon Ezeulu as the priest of a dead god:

> And what is the power of Ulu today? [...] He saved our fathers from the warriors of Abam but he can not save us from the warriors of Abam. Let us drive him away as our neighbors of Aninta drove out Ogba when he left what he was called to do and did other things, when he turned around to kill the people of Aninta instead of their enemies (Arrow of God 160).

Occurring with mid-day clarity, Ezeulu believes it is a vision. And ruminating in his mind, it occurs to him that he is actually devising thoughts of revenge which now come to him as he sits listening to Nwaka. In various assemblies, he had warned them over and over again and Umuaro did not listen. With Nwaka and Ezidemili, the struggle for supremacy must be fought once and for all because "until a man wrestles with one of those who make a path across his homestead, the others will not stop [and] Ezeulu's muscles tingled for the fight" (161).

Akuebue is one man who knows the depth of his friend's bitterness. He believes he knows the priest better than even "his children or his wives. He knew that it was not beyond him [Ezeulu] to die abroad so as to plague his enemies" (165). The white administration held Ezeulu for thirty-two days and when he was freed, he burst into that *unknowable,* belly-deep laughter characteristic of him, and puzzling to hearers: "So the white man is tired' (178). Ezeulu's stature has been enhanced by his reputation for magic, rejection of the offer, and his proud defiance of the Colonials. And to Nwodika who admires him for having pressed the white man's back to the ground, Ezeulu answers, laughing:

> You call this wrestling? No, my clansman. We have not wrestled. We have merely studied each other's hand. I shall come again, but before that I want to wrestle with my own people whose hand I know and who know my hand. I am going home to challenge those who have been poking their fingers into my face to come outside their gate and meet me in combat and whoever throws the other will strip him of his anklet (179).

This becomes a fight to the finish. Perhaps, Ezeulu should have heeded the observation he had made of his son Obika's intrepidness: "It is praiseworthy to be brave and fearless, my son, but sometimes it is better to be a coward. We often stand in the compound of a coward to point at the ruins where a brave man used to live" (11). Ezeulu will not return to Government Hill in Okperi. And so the priest's unplanned imprisonment becomes a catalyst to an explosion of already simmering events in Umuaro. And the struggle that ensues will be and will end in a form Ezeulu does not envision. But, upon his return self-doubt sets in because a large number of people, and some from the enemy village Umunneora come to visit that "thoughts of reconciliation, began albeit timidly, to visit him" (187).

Ogbuefi Ofoka's visit resolves the conflict in Ezeulu's mind. The man summarizes Umuaro's confusion, regarding Ezeulu's actions. Firstly, the priest tells Umuaro not to defy the white man and fight with Okperi. Umuaro defies him and loses the war. Next, Ezeulu himself goes ahead to defy the very white man after sending his son to the white man's school and religion. It is worth noting that Ezeulu's inability to express himself with eloquence is here indicted. His ancestors succeeded because their pragmatism (which the inflexible, taciturn Ezeulu lacks) ensured for them the people's support.

But he does not have unity in Umuaro. While he is imprisoned at Okperi, the full moon comes out. Had he been home, Ezeulu would have eaten the last of the twelve sacred yams that would usher in the planting season. This he refuses to eat. Akuebue reasons with him to no avail. Then ten high-ranking Umuaro men come, but Ezeulu insists that there are three yams yet to be eaten, clearly using his Okperi exile as a weapon with which to fight his enemies. And who are his enemies? They are personified in "Idemili whose envy seeks to destroy me that his python may again come to power." He hears voices, "'Tae Nwanu!' Barked Ulu in his ear, as a spirit would in the ear of an impertinent child. 'Who told you that this was your own fight?'" (191).

But in fighting this personal war with Ezidemili, Nwaka and their cohorts, and by refusing to call the date of the New Yam festival, he hits the people where it will hurt most – in agriculture, their metaphorical economic bloodline. The spokesman of the visiting group, Anichebe Udeozo speaks to him with absolute clarity, devoid of any ambiguity:

> "Ezeulu [...] never has the white man taken the Chief Priest away. These are not the times we used to know and we must meet them as they come or be rolled in the dust. I want you to look around this room and tell me what you see. Do you think there is another Umuaro outside this hut now?"

> "No, you are Umuaro, " said Ezeulu.

> "Yes, we are Umuaro. Therefore, listen to what I am going to say. Umuaro is now asking you to go and eat those remaining yams, today, not tomorrow; and if Ulu says we have committed an abomination, let it be on the heads of the ten of us here. You will be free because we have set you to do it. And the person who sets a child to catch a shrew should also find him water to wash the odour from his hands. We shall find you the water. Umuaro, have I spoken well?"

> "You have said everything. We shall take the punishment." (208-9)

It is at best very disingenuous of Ezeulu to reassure Umuaro of his goodwill and honesty, saying that "it could not be my wish to ruin all these people. It could not be my wish to make the smallest man in Umuaro suffer. But this was not my doing. The gods sometimes use us as a whip." For Umuaro, the issue is one that strikes at the core of their health and prosperity – their very survival depends on a timely harvesting of agricultural produce, and Onenyi Nnanyelugo very succinctly communicates this urgency to Ulu's Chief Priest, "But the harvest is ripe in the soil and must be gathered now or it will be eaten by the sun and the weevils" (207). The men asked for the reason for Ulu's anger, and the appeasement penalty, to which Ezeulu replies, "Ulu did say that two new moons came and went and there was no one to break kolanut to him and Umuaro kept silent" (208).

Nwoga has pointed out that the uniqueness of Ulu as a god is that its authority or function is not determined by taboo, but that it rather allows for "in-built cracks to be determined by any crucial stresses" (*Research in African Literature,* 20). Ezeulu has expressly acknowledged that Umuaro are living in a new age that requires transformations and adjustments, hence his desire to acquire new knowledge through Oduche; hence also his sayings that a new disease can hardly be cured "with everyday herbs" (*Arrow of God* 133), that a "man must dance the dance prevalent in his time" (189), that in the making of a charm, if a chicken can not do, one looks for a goat, or ram or even a bull to march its power (133). Obviously, from these utterances, Ulu can be malleable, and there is room for accommodating the demands of a new age, but the now vengeful Ezeulu resists any ideology he does not himself interpret. According to Ezeulu himself, every charm must be made with an animal of a matching power, and every offence must have its sacrifice. It must indeed be "the end of things if neither a cock nor a goat nor even a bull will do" (133).

Here is a clear case of the Priest seeking punishment and revenge. Umuaro's entreaties to the priest about the fundamental worth and survival of the people fall on deaf ears. The delegates cite numerous examples of customs that have undergone change when they begin to wreak havoc on the people. Finally, they remind the now silent Ezeulu that there used to be a fifth title in Umuaro which also underwent a change – "**the title of king**" (209). Because traditionally, the Igbo regard discussion and consensus as the highest ideals of the political process, Umuaro are unable, as Achebe would say in "Chi in Igbo Cosmology," to "suspend for the convenience of a ruler, limitations which they impose even on their gods?" (*Morning Yet On Creation Day* 103).

But it is obvious that Ezeulu is bent on pushing the limits of his power as Chief Priest, seeking to transform it and himself into Priest-King, styling himself as Ulu's "whip with which to flog Umuaro" (209). In claiming that the god refused any pacification, Ezeulu is claiming a certain knowledge of the mind of Ulu – a certainty which at the beginning of the drama is negated by his tentative searching for such reservoir of knowledge, for the narrator reveals that Ezeulu's mind "never content with shallow satisfactions crept again to the *brinks of knowing*" (4). The implication is that complete knowledge is still out of reach. If he succeeds in apprehending this total knowledge, then Ezeulu and Ulu will be one entity. Interpretively, by isolating Ulu from the people and their cultural practices and placing him in a world to be inhabited only by Ulu and himself, Ezeulu seeks to become the deity himself. This is the ultimate in consummate ambition. Consequently, his refusal to eat the sacred yams produced "such alarm as had not been known in Umuaro in living memory" (211), thus precipitating a crisis whose tragic closure is most heart-wrenching.

Arrow of God as a Classic Aristotelian Tragedy

From Machiavelli, comes the statement that a "Prince has little to fear from conspiracies when his subjects are well-affected towards him, but when they are hostile and hold him in abhorrence, he has then reason to fear everything and every one" (*The Prince*, Chapter XIX). Ezeulu has a lot to fear from his now disaffected subjects, for almost overnight, he "had become something of a public enemy in the eyes of all, and as was to be expected his entire family shared in his guilt" (*Arrow of God* 211). Even his wives can not buy from the market and his family develops a feeling that the "hostility was visibly encircling them all in Ezeulu's compound" (212).

Akuebue valiantly defends his friend whom, even though stubborn, he considers too honest to falsify Ulu's decision. One of the worthiest men of Umuaro, Ogbuefi Ofoka, accuses Ezeulu of wickedness, "sometimes I want to agree with those who say the man has caught his mother's madness[...] today he would rather see the six villages ruined than eat the two yams." He assures Akuebue that "a priest like Ezeulu leads a god to ruin. It has happened before;" and Akuebue in defense of his friend answers swiftly, "Or perhaps a god like Ulu leads a priest to ruin himself" (212). Thus, Ulu and Ezeulu becoming two faces of the same prideful persona, will thrive, rise, or fall together.

Arrow of God satisfies Aristotelian prescription for a great and successful tragedy: a drama that is serious, complete and possessing magnitude[3] in which the hero's fall from grace is not through vice or depravity but from some character flaw or error in judgment. In complexity, the structure of *Arrow of God* should satisfy both Euripides and Aristotle with the novel's intricately interwoven sub-plots replete with ironies and reversals. Achebe's usual economy of words and strong plots contribute to the poignancy of the drama. All these are discernible as the reader witnesses that Umuaro's hatred towards Ezeulu and his family intensifies. When villager Amalu dies, Umuaro blames it on Ezeulu's wickedness. But Ezeulu's tragic flaw is hubris, which following the Greek prescription, occasions his downfall. In fact, Akuebue, while defending Ezeulu's honesty still agrees that his friend is "a proud man and the most stubborn person you know is his messenger" (212). Ezeulu's overweening pride, bordering on willful blindness is as symbolic as the actual stubborn blindness of Sophocles' eponymous Oedipus for it gives a cosmic dimension to both of their characters, isolating them from their people.

Yet, Ezeulu longs for human companionship, some news but gets none until in his repressed pain, he feels like going to the market place to shout out his angst. He begins to consider himself a sacrificial lamb, the kind of scapegoat stance he adopts even on his journey back from Okperi, walking in the rain, heedless of any danger to his health and feeling elated, for the more his suffering, the greater the punishment he would mete out as revenge to his adversaries. And becoming, a figure of sacrifice, he "would not for any reason now see the present trend reversed. He carried more punishment and more suffering than all his fellows. What troubled him now – was that the punishment was not for now alone but for all time" (220). But still he persists in his intransigent inflexibility. The division within Umuaro is now complete. The news his friend Akuebue brings about the Christian strategy of encouraging the natives to carry their offerings to the Christian god who will protect them from Ulu's vengeance, was one of the devastating last blows. Ezeulu confronts Oduche, who reluctantly confirms: "Yes. Our teacher told them so." Ezeulu retorts: "I said why did you not report it to me?" With sadness, Ezeulu realizes the depth of his estrangement from this son: "I called you as a father calls his son and told you to go and be my eye and ear among those people[...] I called you by name and sent you to see and hear for me. I did not know at the time I was sending a goat's skull[...] Go away[...] I have no spirit for talking now" (221).

Ezeulu's gamble has not paid off: "If there is nothing in it you will come back. But if there is something there you will bring home my share" (46), Ezeulu had said to Oduche. But there is something there, and ironically, his son does not bring home Ezeulu's share or what Ezeulu thought was his share. Rather he appears to have lost his son in the process. His dream that night is a premonitory vision of mourners passing behind his compound to bury a man in the bush. Feeling powerless in his dream, he ran to his wives' huts to discover everywhere in ruin, "his compound was deserted[...] all he saw were the ashes of a long dead fire.[...] and a few blades of grass were sprouting on the thatch [of Ugoye's hut]"(222); and then he heard the furious passage of the Ogbazulobodo.

The Unmasking of the "Unknowable"

Because Obika is Umuaro's champion runner, knowing the terrain with landmarks like trees and huts, not leaving "out even one small path from the accustomed route [because] *he knew it without the use of his eyes*" (226), the Amalu family put aside their grievances against Ezeulu to ask his son to run round the town as Ogbazuluobodo in honor of their father's second burial. Obika who "had been having a little fever" begs to stay out of the race, but the bereaved family insists. Obika, described as being "at once blind and full of insight" confesses to agreeing out of cowardice lest in the villagers' grudge against his father, he, Obika, would be accused of trying to wreck the burial of a "village man." His wife, Okuata tries dissuading him but Obika insists on running and he does run, and the villagers were fulsome in their praise. He finishes his run, returns in a projected moment of triumph but collapses, and neither answers, nor gets up.

The song of the *Ayaka* stops abruptly and was succeeded by a frightening silence. When Ezeulu hears voices, his dream comes back to him. Springing up, he takes up his matchet, "What happened to him? Who did this? I said who?" The description of his unutterable sorrow is poignant: The matchet fell from his hand and he slumped down on both knees beside the body. 'My son,' he cried, 'Ulu, were you there when this happened to me?' He hid his face in Obika's chest" (228). Obika's death, the narrator states, "shook Umuaro to the roots; a man like him did not come into the world too often" (229). His god has failed the Chief Priest – the humiliation of this abandonment hurts, and sends him wondering with futility where he had gone wrong:

> What was his offense? Had he not divined the god's will and obeyed it? When was it ever heard that a child was scalded by the piece of yam its own mother put in his palm? What man would send his son with a potsherd to bring fire from a neighbour's hut and then unleash rain on him?[...] What could it point to but the collapse and ruin of all things? (229).

Yet, nowhere does Ezeulu acknowledge responsibility for the conflicts or for his sufferings, which he believes are brought about by other peoples' actions. His hurt wonderings raise the issue of self-misrepresentation. Did Ezeulu misinterpret the dynamics / problematics of power? Does he have real power or is he as the omniscient narrator said at the beginning merely "a watchman," having nothing but "the power of a child over a goat that was said to be his" (3) as long as the goat was alive. And the pointer is that he has been serving but a dead god.

The betrayal by Oduche, hatred by his people, protracted internal Umuaro conflicts, death of his son Obika, desertion by the god Ulu – all culminate in pushing Ezeulu over the edge into an unreachable abyss of insanity. This Schizo has crossed over the limits. He will not recover because not believing that he has anything worth living for, he is unable to go beyond the paranoiac breakdown to find a revolutionary *breakthrough* which seeks to discover flows of desire that can help to achieve a healing process. His Umuaro enemies claim vindication – Ulu has taken their side against a stubborn and ambitious priest. As in the case of Okonkwo, Ezeulu's inflexibility (his Achilles heel) proves to be his undoing for, as the whole of Umuaro said, "No man however great was greater than his people; that no one ever won a judgment against his clan."

But Ulu, the narrator is quick to add, if it abandoned Ezeulu, also brings on its own destruction, for a few days after Obika's death, the Christian church was overflowing with native worshippers and their abundant offerings to the new God. Thus, Umuaro's people desert Ulu, and ritual power shifts to the now triumphant Christian religion which had started making slow but corrosive inroads into traditional beliefs when it taught Oduche and others to denigrate and disbelieve the powers of the python considered sacred, telling them: "you address the python as Father. It is nothing but a snake, the snake that deceived our first mother Eve. If you are afraid to kill it do not count yourself as a Christian" (47). However, the omniscient narrator describes, Ezeulu's madness as a merciful "final act of malevolence" since he is spared coming cruel events, for his mind has already given way, allowing him to live out his days "in the haughty splendor of a demented high priest" (229). In Obika'a actual physical death is prefigured Ezeulu's symbolic rational death. The two, father and son, - actual doubles – now fuse into one tragic entity. The poignancy of Ezeulu's tragic fall is palpable.

Finally, even though Ezeulu, the Chief Priest starts out a principled, truthful man, interested in putting to the test the limits of his power over Umuaro people, he ends up becoming too uncompromising, arrogant, rashly unwise, and even too duplicitous (symbolically assuming as persona the *unknowningness* of the mask) to know when and how to truly bend his principles to accommodate the wishes of his people living in an age of changing mores. In his determination to defeat his enemies, he confuses his identity with that of his god, Ulu. Moreover, he unwisely rejects the offer of collaboration with the Winterbottom administration that would have simultaneously ensured the total defeat of his enemy and secured for him the status of Priest-King. In the end, the story of Ezeulu becomes a cautionary tale of the necessity of putting in place a well-thought-out system of politico / religious, and administrative machinery in which the well-being of the people is paramount. Failing to realize and actualize this leads to the destruction of Ezeulu and his family and the enthronement of an alien religion over Umuaro's traditional beliefs. His people simply abandon their undependable god, Ulu, to worship alien and more tractable gods.

As a heroic personage, Ezeulu's sad end is intricately linked to the communal tragedy of his Igbo society. And at last, readers witness the ruins of the home where a brave man called Ezeulu used to live – an ironic fulfillment to Ezeulu's concern at the beginning of the narrative regarding the rash temperament of his son Obika, embodiment of cultural masculinism. Machiavelli's Prince would have counseled that "a wise prince will evidently rely on what is his own power and not on what is in the power of another. As I have said, he need only take pains to avoid hatred" (*The Prince*, Chapter 15, *Norton Anthology*, 2441). But Ezeulu, not relying on his own power, is unable to avoid being hated by his people. He gambled on reliance on the putative power of a deity who indeed "kills man when life is sweetest," and who is nothing but a dead god or perhaps a god of death.

In Achebe's future works and narratives of nationalism and post-colonialism would be played out the full import of this Christian conquest of the traditional African rituals and religious beliefs as dramatized in both *Things Fall Apart* and *Arrow of God* in which literally, things fall apart and the arrow of the Christian God pierces through African rituals, government and traditions leading to a devalorization of the communities' central symbols (unmasking of the masquerade, demythifying of the evil forest, the new yam, the ikenga, the python), producing general instability and an African world *no longer*, and perhaps never to be again, *at ease*.

Notes

[1] *The Prince* was written in 1513 by Niccolò Machiavelli with the hope of obtaining public office from the Medici. It describes the ruthless political methods of Cesare Borgia, "Il duca Valentino" the favorite son of Pope Alexander VI. This treatise on how to obtain and keep political power has twenty-six chapters. The book presents a cheerless view of humanity as evil, and of people as willing to be deceived. The early Latin title of the book was *De principatibus* – (*Of Princedoms*).

[2] This is recorded in *Things Fall Apart* 137-141. Obierika brought the news of the Whiteman's destruction of Abame a town where having killed a Whiteman called an "albino," the people unwisely tied his bicycle – "iron horse" to a sacred silk cotton tree – a deed that

pointed to their guilt. The numerous links that the narrator has tried to make between Umuofia and Umuaro must be mentioned here.

[3] See excerpts of Aristotle's "Poetics" in *The Norton Anthology of World's Masterpieces*. New York: W.W. Norton, Inc., 1995, 758-762.

Works Cited

Achebe, Chinua. *Arrow of God*. Revised edition. New York: Random House, 1974.

--- *Things Fall Apart*. Revised edition. New York: Doubleday, 1994.

--- "Chi in Igbo Cosmology." In *Morning Yet On Creation Day*. Heinemann, 1975.

Aristotle. "Poetics." In *The Norton's World Masterpieces*. N. Y.: Norton, 1995.

Clavreul, Jean. "Perverse Couple." *Returning to Freud*. Ed. Stuart. New Haven: Yale University Press, 1980.

Deleuze, Gilles and Felix Guattari. *Anti-Oedipus: Capitalism and Schizophrenia*. U.S.A.: University of Minnesota Press. 1968.

Ezewudo, Gabriel. "Christianity, African Traditional Religion and Colonialism: Were Africans pawns or players in the Cultural Encounter?" In *Religion and Society*. Ed. Rose Ure Mezu. -- Baltimore, MD: Black Academy Press, 1998. 43-61.

Gikandi, Simon. "The Language of the Dancing Mask: *Arrow of God*." In *Reading Achebe: Language and Ideology in Fiction*. London: Heinemann 1991. 51-77-100.

3

Conflicts and Notions of Culture and Civilization in *No Longer At Ease*.

> *It is clear to me that an African creative writer who tries to avoid the big social and political issues of contemporary Africa will end up being completely irrelevant — like the absurd man in the proverb who leaves his burning house to pursue a rat fleeing from the flames [...] Take for instance the issue of racial inequality which — whether or not we realize it — is at the very root of Africa's problems and has been for four hundred years*
> (Achebe, *Morning Yet On Creation Day* 78)

> *The white man, the new religion, the soldiers, the new road — they are all part of the same thing[...] The white man [...] does not fight with one weapon alone.* (*Arrow of God* 85)

One central thought runs like a thread through all the writings of Chinua Achebe, and that is: the question of proper governance – the nature of power, the issue of authority and the place of the human being within it. This involves also the responsibilities of government towards the governed as well as the obligations of the citizenry towards government. In *Things Fall Apart*, the issue is broached subjectively, albeit not centrally, in Okonkwo's relations with family and community since the novelist's intention has been well articulated in his essays - to creatively re-establish a legitimate, holistic, pre-colonial civilization to help all Black people regain pride in self and culture ("The Novelist as a Teacher" 45). In *Arrow of God*, the focus is on exploring the limits and limitations of power and the consequences of its unwise application. Underpinning the tragic drama of that story is the putative superiority of an encircling alien civilization.

Now, in Achebe's second novel, *No Longer At Ease*,[1] Obi Okonkwo becomes the subjective medium through which are played out for the first time the conflicts and practical implications arising out of the Christian take-over of African religious thoughts and communal rituals not fully explored in *Things Fall Apart*; and only introduced in *Arrow of God*, and which would be given fuller treatment in the later novels -- *A Man of the People* (1966) and *Anthills of the Savannah* (1988). These novelistic explorations of the nature of power and the quality of government *cum* the governed will eventually culminate in Achebe's brief treatise, *The Trouble with Nigeria* (1983).

Published in 1960, the year of Nigeria's Independence but set in the dying years of the 1950s, *No Longer At Ease* narrates the transition from colonialism to postcolonial identity. Using the novelistic medium, Achebe struggles to craft a discourse of national identity which an educated generation - personified in Obi Okonkwo – requires in order to express the pressures of a pre-Independence Nigeria.

The central issue of *No Longer At Ease* – an effort to forge new instruments of producing social meanings becomes contemporaneous with the very act of writing which interrogates the effects of the new dispensation on the university-trained generation. It is all a matter of a self-described "conscious artist" experimenting with language as a weapon of strength – a new language "still in communion with the ancestral" roots, but altered "to carry the weight" of this new African urban experience ("The African Writer and the English Language" 62).

With *No Longer at Ease*, readers witness first hand the maturation of the Christian missionary activities of which Mr. Brown and Rev. James Smith started in *Things Fall Apart*, and Mr. Goodcountry in *Arrow of God*. Readers also see played out the reality of colonial civil administration policies like those of Mr. Green which were put in place by the District Commissioner - George Allen[2] (*Things Fall Apart*) and Captain Winterbottom, Tony Clarke, Wade, and Wright (*Arrow of God*).

The third novel of a projected trilogy, *No Longer at Ease*, does not have the deep structural complexities of *Arrow of God,* nor a tragic persona comparable in stature to the heroic Okonkwo and Ezeulu. Rather, *No Longer at Ease* meshes the story of Obi Okonkwo, grandson of Okonkwo, and that of his son, Nwoye (christened "Isaac") whose actual story never gets to be told in full[3] (see "The Mezus Visit with the

Achebes"), but is briefly mentioned here and mingled with his son's story.

In *No Longer at Ease*, we move from the communal hinterland of Umuofia and Umuaro to the physical and mental stresses of urban life in Lagos as capital of colonized Nigeria on the threshold of independence. This chapter explores (1) the tensions that exist between the alienating ideals of democracy and a cohesive, community-structured, egalitarian leadership style which the colonial government replaced; (2) the corruption that resides at the core of this new leadership concept - Government; (3) the figures of Obi Okonkwo and Isaac (Nwoye) Okonkwo as actually personifying the stresses/conflicts between these two concepts; (4) tensions in gender relations, and (5), pointers to an uneasy political and economic future of a post-colonial Nigeria on the verge of acquiring political authority.

Western Democratic Ideal versus "Sons of the Soil"

At issue here is the paradoxical duality of Self-Identity and Self-Image – that a putative "superior" culture to sustain its self-image must denigrate as "inferior" the culture it hopes to exploit, thus receiving moral justification for an economic rape. Colonial missionaries and administrators worked co-operatively to promote the ascendancy of Western cultural history over that of colonized African communities. And as Unachukwu tells the Umuaro Otakagu age group, "the white man, the new religion, the soldiers, the new road— they are all part of the same thing[...] The white man [...] does not fight with one weapon alone" (*Arrow of God* 85).

One of Europe's weapons was to denigrate and undercut, at every turn, the educated African witness. It was in Europe's interest to arrogate to itself the title of a superior culture and denigrate, indeed, seek to obliterate the way of life of the Africans. And as Achebe explains in "The African Writer and the Biafran Cause," "no one arrogates to himself the right to order the lives of a whole people unless he takes for granted his own superiority over those people. European colonizers of Africa had no difficulty in taking their own superiority for granted" (79).

Thus, in *Arrow of God*, readers see Wright the engineer hang on the unpaid, youthful age-grade road-workers the label of "black monkeys" – lazy and infantile; he flogs Obika, the boisterous son of the Chief Priest without regard to his status as belonging to the ruling elite of

Umuaro. And in *No Longer at Ease*, Mr. Green, Obi Okonkwo's boss, is the typical European who shows paternalistic generosity to "his Africans": simple-minded natives like Charles his messenger, his steward, garden boys, cooks and drivers - hence the *"I know my natives"* attitude towards those he can easily control. But, he treats with insolent levity and contempt educated Nigerians like Obi who do not, like Mr. Omo, say, "yes, sir" (75) to him. These Europeans do not believe these "African elites," trained to take over from them, have shown adequate gratitude for the privilege of having Western civilization bestowed on them. Mr. Green therefore warns Okonkwo about the fate of a country where in his opinion, "even the educated have not reached the level of thinking about tomorrow" (*No Longer at Ease* 109).

Obi Okonkwo believes Europeans like Mr. Green must have come to Africa with a set agenda – "to bring light to the heart of darkness, to tribal headhunters performing weird ceremonies and unspeakable rites. But when he arrived, Africa played him false. Where was his beloved bush full of human sacrifice?" (121). Achebe definitely makes Okonkwo the mouthpiece of his angst against such writers as Joyce Carey (*Mr. Johnson*; *The African Witch*) and Joseph Conrad (*The Heart of Darkness*) whose novels about Africa had provided Europe with the prevailing negative stereotypes until writers like Achebe stepped in with their "Sons-of-the soil" narratives of Africa's historico-cultural past composed as Canadian novelist and critic Margaret Laurence insists "of real and venerable people, their ancestors, not the figments of missionary and colonialist imagination" (*Long Drums and Canons* 9). In "Colonialist Criticism," Achebe denounces colonialists such as Mr. Green, Winterbottom, George Allen or Joyce Carey and Conrad as being no restorers of Africa's dignity (*Morning Yet On Creation Day*[5] 13).

Eurocentric critics have taken issue with Achebe's recurring parody and mimicry in his novels of the colonizers' discourses. But Gikandi asserts that by retextualizing colonialist ideologies and discourses, Achebe simultaneously appropriates and subverts these discourses and re-presents them as clichs to unenthusiastic African readers who think them prosaic, unoriginal and dead ("Language of the Dancing Mask" 62). Thus, the Eurocentric perspective of racial superiority is diluted, even nullified.

Such a counter-offensive by African writers seeking to validate Africa's past civilization is all the more necessary since the foundational tenet of colonial ideology is that the crop of Christian Western-trained Nigerians / Africans have no sense of "a clear duty," and so are not yet fit to govern themselves, as the words found in John Buchan's 1910 colonialist classic *Prester John* indicate: "That's the difference between white and black, the gift of responsibility" (Achebe, "Colonialist Criticism" 11). Over and over again, Mr. Green hurls these sentiments like bullets at Obi Okonkwo, whom he suspects right from their first encounter to be "bone-lazy" and irresponsible (*No Longer At Ease* 74).

Nevertheless, Obi reluctantly grudgingly recognizes Mr. Green's devotion to duty. This European is at his desk daily, working beyond the call of duty, for a country he obviously dislikes. In Obi Okonkwo's mind, this trait must be part of the ideal of Western democracy, and thus, Mr. Green seems to him like "a man who had some urgent work to do [...] some great and supreme task that must be completed before a final catastrophe intervened" (121). On his part, Mr. Green deplores the attitude of the so-called educated Nigerians whom he finds to be very unpatriotic, ready to milk their country for all they can get. "You know Okonkwo," said Mr. Green,

> I have lived in your country for fifteen years and yet I cannot begin to understand the mentality of the so-called educated Nigerian [...] I think Government is making a terrible mistake in making it so easy for people [...] to have so-called university education. Education for what? To get as much as they can for themselves and their family. Not the least bit interested in the millions of their countrymen who die every day from hunger and disease (132).

But these perks of the civil service, Obi counters, were in the first place put in place long ago for the colonizers' enjoyment – paid leave of absence, car allowance, house allowance, subsidized bank loan, *et cetera*. And why not for the benefit of the educated Nigerians? Understandably, at this stage of the drama, the idealistic Obi comes across as the author's mouthpiece, feeling and verbalizing Achebe's own thoughts that "for a man to go through life swallowing real insults is to lose one's self-respect. Whether we like to face up to it or not Africa has been the most insulted continent in the world" ("The African Writer and the Biafran Cause" 79). And as long as he retains his ideals, Obi Okonkwo, is able to fight back with verve until he comes to compromise all these lofty ideals and morals which form the foundation of his and his generation's ideology of re-inventing an ideal Nigerian nation.

Corruption in Civil Service as Metaphor for Alienation

At the core of Obi's ideals can be found the reality of what the Nigerian / African feels about Western-style government – a system that radically contradicts and even cancels out the indigenous life style that is rooted in communalism by which the people work for their collective well-being while promoting the legitimate, prestige-enhancing ambitions of one another. "The African is corrupt through and through," Mr. Green informs a British Council man. This is a personal and biased opinion on which he bases his comments regarding the frailties of the educated Africans whose only ambition is "to get as much as they can for themselves and their family. Not the least bit interested in the millions of their countrymen who die every day from hunger and disease" (132).

Actually, with urbanization and a centralized, impersonal government, a definite feeling of alienation sets in with the masses who regard themselves as foreigners in the national community. For most Nigerians, at this time, the country is an aggregation of amorphous, unstable cultural bodies which the colonizers had yoked together. Away from the communal terrain, these urban communal settlers congregate for group identity and survival. They save enough money to go back to their native town, build and marry – their success concretized in the physical structures they build in their different villages.

Thus, these "Umuofians" regard themselves as "sojourners" away from home. Unambiguously, they explain to Obi Okonkwo their own space in this urban dispensation: "We are pioneers building up our families and our town and they who build must deny themselves many pleasures" (94). The sacrifices they are willing to make come in the form of observing continence in drink, fiscal discipline, no excessive womanizing, or worse still, no marrying white women for a black man who does this is wasting his time since, the people believe, "her stay with him is like the stay of the moon in the sky. When the time comes she will go" (60). White women they believe will alienate a man from his people. Therefore, in whatever urban, or overseas city these people happen to live, "they inaugurate a local branch of the Umuofia Progressive Union[5]"(5).

These branch associations serve to restore to them a semblance of the cultural oneness - each the brother's keeper - that they have known in their communities and which is their ancestral heritage. Therefore, feeling alienated from government – a Western form of autocracy (in their thinking) whose individualist ethos creates a type of *l'homme isolé* - man isolated from his community - people like the Umuofians have a lack of loyalty or obligation to it.

Seen in this light, precisely what Mr. Green says is ironically true - that different ethnocentric groups devise creative ways of taking all they can from a Government which they consider a national cake – the wealth of the country. Consequently, Obi Okonkwo, the only son of Umuofia to receive European education, embodies all Umuofians' dreams of getting a share of this national cake, for had they not mercilessly taxed themselves to raise the eight hundred pounds needed for his overseas training? And so, they seek to inculcate in the newly-arrived Obi Okonkwo a sense of their oneness with him, reminding him constantly that Western "book" knowledge is good as a *modus vivendi* but insufficient when compared to experience which age and tough living teach. The brash and scoffing Okonkwo who treats with impatience such admonitions will in no time discover the truth of the assertion of the UPU members about the necessity of a disciplined lifestyle: "What the government is paying you is more than enough unless you go into bad ways" (94); or "Lagos is a bad place for a young man. If you follow its sweetness, you will perish."

To prove the point, Obi Okonkwo's kinsman Joseph Okeke who used to go around with several women, appears on Okonkwo's return very sober and disciplined and explains to his educated friend the reason for his new Spartan lifestyle, "Didn't I tell you I was getting married? [...] When you have paid a hundred and thirty pounds bride-price and you are only a second-class clerk, you find you haven't got any more to spare on other women" (47).

It is remarkable that the Umuofia Progressive Union in their assemblies boldly acknowledge their feelings of alienation from their country Nigeria: "We are strangers in this land[6]. If good comes to it may we have a share. But if bad come let it go to the owners of the land who know what gods should be appeased" (7). To drive in the point made earlier, the omniscient narrator explains that in Nigeria, the government is always called "'they.' It was an alien institution and peoples' business was to get as much from it as they could without getting into trouble" (37). And so, when Obi Okonkwo gets caught, he is not considered a criminal, for, says one, "it is all lack of experience." He should not have accepted the money himself: "What others do is to tell you to go and hand it to their houseboy" (7). And so, he is only indicted for being experientially inept in his manner of operation, and for not going for "big game." As some Umuofians opine: "If you want to eat a toad, you should look for a fat and juicy one." Nor do they believe that the white man is himself above corruption for corruption is a universal phenomenon as one Umuofian assures his listeners, "You think white men don't eat bribe? Come to our department. They eat more than black men nowadays" (38).

Part of the UPU angst against Obi Okonkwo is that he fails to help them realize their dream of getting a share of this government – the same kind of dream that Nwodika narrates to Ezeulu and his kinsmen when he bewails Umuaro's lack of presence in White government administration, "Sometimes I feel shame when others ask me where I come from. We [Umuaro] have no share in the market; we have no share in the white man's office. We have no share anywhere" (*Arrow of God* 170).

UPU members wanted Obi to study law in England so that he could, on return, handle all their land cases against their foes, but he preferred to major in English. Disgruntled as the UPU members are with Obi Okonkwo for his anti-communal, individualist ethos, they still stand by him in his disgrace because an only palm fruit does not get lost in the fire, for do other towns not have "four or five or even ten of their sons in Europeans posts in this city. Umuofia has only one" (*No Longer at Ease* 7). That Obi Okonkwo gets caught is attributed to the malicious plotting of their enemies rather than to their kinsman's amoral ethics: "and now our enemies say that even that one is too many for us. But our ancestors will not agree to such a thing" (7). A practical demonstration of their solidarity with any kinsman in trouble is the case of Joshua Udo the messenger who is sacked from his Post Office job and comes to the union for a loan of ten pounds:

> Joshua is now without a job. We have given him ten pounds. But ten pounds does not talk. If you stand a hundred pounds here where I

stand now, it will not talk. That is why we say that he who has people is richer than he who has money. Everyone of us should look out for openings in his department and put in a word for Joshua (91).

Evidently, while the people remain alienated from the government, impersonally referred to as "they," and despite Mr. Green's accusation of a lack of fellow feeling, Umuofians will stand by any kinsman in trouble. Thus, between Mr. Green and UPU members, there exists a vast cultural gulf conditioning their respective *vision de monde*.

No Longer at Ease as a Paradigm of Differing Interpretations of Life

In *No Longer at Ease* can be found multiple, contradictory layers and degrees of un-ease. It can be said that Okonkwo (*Things Fall Apart*) as a lord of the clan is seen to be totally at ease in his culture, and in some respects, epitomizes both its best and its worst, even seeking ways to restore it to its pristine, masculinist, warrior ethos. Even though Okonkwo embodies some of the excesses of his culture, and dies an abominable death by suicide, yet this generation of the Christian era extols the valor and decisiveness of "Ogbuefi Okonkwo who faced the white man single-handed and died in the fight" (*No Longer At Ease* 61). Much as this praise warms the heart of his grandson, yet, Obi Okonkwo is clearly a man defined by, and caught between the two opposing cultural currents which create psychic tension within him.

Okonkwo -- "the Roaring Flame" – calls his son Isaac (Nwoye), "cold, impotent ash", (*Things Fall Apart* 153) believing him to be as degenerate and effeminate as the alien religion that his son comes to embrace. Paradoxically, the tensions are palpable as Isaac comes to be caught between two systems of beliefs, even as he seeks to remain an authentic Christian. For Isaac, Western life and religion produce an ambivalence which in the end ensures his permanent unhappiness. Isaac also is not **at ease** in either the old or the new philosophical dispensations, for while he trains his children to regard food offered by their "pagan" neighbors as "heathen food" (*No Longer at Ease* 67), he would later try unsuccessfully to rationalize his objections to his son's desire to marry Clara Okeke, an Osu, part of the "pagan" tradition of taboos that Christianity has sought without full success to obliterate.

But if Isaac is in spiritual quandary about adherence to certain aspects of traditional beliefs, Achebe the man did not feel confused on finding himself at cultural crossroads. Fifth child of a Catechist and primed full with Christian doctrines, he was regaled with folktales by both his mother and his elder sister. He and his little sister had no qualms about sneaking to their neighbor's house and partaking of "heathen festival meals." He says with candor,

> I never found their rice and stew to have the flavor of idolatry. I was about ten then. If anyone likes to believe that I was torn by spiritual agonies, or stretched on the wrack of my ambivalence, he certainly may suit himself. I do not remember any undue stress. What I remember was a fascination for the ritual and the life on the other arm of the crossroads ("Named for Victoria [...]" 68).

Despite his ambivalence and his firm Christian beliefs, on the issue of the osu system which defines not just self-image but self-identity, Isaac Nwoye Okonkwo will not budge. The narrator compares Isaac Okonkwo's laugh to that of a masked spirit endowed with knowledge beyond human reach, as he tells his son Obi, "You cannot marry the girl" (*No Longer At Ease*, 68). In "Christianity, African Traditional Religion and Colonialism [...]," Reverend Gabriel Ezewudo, presents a definite "insider" summation of the central arguments implicated in cultural-religious issues:

> The point made here is that when matters come down to the existential questions, one's allegiance lies more with the clan, and the prescription of the new religion can be compromised. Now we are confronting fundamental worldviews or basic assumptions of a culture. In terms of the cultural practice raised, the foreign missionaries were in no mood to dialogue with the osu caste system in Igboland. To the present moment, the problem persists in a number of communities despite the overwhelming number of Christians. With regard to social implications, the osu tabu would represent a modern Western equivalent of a parent being told that a son or daughter was heading for a same-sex marriage. The action goes against a hitherto unquestioned institutionalized social norm. (In *Religion and Society* 54-5)

This eloquently captures the limitations that the African worldview imposes on Western Christianity which Obi's newly-acquired European worldview cannot obliterate.

Obi Okonkwo – Idealism and the Language of Social Unease

On his return from his sojourn in England, Obi Okonkwo is brimming over with romantic ideals of governance. It is in England that he discovers his Africanness. He loves his imagined national community, dedicating to it immature, romantic poems. His British education orients him towards shedding his prejudices regarding cultural proscriptions. Back in Lagos, he defines personal authenticity as being natural and acting as behoves a "son-of-the-soil." Regarding himself as part of a second generation of educated Nigerians, he acts out in mannerisms his fantasy of what constitutes a national community by defiantly eating pounded yam and *egusi* soup with his fingers because food tastes better that way – part of his "retour aux sources" routine.

Gikandi points out that what becomes problematic is "Obi's construction of a theory of Nigeria built on a fantasy which he creates merely to counter the colonial fantasies of Africa" ("Writing in the Marginal Space" 86). Gikandi's contention is that prior to Obi's England trip, Nigeria existed in his mind only as an image or sign detached from its reality; but in England, he merely replaces one image with another fantasized one. All these can be read as an effort on Obi's part to recover his space in this new Nigeria while dealing with all the problems imagined or otherwise that can frustrate the achievement of this ideal. And so the problems Achebe presents in the course of the development of his narrative challenge the realism of Obi's romantic, naïve notions of a stable Nigeria built on knowable referents. Upon return, Obi shouts out aloud his desire for an ideal nation with acts designed to disconcert the colonialists as shown, for instance, by his verbally expressed disdain for "**boilèd**" potatoes.

During his welcome ceremony, while everybody is dressed in *agbada* or European suits, Obi, the guest of honor, because of the heat, dresses in shirtsleeves for his first UPU meeting. Thus, begins the process of disenchanting his kinsmen who want him to appear like a proper "been-to." And while the secretary speaks the kind of English that delights the UPU members, with flamboyance and big words – "the kind that filled the mouth like the proverbial dry meat," Obi's English is simple and unimpressive, filled with "is" and "was" (37). Consequently, this exhibition of Obi's brand of European education deepens his peoples' alienation from Government, more especially (in their opinion) "at this momentous epoch in our political evolution" (37). Their apprehension highlights the fact that Nigeria as a political British formulation is still evolving as a political entity in a period of transition from colonial to a postcolonial status.

Contemporaneously, Achebe is also experimenting with forging the proper kind of language suitable for this period of evolutionary transition. The reader discerns the author's attempt to craft this language capable of translating the Nigerian urban unease with all the tensions created by Western-style Government. And Achebe readily admits that his is "a new voice, coming out of Africa and speaking of African experience in a world-wide context" ("The African Writer and the English Language" 61). Because of this experimentation, the language in *No Longer at Ease* is different from, and lacks the dynamic power of *Things Fall Apart,* or *Arrow of God.* The latter novel evinces a language of stable communal entity, firmly grounded in its rituals and cultural symbols which make its heroes seem at ease in their cultural habitat.

But here in Lagos, cultural entities like the Umuofia Progressive Union feel that they are occupying a marginal space that does not fit smoothly into the Western-created entity that answers Nigeria – hence their usual reference to government as **"they."** And so, the author keeps fashioning, with the artistic diligence of an Edogo (*Arrow of God*) carving a mask, the kind of English that will best bring out his message by translating with clarity the peculiar unease of this evolutionary period. As our author again reminds his readers, "a serious writer must look for an animal whose blood can match the power of his offering" ("The African Writer and the English Language" 61).

Equally, empowered by his British education, Obi Okonkwo feels he is a pioneer poised to fashion a new destiny for Nigeria. In his mind, he knows exactly what is wrong with the country, and what solutions to apply. As expressed in a paper he read out to the Nigerian Students' Union in London, Nigerian public service will remain corrupt until an emancipated generation of university-trained graduates replaces the old top Africans like Mr. Omo who have internalized the type of colonial mentality inimical to the shaping of a new Nigerian nation.

His thinking equates enlightenment with idealism and patriotism. He puts his theory into immediate application when he forestalls an act of bribery at the Lagos port. "Dear Old Nigeria" (*No Longer at Ease* 28), he moans at this evidence of the further degeneration of the nation. At Ibadan, he tries but fails to foil another bribery incident as the lorry driver and his conductor try to pay off a policeman. His antics push the driver and passengers to anger and Obi Okonkwo becomes a pariah as the driver berates him, "Why you look the man for face when we want give um two shillings[...] Na him make I no de want carry you book people. Too no na him de worry una. Why you put your nose for matter wey no concern you? Now that policeman go charge me like ten shillings" (50) – which the policeman does; and for the rest of the journey, no one in the lorry speaks to Obi whose frustration mounts as he exclaims condescendingly:

> What an Augean stable! Where does one begin? With the masses? Educate the masses? [...] It would take centuries. A handful of men at the top. Or even one man with vision – an enlightened dictator[...] But what kind of democracy can exist side by side with so much corruption and ignorance (50).

During his job interview, he considers as idiotic the question the only Nigerian on the Commission Board blatantly hurls at him, "Why do you want a job in the civil service? So that you can take bribes?" (46). This man who sleeps through most of the interview and Mr. Omo, the Administrative Assistant to Mr. Green, represent the old brigade at the top at whose feet Okonkwo lays much of the malaise the fledgling nation is suffering.

Critics have described Obi's romance with an ideal nation as an imaginary response to his lack of a community while in England. Obi Okonkwo's high idealism survives until financial pressures dictate first a compromise, then an outright plunge into bribery, corruption and fornication as if to prove true the adage that says, "If you can't beat them, join them." In *The Trouble with Nigeria*, and *Anthills of the Savannah*, Achebe lays the blame for poor governance on the shoulders of the elite class, not on the masses even if the latter group receives appropriate blame.

The process by which Obi Okonkwo falls from his state of grace is one determined by his personal choices, his temper, and lack of maturity. Paid a reasonable sum, as is pointed out to him by members of the UPU, Obi at first thinks his salary more than adequate for his needs. On his first return home to Umuofia, he reassures his father that he will take care of his brother, John's Grammar School fees, plus an allowance of maybe ten pounds, for which his father is grateful. Obi is appointed secretary to the Scholarship Board in charge of screening and recommending potential candidates to be sent overseas. It is a gold mine which if handled judiciously, his kinsmen believe, will yield rich dividends. Irony sets in when Joseph's colleague remarks admiringly, "E go make plenty money there. Every student wan' go England go de see am for house." And Joseph answers with confidence, "E no be like dat. Him na gentleman. No fit take bribe." And the disbelieving colleague rejoins cynically, "Na so" (88-9). When Obi brings out his Morris Oxford car, collects an allowance and rents an apartment, he slides down the slippery slope of the costly lifestyle of an educated civil servant. Suddenly, the money is no longer sufficient for these and other needs which include procuring abortion for Clara which nearly cost her life. His problems mount: car insurance, electricity bill, vehicle license renewal, his brother's school fees, his mother's treatment bills, income tax, leave allowance repayment – and he regrets his rash decision to immediately pay off the UPU loan.

However, Obi's sufferings are self-inflicted. When he jettisons his high ideals and succumbs to bribery and its concomitant evils, his moral degeneracy brings him to the nadir of despair. His mother dies while he is mourning the loss of Clara. But deciding not to go home for the funeral brings further opprobrium on himself, for it is said that a woman who has a son in Government service deserves a better burial. The prediction of Umuofia Progressive Union members has indeed come true about the alienating and corrupting influences of an undisciplined urban lifestyle: "This is what Lagos can do to a young man. He runs after sweet things, dances breast to breast with women and forgets his home and his people?" (81). And the comparison is made with his father Isaac (Nwoye) who also refused to come home for his own father Okonkwo's burial, saying at the time, "those who kill with the machet must die by the matchet" (182). Yet, Obi's self-pitying analysis of the entrapping nature of his high position presents a recognizable terrain that his kinsmen fail to realize, that

> having labored in sweat and tears to enroll their kinsman among the shining elite, they have to keep him there. Having made him a member of an exclusive club whose members greet one another with

"How's the car behaving? did they expect him to turn around and answer, "I'm sorry, but my car is off the road. You see, I couldn't pay my insurance" (113).

In Obi's state of psychic and moral degeneracy, fate steps in and following one tempting slip, his fall from grace is complete. Part of Obi's tragic flaw is his inability to sustain high ideals, and a case in point is the disappointing way he treats Clara.

The Osu Factor

The Umuofians are proud of their historical past. Although the society was egalitarian in structure, among the titled lords of the clan exists a class hierarchy predicated on each person's talent and prowess. Thus the inhabitants of Umuofia exult in their heroic past when the town was the terror of its neighbors "before the white man came and leveled everybody down" (5). The Western equalization of everyone is at the root of the inhabitants' *dis-ease* with urban living, and no where do the free-born find this most destructive as in the osu issue.

Christian religion embodies an equalization process that alienates the people by abrogating everything Umuofia cherishes while approving everything the community abhors. For real-life Igbos and for fictional Umuofia people, the Osu question is an intractable one that has defied a permanent solution. The Osu are a group of people who in the distant past opted to be dedicated to a god, and are therefore considered "not free," and are forced to live in special areas close to the Great Shrine. They would forever be deemed a people set apart - outcasts or Osu - who can neither marry with, nor attend communal assembly with the free-born.

That in Christian socio-religious thought the Osu is considered equal in all ways is part of the people's *dis-ease* with the Christian European body of beliefs now imposed on a conquered people. And this, equalizing principle propagated through Western education is all the more suspect, and alienating when they perceive how individualistic Obi Okonkwo has become, even to the point of flouting traditional taboos in deciding to marry Clara, the girl he meets in England. His friend warns him about the far-reaching and complex consequences of this marriage: "Look at me Obi. What you are going to do concerns not only yourself but your whole family and future

79

generations. If one finger brings oil, it soils the rest. In future, when we are civilized, anybody may marry anybody. But that time has not come. **We of this generation are only pioneers**" (87; my emphasis).

Of course, Joseph's apprehension of the signification of "pioneer" is vastly different from Obi's conception of the word. To Joseph, "pioneer" embodies all of the tensions and stresses of the average Nigerian negotiating the treacherous waters of Western urban living and struggling to fashion both individual and communal identity within the structure. Alienation becomes the leitmotif here when Joseph questions Obi in wonder, "[...] but this is no matter for book. Do you know what an **osu** is?" And remembering that Obi's father Isaac is a Christian catechist, Joseph adds, "But how can you?"

The implication is that his family's Euro-Christian socialization has made Obi a stranger to cultural norms. And still, his kinsman further reminds Obi that in the African traditional system, a favored, successful son owes huge obligations to the larger community, warning him not to be like the child whose first tooth is a decayed one, "What sort of encouragement will your action give to the men and women who collected the [scholarship] money?" This serves to chafe Obi even further. And when the President of the UPU tactfully broaches Obi Okonkwo's intimacy with "a girl of doubtful ancestry" (95), Obi explodes in fury, and drives off ranting and threatening court action, thereby confirming how alienated from his people Western education has made him.

In *Things Fall Apart*, the Osu issue is merely broached as one of the taboos the new religion exploits to undermine African cultural norms, and to discredit the gods of Umuofia. Even the free-born *efulefu* – people considered of no worth who go over to join the new religion – discriminate against the first two Osu Christians. Mr. Kiaga seeks to persuade them that

> [...] before God, there is no slave or free. We are all children of God and we must receive these as our brothers [...] The same God created you and them [traditional Umuofia].

> But they have cast you out like lepers. It is against the will of God who has promised everlasting life to all who believe in his Holy name (*Things Fall Apart* 156-7).

But the component members of the *efulefu* group considered worthless in the enthno-centered Igbo social hierarchy, by receiving validation within colonial religious value system, will emerge as the new leaders of the colonial mentality. But meanwhile, the egalitarian principle of colonial rule is salvatory music to the ears of the Osu, but for traditional Umuofia, it was good riddance to this Christian *efulefu* group. In *No Longer at Ease*, the Osu problem receives more in-depth treatment since it becomes a factor that affects the fortunes of our protagonist Obi Okonkwo. Precisely because Obi Okonkwo is a Christian who regards all people as equal before God, coupled with his British education, he rationalizes some of the cultural taboos as obsolete practices. But when Clara tells him outright, "I can't marry you[...] I am an *osu*" (80-1). His hesitated shout of "nonsense" rather than sounding reassuring serves to underline his terror and emphasize the intractable depth of this system.

His last recourse is his mother with whom he shares a special bond, "If I could convince my mother!" (87), he thinks, but ironically, his modernist perspective will bring him into deep conflict with his Christian parents, especially his mother who tells him blatantly, "If you want to marry this girl, you must wait until I am no more [...] But if you do the thing while I am alive, you will have my blood on your head, because I shall kill myself" (154). In one moment, all Mrs. Hannah Okonkwo's lifelong Christian beliefs crumble before this great threat, and she even threatens Obi with the one anti-Christian act – suicide - "I shall kill myself!" (like Okonkwo). Suicide is a deed viewed as abominable in the eyes of both Umuofia community and the Christian Church. But his mother harbors a clandestine love for Igbo culture. In his school days, she would surreptitiously tell Obi folk tales. Now, refusing to yield to Obi's demand, she never recovers. Readers assume her death shortly after is from apparent heartbreak and disappointment.

Isaac Okonkwo: the Problematics of Being of a Christian within a Traditional Space

In Isaac Okonkwo's life, the strains and tensions generated by the clash of cultures are most visible and he is no longer at ease either in the "occult zone" of Igbo culture or with some of the tenets of Christian doctrines. The similarity to his father becomes ironical. Towards the end, as his secure cultural / spiritual world is collapsing all around him, Okonkwo is able to see with the eyes of a visionary what will eventually occur in both *Things Fall Apart*, *Arrow of God* and the novels of postcolonial Nigeria: "himself and his fathers crowding round their ancestral shrine waiting in vain for worship and sacrifice and finding nothing but ashes of bygone days, and his children the while praying to white man's god" (*Things Fall Apart* 153).

It is a moment filled with revelatory poignancy. Similarly, Isaac, nearing his end, lives out the feelings of mournful helplessness which his own father must have felt at a son's betrayal and abandonment. There were Obi's treacherous ruminations to himself, "What would happen if I stood up and said to him 'Father, I no longer believe in your God?'" (*No Longer at Ease* 65). During family prayer, he read his Bible passage badly, mispronouncing some of the Igbo words.

Initially, Obi really tries to be an ideal son. His first visit home shows Obi that Christianity has not prospered his parents. His father is a bag of bones, and his mother worse looking, and wears "her sadness round his neck like a necklace of stone' (63). Poorly paid as a catechist of the Church Missionary Society, Isaac has a retirement pension of only twenty-five pounds a year. Obi considers this a scandalous reward for nearly thirty years of service. But valiantly, Isaac strives to live by his Christian beliefs. Kolanut must not be "sacrificed to idols" because his is a "Christian house" (*No Longer at Ease* 59). An excellent example of the traditional Community's search for a stable ground within the new Christian dispensation can be seen in Ogbuefi Odogwu's prayer, blessing the kolanut during Obi's welcoming ceremony:

> As a man comes into this world, so will he go out of it. When a titled man dies, his anklets of title are cut so that he will return as he came. The Christians are right when they say that as it was in the beginning it will be in the end (60).

Ogbuefi Odogwu's clever and pragmatic mix of the old and the new gets even Isaac cheering along with the rest. But the community is cognizant of the reality of change. Ogbuefi Odogwu lists the parameters for greatness in bygone days when the codes that defined the heroic were stable. But the old social dispensation has collapsed; and so he emphasizes modernity which exists in new and fluid paradigms of high social status; Odogwu is quick to point to the contrast:

[...] today, greatness has changed its tune. Titles are no longer great, neither are barns or great numbers of wives and children. Greatness is now in the things of the white man. And so we too have changed our tune [recalling Ezeulu's metaphor of the dancing mask who never stays in one place]. We are the first in all the nine villages to send our son to the white man's land (*No Longer at Ease* 62).

Obi must have felt the burden and implications of the expectations being placed on his young shoulder, for he spends the night thinking about his responsibilities since "it was clear that his parents could no longer stand on their own" (69). In his family's and the community's move from traditionalism towards colonial modernity – a world of flux, constantly transforming itself - it is Obi Okonkwo, Western-educated who will be their guidepost, the lighthouse, showing them stable ground. And the bounties of the Christian God, Achebe explains in "Named for Victoria. ." . "were not to be taken lightly---education, paid jobs and many other advantages that nobody in his right mind could underrate" (In *MYOCD* 65). Obi Okonkwo dares not fail.

But he does fail both his people and himself. The multiplicity of the monetary demands on his paycheck (huge in others' eyes but inadequate for his position) tempts him to compromise the ideals he has tried to uphold. His individualism which leads him to reject the UPU offer to postpone repaying the education loan puts him in a tight spot out of which no one can help him, not even the loving, generous Clara.

It can be argued that Obi's emotional troubles propel him into a state of panic and depression, making him vulnerable to temptations. He believed he could elicit the help of his father especially – a man described as being made blind by Christianity, yet known for his generosity evident in his favorite saying that "a man who lived on the banks of the Niger should not wash his hands with spittle" (*No Longer at Ease* 11).

Apparently, Isaac is not too blind not to see the looming tragic implications of his son's contemplated decision. When his son seeks to bully him into submission, Isaac Okonkwo is silent, refusing to fight. Then Obi employs the argument of their being Christians, bringing light to their ancestors who "in their darkness and ignorance called an innocent man *osu*, a thing given to the gods [...] But we have seen the light of the Gospel?" (151).

Designed to persuade his father, it is an argument which his Christian father could himself have understood. But Isaac remains resistant to such Christian arguments, explaining to Obi, "*Osu* is like leprosy in the minds of our people. I beg of you my son not to bring the mark of shame and leprosy unto our family. If you do, your children and your children's children unto the fourth generation will curse your memory [...] Who will marry your daughters? Whose daughters will your sons marry?" (152). The full weight of the irony is here apparent: that Isaac, who as Nwoye, rejected his father's gods to embrace an "alien God," now in his old age, reverses himself in defense of the same cultural taboos such as the *Osu* system - part of a heritage that his own father Okonkwo died defending. The difference between father and son lies in the manner of handling problems. While Okonkwo usually bellows in uncontrollable anger and violence, Isaac speaks softly and with charity but is still as firmly categorical. Patiently narrating the tragic drama of his life with his father Okonkwo, Isaac assures Obi, "I tell you all this so that you may know what it was in those days to become a Christian. I left my father's house, and he placed a curse on me. Because I suffered, I understand Christianity--- more than you will ever do" (157).

The potency of a curse by a heartbroken parent receives impressive cultural validation, for Isaac has lived to see his own son Obi forsake his father's Christian God for values degrading and non-spiritual. It can be argued that Isaac or Obi will be affected by this verbalized ritual authority because they believe in its efficacy (even if subconsciously); conversely, the missionaries in *TFA*'s Umuofia who operate outside the zone of linguistic prohibition of native lore will be unaffected by the malevolence of the "evil forest" because they do not believe in its "sinister forces and powers of darkness" (*TFA* 151).

The tragedy of Obi Okonkwo's life can be traced to a lack of stable, socio-cultural referents. He occupies an intermediate space between traditional life and the modern order. He is in revolt against the colonial order but has loosened his ties with the traditional life. While he romantically cherishes Igbo culture, he wishes to do away with its proscriptions. Caught in the internal tensions generated from two very different cultural currents, Obi "cannot abandon any of the above ties completely," says Gikandi, "nor can he embrace any of them wholly" ("Writing in the marginal space" 96).

Turner further describes Obi's passage in the novel as a rite of passage through "a cultural realm that has few or none of the attributes of the past and the coming state;" and so Obi exists in "liminal entities which are neither here nor there" (*The Ritual Process[...]* 96). Thus, Obi is trapped between the dialectic of difference and identity – unable to erase from his being the colonial heritage he got from his father yet incapable of identifying completely with the belief system of his Igbo ancestors. Like Cervantes' Don Quixote, he vainly tries to shape reality to fit his pre-conceived ideals.

When he fails, he tumbles into an abyss of moral degradation and despair, prompting the tragic, puzzling speculation at his trial from Mr. Justice William Galloway, "I cannot comprehend how a young man of your education and brilliant promise could have done this!" (*No Longer at Ease* 2). Thus, the drama ends on a suspended note, with no expressed resolution or definite conclusion.

Gender Relations - Romance versus Realism

Achebe presents Clara Okeke with some empathy. She represents the new urban African woman, trained overseas just like the man and sufficiently economically independent that she can lend money to the beleaguered Obi Okonkwo. But there it ends. Her character is unrealized and she fades out of the picture abruptly, showing that for the Achebe of the 1950s, the happiness of the woman, or, the realization of her destiny is still peripheral, the focus being entirely on the male and the fate of the emerging nation.

But it is Clara, not Obi who demonstrates a clear understanding of the multiple-headed nature that the *osu* problem poses. If Obi had taken seriously her perception of the realism of the situation, rather than his own romanticization of the issue, the tragedy of their relationship could have been forestalled; and, perhaps, they might have parted in friendship rather than in alienation and hatred.

In England, the issue seems remote, for the traditional mores do not apply so far away. But back in Nigeria, even in Lagos, the issue becomes everybody's problem – Joseph's and as well as the members of UPU. At best, it is duplicitous of Obi to receive Scholarship money from the Union, accept their brotherly support and in a matter that affects the entire community, turn around to claim the privilege of subjective and individualist determinism – a concept that only highlights the alien and destructive nature of colonial intrusion into their communal living. As is said, when one finger brings oil, it soils the rest. But Obi is now completely lost to his people, lacking all respect: "Don't you dare interfere in my affairs again!" he bellows at the President of the Umuofia Progressive Union. Thus, he rejects any claims they may have on him. But **it is their business**, because he is their son – their "only palm fruit;" **they do have a claim over him**, for when his mother dies, they come to condole with him, despite their differences. Also when he goes on trial for corruption, they hire a lawyer to defend him.

It has been argued that by stubbornly insisting on marrying Clara – the same kind of stubbornness he showed as a boy in writing a letter of support to the beleaguered Hitler -- Obi is like a man that challenges his *chi* to a fight. Like his father, Isaac, he flouts conventional mores, but he lacks the integrity of the former. But considered in a different way, his love affair with Clara Okeke represents the only possibility of real happiness he experiences in colonial Nigeria.

Articulate, intelligent, kind and professional, Clara is in fact too good for him, serving as friend and counselor, with the potential to become an ideal wife; she cooks for him and when he is hard-pressed for money, lends him fifty pounds which in his pride, he carelessly leaves in the glove compartment of his car from where young thieves steal it. But the *osu* factor complicates matters for both. Refusing to accept her breaking off the engagement, he leads her on to expect he will take a firmer stand and really fight for her. But at the end, Obi is unable to defy the tears and terror of his mother, nor escape feeling pity for his father. Because of Obi's indecisiveness, he duplicitously involves Clara in a painful ordeal of abortion in which she nearly loses her life.

With Clara out of his life, Obi's moral compass becomes clouded, and he compromises his integrity. When his high ideals are at last put to the test, he fails. However, Clara has already pointed out to him, the compromised nature of his moral judgment when he walks out on Mr. Mark for trying to bribe him into granting an overseas scholarship to his sister. But when the sister Elsie Mark comes to his home unannounced, willing to do anything, he not only entertains her but even gives her a ride to Tinubu Square. Although Clara's presence precludes his going to bed with Miss Mark, she nevertheless points out to him his duplicity and hypocrisy, reminding him that "offering money is not as bad as offering one's body" (*No Longer at Ease* 108). But with Clara out of his life and a convergence of financial emergencies, he succumbs to receiving bribes – the very antithesis of his ideals. Consequently, he fails to disprove Mr. Green's assertion that "the African is corrupt through and through."

Which Way Nigeria?

Nigeria of the 1950s was a problem for which thinkers like Achebe sought to provide a solution using the medium of creative writing as seen in *No Longer at Ease*. In a state of transition from traditionalism through the modernity of colonialism to an independent national identity, the reference poles for the national community were not yet visible. The novels merely presented the problems but not the solutions.

Achebe was treading an uncharted terrain in writing experimentally just as political events were evolving contemporaneously. People were together on these choppy waters. Obi Okonkwo's romantic ideals thus embody the collective desires and dreams for a new Nigeria of his parents, Umuofians, and the colonial government. That Obi fails to realize both his quixotic dreams and their mundane expectations indicates that the writer himself found no adequate solutions for the multiplicity of problems enunciated in the narrative. Like the still evolving African literature itself, the novel becomes a continuum of *Romanesque* reality in which "*mensonge romantique* – romantic lie," in the words of René Girard (whose classic book questions the reality of our desires) merges with "*vérité Romanesque* – romantic truth."

Neither have these socio-political problems disappeared presently. Achebe would further explore in later narratives this preoccupation with the issue of proper governance in the body politic of a country under relentless pressures by colonial intrusion. It is an ongoing task, keeping in mind his observation in the epigraph at the beginning of this chapter: "It is clear to me that an African creative writer who tries to avoid the big social and political issues of contemporary Africa will end up being completely irrelevant (*Morning Yet On Creation Day* 78).

Notes

¹ All citations are from this edition.

² In *Arrow of God,* Winterbottom gave to his new assistant Tony Clarke a copy of *The Pacification of the Primitive Tribes of the Lower Niger* by George Allen, who readers presume was then the District Commissioner planning the outline of his work at the end of *Things Fall Apart.* This is one of the many references that connect *Things Fall Apart* to *Arrow of God* and also to *No Longer at Ease.*

³ In Ezenwa-Ohaeto's *Chinua Achebe,* the author explains the difficulty of moving on with the planned trilogy, "I didn't find enough for Nwoye, so I put it aside and did the third story, Obi. That middle story is still waiting to be written." But the real reason can be found in a *Morning Yet On Creation Day essay,* "Named for Victoria, Queen of England" in which Achebe mentions a perplexity in the moving relationship between his maternal great-grandfather and his own father: "there was something I have not been able to fathom. That was why the middle story in the Okonkwo trilogy as I originally projected it never got written. I had suddenly become aware that in my gallery of ancestral heroes there is an empty place from which an unknown personage seems to have departed" (67). If he could have resolved the riddle of the missing ancestral personage, perhaps Nwoye's persona might have come alive to him.

⁴ *Morning Yet On Creation Day* will hereinafter be known as *MYOCD.*

⁵ The Umuofia Progressive Union will hereinafter be called UPU.

⁶ In an interview with this author, Achebe himself acknowledges his homesickness while in New York, reminding me that even in Nigeria, any child born away from homeland, even in Lagos Nigeria, is regarded as "Nwaofia" – child of the forest (See my 1996 Telephone Interview).

Works Cited

Achebe, Chinua. *No Longer at Ease.* Revised edition. New York: Double Day, 1994.

--- *Arrow of God.* Revised edition. New York: Random House, 1974.

--- *Things Fall Apart*. Revised edition. New York: Doubleday, 1994.

--- *Anthills of the Savannah*. Nigeria: Heinemann, 1988.

--- "The African Writer and the English Language." In *Morning Yet On Creation Day*. London: Heinemann, 1975. 55-62.

--- "The African Writer and the Biafran Cause." In *Morning Yet On Creation Day*. London: Heinemann, 1975. 78-84.

--- "Named for Victoria, Queen of England." *In Morning Yet On Creation Day*. London: Heinemann, 1975. 65-70.

--- "The Novelist as a Teacher." *In Morning Yet On Creation Day*. London: Heinemann, 1975. 42-45.

--- *The Trouble With Nigeria*. Enugu: Fourth Dimension Publishers, 1983.

Ezenwa-Ohaeto. *Chinua Achebe: A Biography*. Indiana University Press, 1997.

Ezewudo, Gabriel. "Christianity, African Traditional Religion and Colonialism: Were Africans pawns or players in the Cultural Encounter?" In *Religion and Society*. Ed. Rose Ure Mezu. MD: Black Academy Press, 1998. 43-61.

Gikandi, Simon. "Writing in the Marginal Space." In *Reading Chinua Achebe: Language and Ideology in Fiction*. London: Heinemann, 1991. 78-100.

Girard, René. *Mensonge romantique, Vérité romanesque*. Paris, France: Edition Gallimard, 1961. (Translated into English *as Deceit, Desire and the Novel*).

Laurence, Margaret. *Long Drums and Canons*. London: Macmillan, 1968.

Turner, Victor W. *The Ritual Process: Structure and Anti-Structure*. Chicago: Aldine, 1969.

4

A Man of the People[1]: The Moral Approach

The point that I want to make is that the creative writer in Independent Nigeria found himself with a new, terrifying problem in his hands. He found that the independence his country was supposed to have won was totally without content. The old white master was still in power. He had got himself a bunch of black stooges to do his dirty work for a commission. ("The African Writer [...] " In Morning Yet on Creation Day - MYOCD[2] - 82)

"The Native intellectual [...] must go on until he has found the seething pot out of which the Learning of the future must emerge." (Fanon, "On National Culture." In The Wretched of the Earth).

The Country was ripe and impatient to shed in violent exercise the lazy folds of flabby skin and fat it had put on the greedy years of indolence. The scandals that were daily exposed in the newspapers – far from causing general depression in the country – produced a feeling akin to festivity (AMOP 113).

O f the many perspectives through which a work of art can be critically examined, the moral approach provides a most suitable platform on which to stand and view the value of both structure and content – meanings – the work has to offer. In using this approach, attention will be paid not to the Juvenalian form of satire that embodies extreme bitterness borne out of despair but rather to the Horatian brand of satire with its maxim as *"aut prodessee aut delectare" - dulce et utile -* "teach and delight" which proclaims that the aim of literature is to instruct even while it entertains, that a work is important not just in its way (form) of saying things but in what it says (content). This approach must be clarified, especially when critics such as Umelo Ojinmah insist on "Achebe's despair about the political mess" with regard to *A Man of the People* (*Chinua Achebe: New Perspectives* 60).

In his many writings, Achebe has never evinced despair with Nigeria / Africa's situation. Rather, in the manner of Horace and Chaucer, he earnestly but laughingly points out issues that create a state of anomy. The reader indeed laughs because of Achebe's narrative tropes, his many verbal twists and dexterous use of proverbs, yet the point is always well-taken. Rather, Achebe himself labels as "foreign, unusable, . . imported from Eastern European countries" the aura of "cosmic sorrow and despair" redolent of Ayi Kwei Armah's *The Beauyful Ones Are Not Yet Born*." African art, he insists, can not afford to go into a phase of despair; may be European art can, but not "ours. The worst we can afford at present is disappointment" (Africa and her writers." In *MYOCD* 24-5).

Anyone really familiar with the author's ideas knows that Achebe shies away from any absolutism. With his characteristic tolerance, and a sort of pragmatism (a trait he attributes to traditional Igbo society), his philosophical ideas always allows room for improvement. Talking to Robert Serumaga, he attributes Africa's post-independence mess to growing pains, "every society has to grow up, every society has to learn its lessons, so I don't despair" (*African Writers Talking* 13).

Evidently, Achebe will naturally subscribe to the Horatian brand of satire which maintains that literature has functions and dysfunctions (and the latter must be corrected gently with humor but not with despair), for while good literature elevates character by holding up the right ideals, bad literature debases human beings whom God has endowed with a reasoning process to enable them to distinguish good from evil. Therefore, when T.S.Eliot issued his dictum that the greatness of literature cannot be determined solely by literary standards, although we must remember that whether it is literature or not can be determined only be literary standards (Religion and Literature, 43), he meant that readers must vigorously and tirelessly criticize works of literature, especially, those which aim at being a mimesis of human life.

Consequently, I believe with T. S. Eliot that what we read affects us whether we want it to or not since "the author of a work of imagination is trying to affect us wholly as human beings, whether he knows it or not; and we are affected by it, as human beings, whether we intend to be or not" (48). I also agree with him that literature should have explicit ethical and theological standards (43). Obviously, by insisting that African art has always been used in the service of humanity, Chinua Achebe braves the charge of didacticism by proving, especially, with his colonial and post-colonial works that he shares this same belief that "literature as a criticism of life" ("applied art" and all) should ultimately have a higher ideal since what we read affects our moral as well as literary existence.

In philosophical discourses on the great moral questions of good versus evil, Karol Wotjyla (known later as Pope John Paul II) insists, as Fanon does in the second opening epigraph above, that we should probe deeply enough into things-as-they-are to help us grasp the way we *ought* to act. And this seems to be the declared goal of Chinua Achebe in *A Man of the People* as he revisits and deconstructs the foundations of the nation's moral life.

The one strong weakness of the novel is that he undertakes no moral reconstructive work. But while Achebe fails to reconstruct and formulate any norms of national leadership, he yet escapes the entrapment and the prison of solipsism – *thinking about thinking about thinking*. Quite in the manner of the great German thinker Max Scheler, Achebe tries to ground the moral problems in the novel in an analysis of the realities of everyday moral choosing, rather than in any abstract fashion. From a philosophical perspective, the moral act is a real act with real consequences because ideas have consequences, for good and for evil. And so, moral choices not only shape the life of an individual, but that of any nation as well since there is an obvious link between democracy and public morality. Consequently, a work of imagination should be scrutinized with set ethical standards in mind. In the light of the foregoing, this chapter uses the moral approach to critically examine Achebe's novel, *A Man of the People*. In considering this book, it will be pertinent to ask the following questions: "What does the writer aim at? How does he make his objectives clear? Does he succeed? Are the aims and results intrinsically worthwhile?" The attempt to answer these questions will constitute the body of this chapter.

In both *Things Fall Apart* and *Arrow of* God, readers witness the devalorization of the central symbols of the traditional communities by the Christian Church (unmasking of the masquerade, demythification of the evil forest, new yam, *ikenga*, python), leading to general unease and instability of the Africans' world. No solutions were provided to fill the resultant cultural lacuna. In *No Longer at Ease*, it has been said that that Achebe's novelistic art was evolving contemporaneously with the general societal life, precisely determined at every moment and at every level.

In *Arrow of God*, Achebe allows readers to feel the frustration and exasperation of Captain Winterbottom as he deals with a people emerging from a disintegrating cultural space into a new and *"unowned"* colonial landscape, requiring a new mode of living and to which the people has no loyalty. Again, in *No Longer at Ease* -- Achebe's first fictional venture away from the Igbo cultural space - Obi Okonkwo as emblematic of the first generation of university-trained Nigerians starts off with fresh ideals but ends up crushed by a mix of bad judgment, unreasonable expectations from his people, and the inescapable socio-cultural tensions generated by the clash of new and old systems. These generate conflict and tension in the social fabric as they collide with the ongoing attempt to formulate a model of proper governance in the body politic. And as we have seen from his many essays that Chinua Achebe believes that to remain relevant, the African creative writer can hardly avoid the big social and political issues of contemporary Africa.

He had approached these from the sidelines in earlier narratives, but now in *A Man of the People*, the story comes to have mimetic and polysemous functions for Achebe dives straight up to the top and into the heart of Government to find out why the nation's hard-earned independence has within seven years become a sham. An interpretive approach should ground Achebe's philosophical thinking on such basic, hardy, perennial questions as: what is a human being? What is human nature, and how are we to understand its dynamics? What, if anything, is the point and goal of human life? Understanding these properly would reveal the truth about the human person, which is a hunger for true freedom – personal and national aspiration to true freedom and Civil Rights. Again, Achebe insists that "most of what needs to be done can best be tackled by ourselves, the owners" ("Colonialist Criticism" in *Morning Yet On Creation Day*[2] 18). Henceforth, he makes it difficult for any African writer to ignore the consequences of postcolonial misrule by indigenous African leaders.

With *A Man of the People* (published in 1966) Achebe, along with other Nigerians, is thrown into the maelstrom of a postcolonial Nigeria struggling for life in the murky waters unleashed by the nation's 1960 independence. The drama is a satiric, political tragi-comedy, describing the disintegration of a civil order riddled with abuses, of a government that has abdicated its responsibilities to the people in preference to personal gains, and of a citizenry who, when not actively collaborating with the people in power to defraud their very nation, show incredible indifference and resignation -- their whole philosophy of life being marked by stark cynical materialism.

Achebe accepts that *A Man of the People* is "a rather serious indictment [...] of post-independence Africa" (*African Writers Talking* 13). In the novel, he offers readers an *unidealized* protagonist, Odili Samalu who becomes our compass as we navigate this treacherous, corrupt yet sometimes dazzlingly flamboyant politico-social terrain; simultaneously, the protagonist is undergoing a process of individuation even as the cataclysmic events of the novel unfold.

Despite Odili's liabilities as protagonist-narrator, he remains an indispensable quarry for insights into the workings of Government. Had he not been close to Chief Nanga, he would, like us, not have any "hard kernel of fact" with which to indict the government in power; but by "sitting at Chief Nanga's feet," he receives enlightenment, for as Odili explains: "many things began to crystallize out of the mist— some of the emergent forms were not nearly as ugly as I had suspected but many seemed much worse [...] . I was too fascinated by the almost ritual lifting of the clouds" (*A Man of the People* 45).

At the end, Odili achieves some moral clarity which he likens symbolically to an "unveiling of the white dome of Kilmanjaro at sunset" (45)-- albeit with a tainted idealism. At the end also, the reader is thoroughly educated without any illusions as to why and how "the rain came to beat us." The moral philosophy of the writer which seeks Fanon's "seething pod out of which the learning of the future must emerge," although hazy in certain aspects, finally emerges in its total form with clarity and a great deal of prophetic insights as to future events. Consequently, this chapter posits that in *A Man of the people*, corruption exists in many forms - moral, socio-economic and political, and is to be found rampant on three levels: (1) **governmental**, (2) **individual** (though more often the two overlap and merge) and (3)

societal, and will be considered accordingly in my search for the ethical standards which Achebe has demonstrated in the book.

Corruption in Government – Unleashed Chaos: A Threat to Human Freedom

As often stated in previous chapters, because traditional Igbo/Africans have always had their cultural–religious life structured along moral lines, they could operate daily within the society's stable and "**known**" moral-values code; but the postcolonial, socio-political "new order" is not "known" and demands no specified allegiances, nor are there specific punitive measures for moral lapses which have received acceptance by consensus of members in the socio-juridical hierarchy. Therefore, this new playing field becomes a free-for-all in which the prevailing ideology is one of "survival–of–the-fittest."

The new generation of Western-trained indigenes like Obi Okonkwo of *No Longer at Ease* show their confused ideological state and end up just like him. Then emerges another type – of the class of Mr. Nanga - who go into government service and politics with a huge libidinous proclivity and for unscrupulous reasons: money, prestige, glamour and lust for power. Once in government, corruption becomes endemic and is there to stay. As Achebe explains to Serumaga, the postcolonial new-order was one in which "the worst elements of the old are retained and some of the worst of the new are added on to them" (*African Writers on African Writing* 8); or, in other words, the postcolonial order exacerbated the worst of the colonial inheritance, creating an artificial crust of "*they*." Still to the ordinary people, it represented the strangeness of the "*other*."

Readers of Achebe's works met this type in *Arrow of God* in the person of James Ikedi, one of the first indigenes to receive missionary education whom Winterbottom considers sufficiently intelligent to be appointed Warrant Chief for Okperi. But Ikedi abuses his office, cleverly colluding with other native functionaries to receive proceeds from illegal taxation, appropriating any woman he fancies without paying bride-price. Recalled from suspension, Ikedi organizes an even greater scheme of "mass extortion," cleverly covering his tracks. In the end, he styles himself "an obi or king, so that he was now called His Highness Ikedi the First, Obi of Okperi (*Arrow of God* 57-9). Thus, the clever and flamboyant Ikedi becomes an early prototype of the breed of corrupt politicians such as Chief Nanga that emerged all over post-independent Africa.

With regard to these creations of the new postcolonial order, Ojinmah makes a valid point: that since most of those who worked with the colonial masters and missionaries were mostly *efulefu* – worthless, largely untitled people and outcasts – they could oppress and exploit the people without compunction, having no regard for the culture of the society that had previously looked upon them with contempt. And the communities by thinking that they have no viable recourse to redress the absolutism of the power wielded over them, become indifferent, apathetic, or collude with their defrauders until, in the words of the Ananta villagers who indict their exploiter Josiah's last act, the defrauders "take enough for the owner to see."

And so, in *A Man of the People*, the government is introduced to the reader by what I will refer to as the "Case of the Minted Fifteen Million Pounds." Following an economic crisis occasioned by a slump in the international coffee market, Dr. Makinde, the minister of Finance - a first-rate economist with a Ph.D., advises a cut-back in the money paid coffee planters. The government, determined to cling to power at all costs, orders the National Bank to print fifteen million pounds.

Thus is introduced a government that lacks economic and political morality; that blatantly lies to its people. All the ministers who oppose this unethical proposal are fired, and thoroughly disgraced as "traitors" collaborating with "foreign saboteurs to destroy the new nation" (*A Man of the People* 4); some are beaten up, or killed by hired thugs. The press (portrayed as very easily bought) is used to besmirch the integrity of the opponents, while the government falls back on the age-old but safe slogan of preservation of the culture.

The anti-intellectual government damns "the decadent stooges versed in text book economics[...] with their expensive university education which only alienates an African from his rich and ancient culture and puts him above his people" (*AMOP* 4). Here, one sees in action reverse morality, or, what Edmund Fuller terms counter-Puritanism whereby criminals and defrauders of the Nation become heroes, "defenders" of a "rich and ancient culture," and instead of being punished, they the miscreants denigrate, besmirch and victimize the non-criminal and honest men. Their brand of totalitarian politics strip men and women of the power of their choice, of responsibility and thus of their humanity. Certainly, the author uses the narrator to engage into the fray on the side of educated Africans even with their "Oxford, Cambridge or Harvard degrees."

Achebe's stance accords with what Odili believes is "the same general anti-intellectual feeling in the country" by which Nanga could in 1948 admit to "a certain secret yearning for higher education [while] in 1964 he was valiantly proving that a man like him was better without it" (*AMOP* 29) – a stance that will receive more in-depth exploration in *Anthills of the Savannah*. Yet, Nanga with characteristic astute charm would turn round, beaming at an admirer who acclaims him as "owner of book." Because the reign of mediocrity is upon us, the author's intention as the moral guide is manifestly clear. If by the choices we make, there is no tether, no restraint on what we do, then raw force takes over our world / nation; and with sufficient force, irrationalism is let loose. Then, freedom or the truth of the human person -- and by extension, of the nation -- becomes a function of power, and not an expression of things as they *ought* to be.

Even narrator Odili can *choose* to be duplicitous when it suits him. He shows this duplicity when he attends a book signing with Chief Nanga. There, Odili greets Jallio, author of *The Song of the Black Bird* who clearly does not remember him from college, and Odili is peeved. And so, while Chief Nanga is castigating the writer for his "improper" non-conformist dressing, Odili is pleased "to see Jallio deflated" (*AMOP* 70), even though he empathizes with him as a man of ideas. For, Odili, who has novelistic ambitions, belongs like Jallio to the class now being pilloried -- "the Western-educated and snobbish intellectuals who will not hesitate to sell their mothers for a mess of pottage" (6).

Having dethroned its intellectual leadership, the government then proceeds to fill the vacant posts with men who shamelessly organize a thorough milking of the treasury, practicing corruption in all its forms: bribery, graft, nepotism, et cetera. It is in such an atmosphere of xenophobia and media hysteria that men like Micah Nanga, a former teacher, becomes Chief the Honorable M.A.Nanga, MP (*Member of Parliament*). In fact, during the crisis, he led the pack of back-bench hounds shouting, "They deserved to be hanged" (5).

The narrator's linguistic discourse is replete with apt metaphors: Nanga is described with the use of an extended metaphor of bestialization: he "had yapped and snarled for the meaty prize" (7). The beleaguered Finance Minister is described as "tall, calm, sorrowful and superior" (*AMOP* 6) in contrast with the "most unedifying spectacle" of the less uneducated politicians who like over-starved beasts would gore the entrails of the nation to enrich themselves. In doing so, they would preserve their position by any means necessary – thuggery, blackmail, intimidation and murder. Since the colonial structure had displaced, with no viable replacement, the traditional mores of leadership by consensus with its code of mutual coexistence and the paramount nature of the wellbeing of the community over individual advancement, Chief Nanga epitomizes all that traditional society abhors – selfishness, outsized ambition, graft and corruption.

One could hear Ezeani, the priest of Ani berating Okonkwo who beats Ojiugo during the Week of Peace for jeopardizing the well-being of the entire Umuofia (*Things Fall Apart*). One could imagine Chief Nwaka of Umunneora, Ezeulu's arch enemy, strutting up and down in the village Assembly hall verbally decimating Ezeulu as he imputes kingly ambitions to the Chief Priest's actions. Making light of Ezeulu's priestly wisdom, Nwaka challenges the exclusivity of his wisdom by saying: "'Wisdom is like a goatskin bag; every man carries his own. Knowledge of the land is also like that and "all the six villages stood behind Nwaka" (*Arrow of God* 16-17). Even though Umuaro loses the war with Okperi, Nwaka carries the day, for as that narrator insists, "no man however great was greater than his people; no one ever won judgment against his clan" (*Arrow of God* 230).

But in *A Man of the People,* there exist no such urban checks and balances to curb politicians' excesses; rather the people tamely go along, until politicians come to see their posts as their birthright, and their fellow citizens as objects bereft of natural rights and freedoms, economic slaves to be manipulated. In "Goodness and Evil," a lecture series (1957–1959) by Karol Wotjyla at Jagiellonian University, the then Bishop and future Pope John Paul II examines the way that moral norms grow in human beings through moral actions; his ideas attempt to introduce an objective moral standard into conversation with the experience of "personal" happiness and societal peace which derive and grow from acting well. Wojytla's "personalist norm" argues that the moral imperative to avoid "using" (read – exploiting) others is the ethical basis of real freedom, because it allows us to interact with others without reducing them to objects by manipulating them (Weigel, *Witness to Hope* 139-41). These ideas, the Nangas and Kokos understand so well that they find ways to subvert their usefulness to the citizenry.

Two sets of morality separate these politicians from the masses. The practice of double standards is shown in the "Case of the Poisoned Coffee via OHMS" dramatized in the house of Chief the Hon. Simon Koko, Minister for Overseas Training. The Government had mounted a full-scale campaign to promote the consumption of locally made products. True patriots were encouraged to buy. This practice would lead to the economic emancipation of the country.

When the imported Nescafe brand of coffee normally prepared for Hon. Simon Koko, Minister for Overseas Training runs out, unable to lay hands immediately on another tin, the cook prepares the OHMS alias "Our Home Made Stuff" brand for the Minister. Then follows the comic scene where because of the unusual taste of the local coffee, the Minister dramatically jumps out of his seat shouting, "They have killed me. They have poisoned my coffee" (37-8).

The comic element resides in the swift action-response and words of the cook who grabbing the coffee cup, drinks every drop querying with surprise, "Why I go kill my master. Abi my head no correct?" (39). Thus, Achebe uses irony to drive home the fact that there are two standards - one leading to the "economic emancipation" of the governed, the other applicable to the leaders who rather relish their economic kleptocracy. *"Ridentem dicere verum* -- speak the truth laughing,*"* Achebe humorously employs this dictum to show up the moral bankruptcy of the politicians in Government. And the fact that Odili does accompany Chief Nanga to Minister Koko's house for Nanga to arrange for a post-graduate scholarship for Odili, removes some moral sheen from the objectivity of the narrator's later denunciation of political corruption.

If a free press represents the conscience of any nation, then the unnamed nation depicted in *A Man of the People* is in trouble for its press is the private property of these unscrupulous politicians. Bribery has become so systemic and blatant that Chief Nanga, even as Odili looks on, gives "a dash" of five pounds to a greasy looking editor who has some dirt on him because "if I don't give him something now, tomorrow he will go and write rubbish about me" (47). To the Minister of Public Construction, Chief Nanga says reassuringly, "Don't worry about the Press, I will make sure they don't publish it" (*AMOP* 48). When Odili decides to run for Chief Nanga's constituency seat, the national radio system blanks him out, not saying "a single word about the existence of our new party even though we had kept them fully informed of our activities" (147).

Punitive retribution swiftly follows. Over the radio, the news comes that his father, Mr. Hezekiah Samalu has been removed from his position as Chairman of the Urua branch of the P.O.P. To put a tether on such ablatant corruption, other political parties such as the Common People's Convention (C.P.C) are started. Odili joins Max's C.P.C., impressed with Max's prophecy of a looming "blow-up. But because C.P.C. is not a viable alternative, nor does it provide any meaningful alternate direction, natives like Couple call it "the third and youngest" of the vultures (*AMOP* 140).

The narrative makes it clear that these politicians brook no opposition, seeking to retain their parliamentary and ministerial seats by the prestige of being returned "unopposed." Thus, Chief Koko bribes Max to step down with an offer of one thousand pounds which Max accepts, but he does not keep his promise. Odili, surprised at this double dealing, remonstrates with Max about his lack of moral ideals – a fact that makes their party look indeed like a third vulture. But Max, defending his action, resorts to sophistry: "the paper I signed has no legal force whatsoever and we needed the money." With left-over idealism, Odili replies, "It had a moral force. I thought we wanted our fight to be clean." Prophetically, he tells Max, "You had better look out. They will be even more vicious from now on and people will say they have cause" (142). And Odili will be proved right by later events.

Orchestrated by the opposition Progressive Alliance Party (P.A.P), there are revelations and scandals galore -- of Government's corrupt practices: collaboration between the Minister of Foreign Trade and the foreign firm of British Amalgamated to sabotage the economy, kickbacks in the form of luxury houses built for Ministers such as Chief Nanga and held in the name of his wife and other relatives. The Cabinet is split and members call for one another's resignation. Trade and Civil Service Unions organize strikes; the country is plunged into chaos, and the government is forced to not only resign but to schedule another election. The stage is thus set for the final reckoning. In the matter of ministers resigning out of a sense of integrity, Max's words to Odili about African politicians reveal stark realism: African political culprits do not resign. "We must face certain facts," says Max: "You take a man like Nanga on a salary of four thousand plus all the – you know. You know what his salary was as an elementary school teacher? Perhaps no more than eight pounds a month. Now do you expect a man like that to resign on a matter of principle?"

These erstwhile comfortable positions created by colonial administrators for themselves have proved, for the half-educated, corrupt breed of native leaders, too much of a comfortable bait for them to resist. Therefore, Nanga, in turn seeking to be returned unopposed, goes to Odili's home town of Urua and offers him two hundred and fifty pounds – an offer Odili at last, refuses with added insult.

Thus, Odili shows some moral fiber, believing also that Max's lack of it "jeopardizes our moral position, our ability to inspire that kind of terror which I had seen in Nanga's eyes despite all his grandiloquent bluff, and "which in the end was our society's only hope of salvation" (144). Odili's rejection and launching of the Ananta branch of the C.P.C. bring reprisals: his father's tax is re- assessed for an alleged income of five hundred pounds "derived from business[...] . Then, at the weekend, seven Public Works lorries arrived at the village and began to cart away the pipes they had deposited several months earlier for our projected Rural Water Scheme" (149). Reminiscently, readers note that Chief Nanga's many confessions about the rigors and worthlessness of his job are not meant to be taking seriously:

> "I no de keep anini for myself, na so so troway. If some person come to you and say 'I wan' make you Minister' make you run like blazes comot. Na true word I tell you. To God who made me. Minister de sweet for eye but too much katakata de for inside. Believe me sincerely" (16).

Obviously, he is not to be believed "sincerely," for when Odili issues the challenge, asking him to vacate his seat, Nanga resorts to "katakata" and brings down on Odili the full weight of his official post. And so, through blackmail, intimidation, bribery and harassment, "they," the corrupt politicians seek to perpetuate themselves in total power which their government positions assure them.

Led by a Government totally bereft of ideals or moral force, the country, says Achebe reprising the words of the third epigraph of this chapter, "was ripe and impatient to shed in violent exercise, the lazy folds of flabby skin and fat it had put on in the greedy years of indolence" (113). The ensuing election is singularly marked by vicious thuggery, buying off of opponents by Ministers bent on being returned unopposed. Party hoodlums such as Chief Nanga's Youth Vanguard alias **Nangavanga** mercilessly beat up their opponents. And when Odili Samalu crashes Chief Nanga's inaugural campaign celebration, Josiah tips off the chief who is on the podium. Between Nanga and his thugs, Odili is physically assaulted, and has his skull cracked. For days, he hovers between life and death.

Incarcerated in the hospital by partisan policemen, he remains in a sick haze until the election is completed with its attendant rigging of ballot boxes, and other malpractices. For his part, Max goes to verify the truth of election rigging by Chief Koko's wife whose Women's wing members are said to be stuffing ballot papers in their brassieres. But, the said investigation results in Max being run over by one of Chief Koko's jeeps. Eunice, Max's fiancé, reportedly takes out a pistol from her revolver and pumps two bullets into Chief Koko's chest. At this, fighting breaks out, leading to social mayhem.

Undaunted, the government nominates Chief Koko's widow senator, and eventually she is made Minister for Women's Affairs, while Chief Nanga is reappointed into the Cabinet. But violence begets violence, goes the adage and in the natural order of things, what observes no moral restraints must of necessity end in self-annihilation. Though the government wins the election by fraud, the forces of disorder and chaos have been unleashed. Having tasted power and blood, and spurred on by greed and unemployment, the people go on the rampage and ruin their masters. As the narrator relates it, "what happened was simply that unruly mobs and private armies having tasted blood and power during the election had got out of hand and ruined their masters and employers" (*AMOP* 162). Such total lawlessness ushers in the first military intervention, and the army takes over the reins of power.

For Odili, the ambition to write in the novelistic genre has to do with the need to represent issues and events in the story so as to recast himself in a better light, to rewrite Self for greater apprehension. But

Achebe, as author sees with clarity and no ambiguity that every nation must have ethical standards. Extending the metaphor of "the rain," he expounds on the greed, the lust for absolute power and the intolerance of any opposition that had brought African politicians and their nations to a moral impasse:

> A man who has just come from the rain and dried his body and put on dry clothes is more reluctant to go out again than another who has been indoors all the time. The trouble with our nation was that none of us had been indoors long enough to be able to say, 'To hell with it.' We had all been in the rain together until yesterday. Then a handful of us – the smart and the lucky and hardly ever the best – had scrambled for the shelters our former rulers left, and taken it over and barricaded themselves in it. And from within they sought to persuade the rest through loudspeakers, that the first phase of the struggle had been won and that the next phase – the extension of our house – was even more important and called for new and original tactics; it required that all argument should cease and the whole people speak with one voice and that anymore dissent and argument outside the door of the shelter would subvert and bring down the house *(AMOP* 42).

In the thinking of these political *arrivistes*, postcolonial government is nether an off-shoot nor an extension of traditional society with its known set of ethical standards. Therefore, modern government becomes synonymous with absolutism - a concept that traditional society which places the communal interests first actually abhors. Achebe, believing that the independence of African countries was without content, regards corrupt politicians as "a bunch of black stooges" working for the "old white master [who] was still in power" (*MYOCD* 82). Speaking to Serumaga, Achebe confirms the flagrant abuse of the democratic process:

> If you take an example of Nigeria, which is the place I know best, things had got to such a point politically that there was no other answer—no way you could resolve this impasse politically. The political machine had been so abused that which ever way you pressed it, it produced the same results; and therefore, you wanted another force, another force just had to come in. (*African Writers Talking* 13-4).

It is this speech that Max summarizes in saying, "It's bound to come [the blow-up]. I don't know how or, when but it's got to come"

(*AMOP* 90). Failing to see the content of the national independence, nor of its benefits to the masses, the author takes sides and pitches good and evil into conflict. As Fuller states, the principle of conflict is at the heart of all dramatic action, and almost always turns up some aspect of the struggle between good and evil. When, at last, a cynical, disillusioned populace comes to believe that "the fat-dripping, gummy, eat-and-let-eat" (*AMOP* 167) government has taken "enough for the people to see," that life-altering "blow-up" at last comes in the form of a military force -- *coup d'état*. Because acts have consequences, for good and evil, the moral approach demands that crime be punished and that evil must never be allowed to thrive and prosper. And so, prophetically, a corrupt government comes to a sordid end with all the Ministers in flight. Yet, this is merely, an expository effort, not a reconstructive and formulative moral effort by Chinua Achebe.

The Power to Corrupt at an Individual Level

Our narrator, Odili Samalu, enters the story possessing, at the beginning, some ethical standards inspired by youthful idealism. As a prospective novelist, he chooses the flashback as a narrative technique – a medium that demands a rethinking, that clarifies for him his motives and issues involved in the story. At the time the story opens, he is a young grammar school teacher, whose school is feverishly awaiting the visit of Chief the Honorable M. Nanga. Odili is trying to instigate a boycott of standing in a queue by teachers, but with no success for a colleague, Andrew Kadibe refuses to join since the Minister comes from his own village – a fact that Odili terms "primitive loyalty" (9).

Odili recalls his first disillusionment with government and its process during the "case of the minted fifteen million pounds." It is to achieve a measure of independence that he forgoes a civil service job to teach in a rural school. In spite of the prevailing principle of it didn't matter "*what* you knew but *who* you know" (19) in the country, he intends to continue to rely on his educational merit to obtain a post-graduate scholarship, the important thing being the opportunity of visiting Europe which in itself must be a big education (19), he believes.

Eventually, Odili meets Chief Nanga, a very flamboyant politician who "has easy charm and country-wide popularity" (36) because he knows how to work the crowd, and his constituency. Odili is immediately seduced by the Chief's remarkable memory of remembering him as student, fifteen years later. To be so easily impressed speaks to Odili's naïveté and a tendency to doubt himself; he begins to cast doubt on his own ethical standards, for, because of Chief Nanga's affability and charm, Odili who earlier had accused Kadibe of "primitive loyalty" now begins to wonder if, perhaps, he has "been applying to politics stringent standards that didn't belong to it" (10).

As if to prove he has been misunderstood, Chief Nanga proceeds to issue an invitation to Odili to come to the capital for a strategic post in the civil service so that their people can get a piece of the national cake. And since the people view government as an alien presence anyway, their attitude is to get as much out of it as they possibly can. Odili falls into this trap, by accepting the Minister's invitation and going back on his principles. It is an attitude that is prevalent in the entire book, for even Edna's father advises him,

> my in-law is like a bull, and your challenge is like the challenge of a tick to a bull[...] I hear that they have given you much money to use in fighting my in-law. If you have sense in your belly you will carry the money into your bed-chamber and stow it away and do something with it. It is your own good luck (120).

Chief Nanga's invitation comes with a promise to help him get a post-graduate scholarship. The luxury of Chief Nanga's house with its "seven bedrooms and seven bathrooms, one for every day of the week" takes his breath away. He forgets to criticize the Chief's lack of moral norms; in fact, he envies him this position:

> I was simply hypnotized by the luxury of the great suite assigned to me. When I lay down in the double bed that seemed to ride on a cushion of air, and switched on the reading lamp and saw all the beautiful furniture anew from the lying down position and looked beyond the door to the gleaming bathroom and the towels as large as a lappa I had to confess that if I were at that moment made a minister, I would be most anxious to remain one for ever (*AMOP* 42).

Thus, it is easy to understand the charge of duplicity often labeled at this narrator. Odili is the representative of the young idealist, equally as prone to corruptibility as Chief Nanga and his ilk. He readily imitates Chief Nanga's libidinous lifestyle, for he casually sleeps with Jean, the married American, after only a day's encounter;

he easily enjoys the prestige of riding in long, imported Cadillacs, as well as the sensual life of adultery and flighty conversations with women.

Thus, Odili shows a weakness of being easily seduced by the same materialistic pathos to which the politicians have fallen prey. In time, he comes to enjoy even the brand-new Volkswagen given by the C.P.C. and other accoutrements of official political campaigns such as bodyguards / thugs, and party money. Early on, Odili jokes with his girl friend Elsie about swopping girl friends with the married and elderly Nanga for whom he asks Elsie to procure a date. For selfish reasons, he exults at the news of Mrs. Nanga's visit home "as no married woman, however accommodating would view kindly the sort of plans I had in mind [...] not even a self-contained guest suite such as I was now occupying would make it look well since Elsie will not want other women to hold a low opinion of her *moral*" (44).

Again, Karol Wotjyla's 1957-59 Post-Graduate Seminar lecture series (published in 1960 as *Love and Responsibility*) try to make moral sense regarding human sexuality. Examining the ethics of marital chastity and sexual love, *Love and Responsibility* sees these as expressions of fundamental moral truths; he posits that the best approach to sexual morality is in the context of "love and responsibility" because love is an expression of personal responsibility, responsibility to another human being, and responsibility to God. Sexual love embodying a genuine and mutual giving symbolizes genuine freedom. Thus, when my freedom freely encounters your freedom, we both seek something that is truly good, and which we both recognize as good (*Witness to Hope* 141).

Applying this thesis to the corrupt political *milieux* of *A Man of the People,* one sees that neither Odili nor Nanga and his ilk know, recognize or accept the responsibility of love, for Nanga and the American woman Jean are adulterous and Odili, Elsie, Nanga use one another as objects of pleasure, commerce and boost to self-love. Therefore, one can validly question Odili's seemingly adaptable and convenient sense of morality -- one that can easily be shelved aside or summoned up at will. Certainly, Odili may not be as bad as Chiefs Nanga and Koko but he is far from being an ideal ethical hero, and he knows it.

Tainted ideals - Nanga Steals Elsie and Odili Vows Revenge

It can hardly be said that Odili's foray into politics is as a result of extreme patriotism or out of any ethical consideration. As has been shown earlier, he is enjoying his stay at Chief Nanga's guesthouse. Indeed, he shuts his eyes and closes his moral conscience to some of the Chief's shenanigans, for does he not go with him to Chief Koko's house to arrange a post-graduate scholarship, contrary to his earlier monologue about "a person like me who simply could not stoop to lick any big man's boots," and that the reason he is stuck in a "bush private school instead of a smart civil service job with car, free housing, etc." is to give himself "a certain amount of autonomy." Yet, when Chief Nanga singles him out for recognition, he is flattered and accepts his invitation. And party big wig, Mrs. Eleanor satirically warns him of the pitfalls, "I kin see you na good boy. Make you no gree am spoil you. Me I no de for dis bed-room and bath-room business" (*AMOP* 20).

And Odili is impressed with Chief Nanga's panache and impatience with **modesty** (which to politicians is synonymous with **hypocrisy**). As Odili speculates, this is the reason for the success of men like Nanga while "starry-eyed idealists strove vaingloriously to bring into politics, niceties and delicate refinements that belonged elsewhere" (12). Odili's moral sensibilities are plastic enough to withstand the revelation that Chief Nanga, at a cost of six thousand pounds each, "had ordered ten luxury buses" to ply the proposed new road for Anata: "I got to know about this road which, incidentally, passes through my own village of Urua. At that time, I was **naturally** sympathetic to Chief Nanga's plans for it" (48). Odili also accommodates the four-story structure that the European building firm of Antonio & Sons to whom Nanga had recently given the half-million pound contract to build the National Academy of Arts and Sciences is erecting for Chief Nanga in Anata. And so, because of partisan interests, Odili is "naturally" sympathetic.

In addition to his compromised idealism, Odili is a young man whose marked sensualism makes him susceptible to Chief Nanga's loose lifestyle. Also, he overlooks the fact that Barrister Mrs. Agnes Akilo, despite her veneer of sophistication is Chief Nanga's girlfriend. In fact, Odili overcomes his earlier awkwardness before this intellectual woman by telling himself, "After all, Chief Nanga who was barely literate was probably going to sleep with her that night" (*AMOP*

53). It is hardly illuminating to hear him recount the sexual exploits of his schoolmate, the English Honor student alias Irresponsible; or, that he confesses to meeting and sleeping with Elsie "within an hour though he acknowledges that this revelation might prejudice anyone against her" (27). Yet, when Chief Nanga makes a fool of him, Odili shows his affront, "As for Elsie, I should have known that she was a common harlot" (80).

These incidents highlight the strain of chauvinism in Odili -- that only by denigrating a woman's honor can he reinforce his belief in his manhood. For this reason, feminists have theorized that for men, a woman's truth or integrity is predicated on her chastity. Even Eunice, Max's fiancé, a very educated woman – a lawyer trained at the London School of Economics seems undesirable because she exudes "the confidence of a beautiful woman **who has brains as well, which I find a little intimidating**" (*AMOP* 89). And so, our budding intellectual who has writing ambitions prefers less intimidating women such as Elsie, his girlfriend, and later the "virginal" Edna – "a girl looking as though she was waiting to be taken back to the convent " (105) -- who he thinks should not be anybody's "second wife," but rather his own.

The point at issue is that but for the fall-out with Chief Nanga over Elsie, Odili's ideals about governance would have remained stillborn. The comical scene where he and Chief Nanga play a cat and mouse game of waiting to take Elsie to bed becomes the deciding factor. Here, also, Odili shows the same hypocrisy, and misogyny as Nanga. To Chief Nanga who asks him to explain the nature of his relationship with Elsie, he exclaims, "You mean about marriage [...] Good Lord, she is just a good time girl." Yet, he admits that it is "grossly unfair" to call Elsie "simply a good time girl" (*AMOP* 66). But, his pride is shattered when he hears laughter behind the closed doors, and Elsie "deliriously screaming" his name. He gives a graphic description: "A sort of paralysis had spread over my limbs, while and intense pressure was building up inside my chest[...] . A strong revulsion and hatred swept over me and I turned sharply away and went down the stairs for the last time" (78). Chief Nanga tries to reason with him,

> but you told me you were not serious with her; I asked you because I do not like misunderstanding [...] Don't be childish, Odili, [...] But anyway I am sorry if you were offended; the mistake is mine. I tender an unreserved apology. If you like I can bring you six girls

this evening. You go do the thing sotay you go beg say you no want again. Ha, ha, ha! (*AMOP* 81*).*

In the decadent circles of these high government officials, girls are a dime a dozen – a quantifiable commodity, about whom men should not fall out, for after all, are they all not Chanticleers who rule the henhouse? But when Odili proves difficult, the Minister gets angry, "Look here, Odili. I will not stomach any nonsense from any small boy for the sake of a common woman, you hear?" (*AMOP* 81). Thereafter, they become mortal enemies. Quickly, Odili packs out of the house and goes looking for a classmate from his Grammar school days, Maxwell Kulamo -- alias Cool Max –a lawyer whom he now remembers after he "could no longer enjoy the flesh-pots of Chief Nanga's house" (*AMOP* 83).

Any wonder as to what Odili would do were circumstances reversed is answered by his early candid admission that given the unparalleled and hypnotic luxury of Chief Nanga's house, as Minister, he would be "most anxious to remain one for ever" (42). The incident with Chief Nanga marks a significant turning point. Odili now undergoes a process of individuation, which involves a psychological growing up; it also involves a process of discovering those aspects of self that make one an individual distinguishable from all others. His journey through the morass of a murky political arena will bring him to a state of self-recognition, and to maturity. His eyes have now been opened to evil. He has been introduced into a world of easy infidelity, political chicanery and total lack of virtue and is completely disillusioned, knowing definitely what he does not want, and where he does not belong. Thus, he journeys from the "alienating" mores of the city back to the familiar, reassuring terrain of his village.

Henceforth, his life becomes purposeful as he joins forces with Maxwell and a new political party – the Common Peoples' Convention (CPC). Events in the novel move with equal rapidity. Odili is the CPC's new representative in Urua and Anata. Here, the revenge motif surfaces as Odili feels the heavy weight of the previous night's humiliation. His Ego and concept of himself as a man are severely threatened:

> What mattered is that a man has treated me as no man had a right to
> treat another – not even if he were master and the other slave; and
> my manhood required that I make him pay for his insult in full

measure. In flesh and blood terms, I realized that I must go back, seek out Nanga's intended parlour-wife and give her the works full and proper *(AMOP 86)*.

Only by stealing Chief Nanga's affianced bride, Edna, would his bruised ego be assuaged. But it must be pointed out that "Elsie" does not really equate "Edna" for Odili never has pretended that Elsie is anything but a "plaything" to him, hence his confession to Nanga that his intentions are not serious. From here on, he courts Edna assiduously but surreptitiously. Hopefully, because of his travails, Odili has sufficiently matured to redefine sexual morality as a concept that transforms sex from something that just happens into something that expresses human dignity (*Witness to Hope* 142).

Sex that just happens such as the adulterous affairs of Odili, Nanga and company is dehumanizing sex. The moral perspective abhors the demeaning of women into objects of male sexual pleasure, even when women themselves misguidedly lay claims to such a "liberation." And after all Odili has been through, it is hoped that this intellectual-narrator will recognize that relations with Edna should equate love between two persons – two freedoms – "seeking personal and common goods together" in a union that is "fully human and fully humanizing" (142).

Thereafter, fully engaged into the process, Odili plunges headlong into politics, as a means of exacting full and satisfactory revenge. The element of revenge heavily taints the "morality," "idealism" and objectivity of Odili, as narrator. But, he translates into practical reality his decision to fight Chief Nanga to the finish, while the former uses the full weight of established political machine to crush him. Odili makes a start by traveling home with a Volkswagen , eight hundred pounds and promises of more to come.

As usual, many people warn him about the near-impossibility of this venture. His father, for instance, wonders out loud, "So you want to really fight Chief Nanga, my son, why don't you fight where your pieces could be gathered. If the money he was offering was too small why did you not say so?" (*AMOP* 135). Equally, his bodyguards ask Odili if he thinks "na so so talk you go take win Chief Nanga. If Government no give you money for election make you go tell them no be san sand we de take do am" (127). Failing to bribe off Odili, Chief Nanga laughingly mocks him,

I am not afraid of you. Every goat and every fowl in this country knows that you will fail woefully. You will lose your deposit and disgrace yourself. I am only giving you this money because I feel that after all the years of service to my people I deserve to be elected unopposed so that my detractors in Bori will know that I have my people solidly behind me (133*).

Evidently, upstaging the established Chief Nanga whose political machine has total control of the community is not something easily accomplished. Odili never even gets to stand against Chief Nanga at the polls, for he is fighting for his life at the hospital. His car is burnt by Nanga's thugs. Yet, Odili comes out of the entire fracas smelling nicely - his moral and ethical standards coming into sharp and clear definitional focus and thus, he stands poised to come of age.

There is an appealing naïveté to his ethical standards. Even Maxwell Kalome, his friend and party founder, who of all the characters in the novel, shows political maturity, disappoints him when he accepts the proffered one thousand pounds from Chief Koko and instead of stepping down for the Minister uses it to fund his campaign. Max laughs at the shocked incredulity shown by Odili who protests that receiving money had a moral force (142) because Max's action had jeopardized our moral position [...] which in the end was our society's only hope of salvation (144). The impression comes across that the author shares this moral conviction of leadership by example.

Another gain for our *unidealized* hero is the resolution of Odili's redefined relationship with his father. Their conflict stems from the latter's lack of restraint, an endless desire for wives and children for whom he can not provide, and his stark materialism in seeking personal gains out of every situation. At the end, Odili sees the moral fiber of which his father is made, when the old man stands firm in the face of punitive, vindictive political measures meted out against him by Chief Nanga.

As regards gender relations in this novel, the tender, romantic, wooing scenes with Edna emphasize that Odili idealizes his women. So does Achebe, as usual. Not for Odili, the emancipated lady lawyer who sleeps with illiterate Chief Nnaga for twenty-five pounds (143), nor Elsie of the easy virtue; not even Eunice, sophisticated in the nail varnish and eyebrow-shadow-line way (143); these women with brains, readers now know, intimidate Odili. He goes for the "unspoilt" beauty of Edna who looked as though they had stopped by some convent on their way and offered her a life, although on feeling her rejection of him, he reverts to his ungallant self by calling her, "beautiful empty head," and "a girl who has no more education than lower Elementary" (149).

At the end, our protagonist, always ready to compromise his principles when an occasion warrants it, decides to pay Edna's bride price by borrowing from the C.P.C. funds still in his hands, proving once more that his ideals remain tainted, even if better than the ethics of his opponents. Yet, the travails of the young woman, Edna as trophy for victorious men, as revenge tool is symbolic and constitutes an indictment against society's inequitable treatment of women through a system whereby greedy parents sell off their daughter to the richest bidder.

The character of Edna's father collapses the persona of the narrator into that of the author, for both writers' portrait of the greedy father represents the moral indictment of the cultural marriage mores pushed to excess. Since Odili's ethical convictions finally crystallized somewhat, even if still tainted, one readily forgives his earlier, aimless drifting and sensuality because he has shown himself capable of aspiring to that higher ideal which Achebe wants African intellectuals to achieve in the effort to reform and reeducate African nations. Odili like Achebe points to the tool needed to realize this dream – moral regeneration involving the best type of education. He also underscores pragmatism as a necessary quality – fight but stay alive so that "you outlive your present annoyance. *The great thing, as the old people have told us, is reminiscence,* and only those who survive can have it" (162). In *Anthills of the Savannah*, "reminiscence" equates "the story" and only story tellers – writers – are equipped by their skills to tell what happened.

Chief the Honorable M. A. Nanga, MP is the archetypal embodiment of the falsest values that can bedevil any nation - a fraudulent, amoral arriviste, a demagogic universal charmer. As portrayed in the novel, he is the embodiment of corruption in all its worst forms and he has no redeeming features. A man with double stands, he declares to Odili, "if some person come to you and say I wan make you Minister, make you run like blazes comot," (16) but he still relishes the prospect of a conferment of Doctor of Laws, LL.D. - "you no see say the title fit my name pem" (21). Though he shows paternalistic benevolence to him Odili aptly points out to Andrew that a man like Chief Nanga does not care two hoots about the outside world. He is more concerned with retaining his hold on his constituency and there he is adept (26). Not only is he unfaithful to his wife, he lodges his paramours in his wife's bedroom. Emotionally immature, when he takes over Odili's girlfriend, he meets his Waterloo as the enraged young man, spurred on by revenge and a deflated ego, stakes all his youthful energies towards pulling him down. He is, in fact, what Edna appropriately calls him, "a bush, jaguda man, with all his money" (165). And when the army struck, he is seen escaping dressed like a fisherman.

For Chief Nanga, the mainspring of political action was personal gain which was more in line with the general feeling in the country than the high-minded thinking of fellows like Max and I (128), Odili confesses. Introducing Chief Nanga to the reader, Odili says he led the pack of back-bench hounds straining their leash to get at their victims during the trial in parliament of the dissenting Ministers. The animal-like imagery continues. Nanga shares in the delusive laughter of the hungry hyena and yapped and snarled so shamelessly for the meaty prize which is the vacant post of Minister to which he is eventually appointed. For him and his ilk, the attraction is women, cars, landed property (87) and Max prophesies:

> the blow-up, it's bound to come. I don't know how or when but it's got to come; you simply cannot have this stagnation and corruption going on indefinitely (90)·

The same situation exists even in Nigeria of today which proves the fact that human beings never learn anything from history. When opposition sets in, Nanga resorts to his usual tactics. He intimidates, he tries to buy off the intractable Odili because "I feel that after all my years of service to my people, I deserve to be elected unopposed"(132). When that fails, he employs thuggery.

Odili is mercilessly beaten up, thus ensuring his being elected unopposed. And since actions must have consequences, nemesis catches up with Nanga as he is "trying to escape by canoe dressed like a fisherman. And, says Odili with poetic justice, "so ended the fat - dripping, gummy, eat-and-let eat regime, you chop me self I chop, palaver finish" (167). However, to the very end, Odili is unable to state unequivocally that his motivation is only political idealism. He started off with the intention to hurt Chief Nanga but then, he got caught up in the romantic idealism of the events as they were unfolding. Quite honestly recognizing the confused nature of his motivations, his retrospective writing serves as therapeutic self-analysis:

> Having got so far in my self-analysis I had to ask myself one question. How important was any political activity in its own right? It was difficult to say; things seemed so mixed up; my revenge, my new political activity, my new ambition and the girl. And perhaps it was just as well that my motives should entangle and reinforce one another. For I was not so naïve as to imagine that loving Edna was enough to wrench her form a minister. True, I had other advantages like youth and education but those were nothing beside wealth and position and the authority of a greedy father (*AMOP* 121).

The fortuitous reinforcement to his wooing which he receives is the timely *coup d'état* that sacks the corrupt politicians.

Ethical Standards on Societal Level

It is often said that a nation gets the government and leaders it deserves. This saying is truly borne out in the case of the society portrayed by Achebe in *A Man of the People*. Deep entrenchment in materialism on the part of Government leaders has rendered the people not only indifferent and apathetic to the misrule and corruption, but cynical as well. Therefore, a disillusioned citizenry with no moral guidance from the leadership decide to become active collaborators with the defrauders of their nation. After all, they think, it is the "white man's rule."

Readers remember how in *No Longer at Ease*, members of the Umuofia Progressive Union see in Obi Okonkwo their passport to getting a share of the "national cake," for according to them, "many towns have four or five or even ten of their sons in European posts[...] Umuofia has only one." And they would quote an appropriate native proverb to illustrate their thought -- "he who has people is richer than he who has money" (*NLAE* 91). Odili despairs of the attitude of the masses who are "not only ignorant but cynical. Tell them that this man had used his position to enrich himself and they would ask you - as my father did – "if you thought that a sensible man would spit out the juicy morsel that good fortune placed in his mouth" (*AMOP* 2).

Hezekiah Samalu's attitude to political activities agrees with that of the general populace – that personal profit is the mainspring of political action and to that extent, he is somewhat mollified by what his son has got out of it – a car, and a name. Odili encounters this attitude every where he goes. People have no qualms defrauding the government, or sharing in the fruits of fraudulent activities.

Regarding Chief Nanga, his prospective in-law, Edna's father declares: "Leave me and my in-law. He will bring and bring and bring and I will eat until I am tired because this is the time to enjoy an in-law, not when he has claimed his wife and gone away" (103). With wry empirical wisdom he dissuades Odili from contesting the election: If you have sense in your belly, you will carry the money into your bed-chamber and stow it away and do something useful with it (119). And so, after the debacle, when Odili goes to start ceremonies on Edna, her father simply refused to believe that he had lost a chief and Minister as son-in-law and must now settle for this crazy boy who had bought a tortoise and called it a car (165).

With such a mindset, an accomplished politician like Chief Nanga who speaks the language of the people will fit into his society very snugly. He owns his constituency and all of its agencies of government. For the masses, his promise to get them a share of the "national cake" is a most potent tool of persuasion. In the eyes of the general populace, there is a disconnection between the people and government. Politics, and issues concerning governance are regarded as "their affair." Interpreters, court messengers, warrant chiefs, and now ministers are all considered go-between the people and colonial government, and they were generally hated for their ruthlessness, high-handedness and proclivity to milk the people. Odili, the son of "a retired District Interpreter" discovers how much hated such government officials are when a classmate's father, on discovering whose son he is, tells him squarely, "You cannot stay in my house [...] I don't blame you, my son, or you either, because no one has told you. But know it from today that no son of Hezekiah Samalu's shelters in my house" (*AMOP* 33-4).

Listening to her husband's denunciation of Odili whom he suspects intends to contest the political seat of the rich Chief Nanga, Edna's mother shrugs in disinterest, saying, "What is my share in that? They are both white man's people and they know what is what between them. What do I know?" (119). In fact, Mrs. Nanga herself shows her disdain for the emptiness of the white man's Embassy parties, as she queries derisively, "What can you enjoy there? *Nine pence talk and three pence food.* 'Hallo, hawa you. Nice, to see you again.' All na lie lie" (*AMOP* 41; my emphasis). This kind of disconnect creates apathy within the populace who see government as the "white man's" system, and therefore not their concern, even if their own sons and daughters are in the game.

Even as he makes fun of all their outrageous beliefs and statements, the reader still feels the resignation and pained wonder of the author at a populace so collaborative, so equally opportunistic and willing to be used when he makes the couple from Urna confess to Odili and his people, "we know they are eating, but we are eating too." The people of Urua break away from the larger Anata community to support Odili because of feelings of kinship. This ethnic partisanship, Max exploits as he reminds them during the launching of the local the C.P.C.: "Last time you elected a Member of Parliament from Anata. Now, it is your time here in Urua. A goat does not eat into the hen's stomach no matter how friendly the two may be. Ours is ours but mine is mine. I present as my party's candidate your own son, Odili Samalu" (140).

This is a strategy the finicky Odili believes is unworthy of Max, but that is the rhetoric the people want to hear; and it proves effective. The C.P.C. as a party is hastily put together, with no sure means of funding. Their motives are idealistic but the leaders who come from the same cultural stock compromise these ideals. Some of their leaders are junior ministers unwilling to operate openly who covertly give them information from inside the corrupt system. This evidence of frustration should compel these men if they have principles to resign, Odili says, at which Max laughs at the naïve Odili: "Resign? Where do you think you are – Britain or something? Don't be funny, Odili" (*AMOP* 93). Max accepts Chief Koko's bribe, and the C.P.C. adopts many of the same strategies as the parties against which they are fighting. However, a challenge has been successfully thrown, and events, once started, acquire a life and momentum of their own, resulting in a cataclysm.

So, the ensuing free-for-all during the elections brings out the worst traits of the people. They go on a rampage as thugs, looters, and adulators of the rich and powerful. Consequently, when the end does come, Odili is able to say with realistic honesty about a people he knows so well: "No, the people had nothing to do with the fall of our Government. This is a people fickle and two-faced, for overnight, everyone began to shake their heads at the excesses of the last regime, at its graft, oppression and corrupt government: newspapers, the radio, the hitherto silent intellectuals and civil servants - everybody said what a terrible lot" (162-6).

A Man of the People does not have the structurally cohesive perfection of *Things Fall Apart*, nor the hauntingly tragic undertones of *Arrow of God* nor the timeless rhythmic tone and fluid movement of these two tradition-based novels; but it has a perennial theme: exposition of the ills of society; and while Achebe does not prescribe a cure, Odili acting as the author's persona, predicts the consequence for moral turpitude -- a coup - which actually comes to pass in Nigeria shortly after the book's publication. For the heavy emotions induced by the intolerable events of the story, the coup provides a cathartic effect. As an *engagé* writer, Achebe enters fully and humorously into the novel's perspective as he traces the economic, political and moral breakdown of a nation with sympathy and amusing mockery. Achebe's *A Man of the People* was scheduled for general release on January 17, 1966. Ezenwa-Ohaeto records that on Friday, January 14, during a meeting of the Society of Nigerian Authors held in Lagos, the author lent his advance copy of the book to his friend J.P. Clark who was said to have remarked enthusiastically, "Chinua, I *know* you are a prophet. Everything in this book has happened except a military coup" (*Chinua Achebe* 109).

By the morning of January 15, 1966 the first Nigerian military *coup d'état* had taken place. So timely and so coincidental were the book's prophetic ending, and the actual coup that did occur in Nigeria, that the authorities eventually called the author in for questioning to find out if he had had previous knowledge of the coup plans. But, prior to the one that did occur in Nigeria, there had been examples of military take-overs of governments in some African nation – in Ghana, for instance. Possibly, Achebe meant this conclusion to be a lesson for all the real-life election swindle, violence, anger, frustration, and general mayhem going on at that time in Western Nigeria. It also serves as an indictment of the African masses for their participatory guilt which was helping to destabilize the rest of the country. And it worked in the case of Nigeria.

In *A Man of the People*, Chinua Achebe has delineated a set of critical standards by which enlightened citizens should hold their leaders morally accountable. As a writer with moral standards, he seeks to recall his people to a sense of individual dignity and collective responsibility, exorcising the fear, anomie and hopelessness that have previously prevented the "we" of society from coalescing against the defrauding "they." His warning seems to be that if leaders become unheeding and take too much for "the owner to see," the consequence can be as sweepingly devastating as the book foretells. Thus, it is evident that the author succeeds in clearly setting out his objectives and; and he is quite successful in this effort because he pitches into conflict good and evil as these are the constituent elements of morality. Clearly, he takes sides, assigns blame.

In fulfilling Edmund Fuller's belief that "no valid compassion can exist without a moral framework" ("The New Compassion in the American Novel" 61), Chinua Achebe, novelist, philosopher and compassionate ethicist justifies the moral approach which expects literature to instruct as well as to entertain. Consequently, along with T. S. Eliot, I conclude by reiterating the need for moral "norms: we shall certainly continue to read the best of its kind of what our time provides, but we must tirelessly criticize it according to our principles and not merely according to the principles admitted by writers and by critics, who discuss it in the press" (55). Love and responsibility remain urgent, moral imperatives for the successful, peaceful, and just governance and survival of any nation. The ethos of sacrifice will help combat the kind of lethargy which permitted, by tacit or overt consent, the continued imposition of an alien (to the natives) and fraudulent form of political control on public governance. These ethical norms define "the high standards of human dignity, objectively and personally" (*Witness to Hope* 143).

Notes

[1] *A Man of the People* (London: Heinemann 1966) will henceforth be referred to as *AMOP*. All citations are from this edition.

[2] *Morning Yet On Creation Day* will hereinafter be known as *MYOCD*.

Works Cited

Achebe, Chinua. *A Man of the People.* London: Heinemann, 1966.

--- *Arrow of God.* Revised edition. New York: Random House, 1974.

--- *Things Fall Apart.* Revised edition. New York: Doubleday, 1994.

--- *Anthills of the Savannah.* Nigeria: Heinemann, 1988.

--- *No Longer at Ease.* Revised edition. New York: Double Day, 1994.

--- "The African Writer and the English Language." In *Morning Yet On Creation Day.* London: Heinemann, 1975. 55-62.

--- "The African Writer and the Biafran Cause." In *MorningYet On Creation Day.* London: Heinemann, 1975. 78-84.

--- "Named for Victoria, Queen of England." In *Morning Yet On Creation Day.* London: Heinemann, 1975. 65-70.

--- "The Novelist as a Teacher." In *Morning Yet On Creation Day.* London: Heinemann, 1975. 42-45.

--- *The Trouble with Nigeria.* Enugu: Fourth Dimension Publishers, 1983.

Duerden, Dennis and Cosmo Pietese, eds. *African Writers Talking.* London, Heinemann, 1972.

Eliot, T.S. "Religion and Literature in Wilbur Scott." *Five Approaches of Literary Criticism.* New York: Macmillan Co., 1962.

Ezenwa-Ohaeto. *Chinua Achebe: A Biography.* Indiana University Press, 1997.

Ezewudo, Gabriel. "Christianity, African Traditional Religion and Colonialism: Were Africans pawns or players in the Cultural Encounter?" In *Religion and Society.* Ed. Rose Ure Mezu. MD: Black Academy Press, 1998. 43-61.

Fuller, Edmund. "The New Compassion in the American Novel" in Wilbur Scott. *Five Approaches of Literary Criticism.* New York: Macmillan Co., 1962.

Gikandi, Simon. "Writing in the Marginal Space." In *Reading Chinua Achebe: Language and Ideology in Fiction*. London: Heinemann, 1991. 78-100.

Killam, G.D., ed. *African Writers on African Writing*. London, Heinemann, 1973.

Laurence, Margaret. *Long Drums and Canons*. London: Macmillan, 1968.

Ojinmah, Umelo. Chinua Achebe: *New Perspectives*. Ibadan, Nigeria: Spectrum Books, 1991.

Weigel, George. *Witness to Hope: A Biography of Pope John Paul I1 1920-2005*. New York: Harper Collins, 2005.

5

Achebe's *Anthills of the Savannah*: A Writer and his Ideas

It is the storyteller, in fact, who makes us what we are, who creates history. The storyteller creates the memory that the survivors must have – otherwise their surviving would have no meaning.

(Chinua Achebe *in "Interview with Bill Moyers"* 337)

C hinua Achebe's fifth novel, *Anthills of the Savannah*[1] (1978) is a complex but highly readable political and ideological work - complex because it seems to be the product of decades of lived, felt and carefully thought-about-feelings on a number of very cogent issues plaguing modern Africa and its peoples; yet highly readable because of its lyricism, such endearingly familiar, earthy, witty Nigerian humor that has one reeling with laughter at intervals during any rereading, with swift changes in narrative locus and voices. It is a tightly controlled, sparsely-constructed drama that stuns as events hurtle towards a dramatic and inevitable conclusion.

Yet the language is sophisticated as it shows Achebe at the acme of his intellectual growth having at his disposal all the best narrative tropes of Western and African literary traditions; in fact, he is almost unapologetically exhibitionist in his intellectualism as he must be if he has to realistically handle the character of Ikem Osodi, the intellectual artist, writer, activist and catalyst to social and political change. It is no longer the deceptively simple, even if carefully crafted language of *Things Fall Apart*; rather, it is a language that displays realism in dialogue, and humor in the "lingo" of the ordinary working-class with all its earthiness and practical insights; a language indicative of the kind of real and tough living which forces Chris Oriko to humbly acknowledge after barely emerging safely from the firing lines of police and army check-points, "I must remember that [...] to succeed as small man no be small thing" (194). Achebe uses both formal and pidgin (creolized) English to mediate between the elite and non-elite categories of his characters, skillfully capturing the nuances of power corruption. The protagonist, Sam - a now matured Chief Nanga - is depicted as a dictator possessing an incredible humor reminiscent of actual civilian leaders of the Second Civilian Republic in Nigeria (1979-1983), in which the antics and back-stabbing sycophancy of the commissioners strongly resembled the kind described in the novel.

Certainly, the Horatian dictum - *dulce et utile* - instructing with humor - serves Achebe's purpose rather than any grim Juvenalian satire; yet this is a language that becomes almost obscure in its sheer poetry and in the mysticism of its cultural myths and historical legends. Ezenwa-Ohaeto attributes the tension in *Anthills of the Savannah* to the fact that the storyline "is woven with thematic strands that include love, hate, passion, friendship [and] hope;[...]shows that even the most devastating political and emotional turmoil gives way to renewal" (*Chinua Achebe: a Biography* 252). On his part, Somalian novelist Nuruddin Farah describes *Anthills of the Savannah* as "a rich treasure of transferred meanings[...][with] a great deal of poetry in it and the quality of the writing charged with informedness, an awareness of high things and high thoughts" (in *Chinua Achebe: a Biography* 252-3).

To Achebe, as to African American writers such as Toni Morrison or even Paule Marshall for whom writing is also a time-consuming project, such lyricism and power of language are not achieved easily; it is a craft to be worked on, and honed to a superlative level. Marshall actually confesses in an interview that "one of the reasons it takes me such a long time to get a book done is that I'm not only struggling with my sense of reality, but I'm also struggling to find the style, the language, the tone that is in keeping with the material. It's in the process of writing that things get illumined" ("American Fiction Series" 2). A similar pursuit of excellence possibly accounts for the length of time Achebe's fourth novel took in coming out since for him writing carries weighty responsibilities.

The potency of his writing therefore is indicated by his language which achieves variety as he hides under different *personae*; its peals resonate, signify and convey clearly the ideological issues that agitate the novelist. Consequently, this study sets out to examine sequentially the following issues:

I.   The ideal political structure that can best serve the peculiar realities of post-Independence Kangan (Nigeria/ Africa);

II. How to effect a re-orientation in the acquired tastes, opinions and attitudes of the people towards governance, the governed and their responsibilities to the nation state;

III. Role of the woman in the structure of the nation;

IV. What it means to be a creative writer in society - nature of writing and its goals, its claims to artistic merit.

Achebe's *Anthills* is a socio-politico-ideological work. Its characters, Chris and Ikem, *alter egos* of the writer, successfully convey his anguish at the destiny of a people who "have messed up their chances so often that their situation needs to be examined with greater seriousness." The author makes it clear that post-colonial African nations, especially Nigeria (represented possibly by the fictive Kangan Republic) have made a mess of their political heritage.

The destiny and direction of a people are grave responsibilities, and it has already been surmised that because of these, *Anthills of the Savannah* had to be carefully crafted. Achebe subsumes in this latest novel, his earlier concerns about the body politic of Africa/Nigeria and their citizenry - the failure of leadership and of a system - that prompted the essay, *The Trouble with Nigeria* (1983). Achebe is still not being prescriptive - for his ideological pundit, Ikem Osodi, maintains that "a writer wants to ask questions. These damned fellows want him to give answers. Writers don't give prescriptions. They give headaches" (158-161). This presentational posture goes beyond that found in his 1966 political satire, *A Man of the People* because Achebe tosses around the problem of leadership and accountability long enough to force his listeners to re-examine their beliefs and (as the saying goes, "the unexamined life is not worth living" *Anthills* 158)), discern their misconceptions and then think long and hard about other viable alternatives. In this regard, Ikem plays the role of the Athenian gadfly, Socrates, whose "goal was to make people aware of their assumptions about what they thought they knew[...] so that they might begin the pursuit of knowledge in the proper way" (*The Humanities* 164).

Ikem as a writer, functioning as the people's conscience-keeper, aims primarily at making his audience "think. I cannot prescribe your pet textbook revolution. As a writer I aspire only to widen the scope of self-examination. I don't want to foreclose it with a catchy, half-baked orthodoxy" (*Anthills* 158), he insists. Again, as did happen to Socrates, Ikem stings his enemies' consciences into such desperate straits that they arrest him and put him to death to neutralize his influence on the populace. But as will always happen, Ikem's secret murder becomes the catalyst needed for social unrest and an eventual *coup d'état*. But while he lives on the pages of *Anthills*, Ikem largely embodies Achebe's search for a workable political formula for Kangan and, by extension, for Nigeria/Africa.

The ideal political structure for post-independence Nigeria and Africa

Achebe's concerns are not with the neo-imperialist economic manipulation of the Western powers (although he does not ignore this, as Ikem explains to his University audience - "Please don't get me wrong. I do not deny that external factors are still at the root of many of our problems" 158), but Achebe, like Ikem, is more interested in guiding his audience towards fashioning an ideal political ideology by examining why the earlier experiments have failed and at what point "the rain began to beat us." He indicts government as a system, and its leadership in particular which presently operates a system of Black-on-Black oppression where power has been transferred to an indigenous governing class bent on perpetuating the elitist pretensions of their erstwhile political masters. The inability of civilians to govern peacefully seems to have ensured in perpetuity, the ascendancy of a military class unversed in the intricacies of government, who "come to power without any preparation for leadership[...] terrified of [the] new job" and with no agenda (12), a rulership who entrench a "butt-licking" mediocrity by appointing to offices only their friends and relations to "kow-tow" to them in servile, spineless sycophancy.

The newly constituted military African upper class are leaders who "openly looted our treasury, whose effrontery soiled our national conscience" (42) and [who] unleash on the defenseless masses a reign of terror, rather than re-establish internal links with the country's dispossessed whose "bruised heart[...]throbs painfully at the core of the nation's being" (141). Such are the "misshapen freaks like Amin and Bokassa sired on Africa by Europe" (52). And so, Africa seems locked in an unprogressive, tyrannical circle of ignorance and backwardness akin to the symbolic triple evil - drought, famine and neglect - inflicted on the Abazon people, a place and a people lyrically feted in Ikem's "Hymn to the Sun" (30-3).

Whereas all it really takes to give good governance is attention to people's needs as simple and basic as "water which is free from Guinea worm"(73), good road network for effective communication and transportation of food *and the like*, great sums are instead squandered and embezzled in the execution of monumental projects. Beatrice denounces, for instance, the forty-five million refurbishment of the presidential retreat as "irresponsibly extravagant in our circumstances." Assuming different postures and seeking to maintain balance (an important issue in Achebe's writings), the writer Chris even makes an apologia for the necessity of grandiose structures such as those that often ennoble nations - the cathedrals of Europe, the Taj Mahal of India, the pyramids of Egypt, *et al* - all raised on the backs of starving serfs - "[o]ur present rulers in Africa are in every sense late-flowering medieval monarchs, even the Marxists among them" (74) such as Nkrumah whom Mazrui called "a Stalinist Czar."

Consequently, Military leadership, whose excesses surpass those of the Civilians, often forget the people they are meant to govern, and instead exhibit naked, unbridled abuse of power as seen in the vengeful intimidation of the people of Bassa province who, for failing to vote in the President-for-life referendum, have their water bore-holes closed "so that you [the Abazon people] will know what it means to offend the sun.

You will suffer so much that in your next reincarnation, you will need no one to tell you to say yes whether the matter is clear to you or not" (127). These excesses manifest themselves in the use of civilian front men such as Alhaji Mahmoud for personal enrichment, the arrest and murder of Ikem, the army Sergeant's noon-day brazen attempt at rape, and his shooting of Chris.

Ultimately, Achebe with this novel indicts the unending intervention of the military in African political affairs. As Ojinmah notes, Achebe questions the very humanity of military dictators who "[h]aving become exposed to the perquisite privileges of their office were quick to change track, to decide that remaining in power for ever was better than going back to the humdrum existence of barrack life [...] to [them] human life has become worthless" (*Chinua Achebe: New Perspectives* 90-1). Thus, even the people forget the habit of governing themselves.

To oppose this penchant for military opportunism, the novelist uses an idealist, Ikem Osodi, a journalist. Ikem is determined not to be the devotee of "single-minded demi-gods," but to be multi-faceted like Walt Whitman's "multitudes" and examine issues from all sides, seeing both "the blot of villainy in the beloved oppressed" (*Anthills* 100-1) and yet granting, no matter how faint, a "glimmer of humanity to the hated oppressor." Ikem as an artist refuses to be partisan or to espouse any one ideology since "all certitude must now be suspect[...] Reform may be a dirty word then but it begins to look more and more like the most promising route to success in the real world" (99). Using Beatrice as a sounding board, and a medium of clarifying his clouded ideological thoughts, Ikem offers no redemptive ideology, no extreme radicalism, only a hazy conservative reformism of orthodoxy, for says Ikem, "society is an extension of the individual. We can only hope to rearrange some details in the periphery of the human personality. Any disturbance of its core is an invitation to disaster"(100). These anguished ruminations of a writer-philosopher at crossroads take place amid a rumbling background of a raging storm, "violent thunder and flashing distanced and muted as in a movie" mirroring his own internal turmoil. Ikem takes the reader along the tortuous pathway of his philosophical peregrination. With the dying of the storm and the insight gained from Beatrice, his ideological vision somewhat clarified, Ikem decides on a mode of action.

Achebe's political ideology has always hinged on the conviction that between the state and its citizenry, there is an unwritten social contract. The state as a governing system organizes society ideally to give to the governed a measure of stability, "peace and justice, and the citizen in return agrees to perform its patriotic duties" (*The Trouble with Nigeria* 15). Therefore, leadership must not renege on this agreement, because since power derives from the people, whoever wields it should be accountable to the people, or face great peril. Ignoring this vital fact produces a leader of the like of Sam who personalizes public office in himself: "You see if Entebbe happens here, it's me the world will laugh at[...]. It's not your funeral but mine[...]so, I don't fool around. I take precautions" (*Anthills* 15-6). Invariably, the precautions take the form of intimidation and other excesses.

Conscious of the isolating potential of power, Achebe throws to Ikem a life-line in the person of the uneducated Elewa who constitutes a link between the world of the haves and the have-nots. Through his illiterate girlfriend, Ikem therefore makes contact with the masses: taxi drivers, market union members. Contact with them revivifies him and he is sufficiently recharged by a visit from the "'earth' people" - members of the taxi cab union. Next, he meets with the leaders of the demonstrating group from the neglected Abazon province of the mythical Kangan Republic (fictionalized name for Nigeria), and later with the students, since progress without these groups is impossible. Ikem realizes that his job as editor of the *Gazette*, while giving him the needed outlet for some trenchant critiques of corrupt governance and retrogressive issues such as the scandalous spectacle of the public execution of armed robbers, *et cetera*, has also removed him from concretely knowing the people for whom good governance is meant.

We already know from Beatrice that Ikem profoundly respects peasants, market women and intellectual women - the first two being the mainstay of the economy in both the rural and urban towns. He now interprets the correct meaning of "Public affairs" as presently run to be nothing more than "the closed transactions of soldiers-turned-politicians, with their cohorts in business and the bureaucracy." Ikem consequently attempts to forge vital links with the "poor and dispossessed of this country, with the bruised heart that throbs painfully at the core of the nation's being" (141). When rulers enthrone misrule, they also strike at the core of their own being.

At this juncture, a comparison with *A Man of the People* becomes inevitable, for in *Anthills*, despite Ikem's denunciatory rhetoric, Achebe actually evinces more evident sympathy for the masses than in *A Man of the People*. The latter novel depicted the masses with bitter cynicism, as seen in Odili's trenchant commentary, "they [the masses] were not only ignorant but cynical. Tell them that this man had used his position to enrich himself and they would ask you - as my father did - if you thought a sensible man would spit out the juicy morsel that good fortune placed in his mouth" (2). In fact, Odili bitterly derides the many women dancing groups - a constant feature in any Nigerian celebration - as "silly, ignorant villagers dancing themselves lame" to honor the defrauders of the economy who sound the death-knell to the country's progress.

In Odili's opinion, and we guess, the author's, the masses are willing collaborators in the game of hypocrisy played by the likes of the bombastic Chief the Honorable M.A. Nanga, M.P. One despairs of a people who think not of giving to the nation but of getting their own share of the 'national cake' as the Urua people put it to Odili:

> 'The village of Anata has already eaten, now they must make way for us to reach the plate. But I want to tell our son one thing: he should tell them that we are waiting here like a baby cutting its first tooth; anyone who wants to look at our first tooth should know that his bag should be heavy. Have I spoken well?'

> 'Yes,' answered the crowd as they began to disperse.
>
> (*A Man of the People* 141).

It is a collective act, then, this mass collusion with corrupt leadership. Odili thus locates the site of his anguish in the willing collaboration of the people with the corrupt leaders like Chief Nanga "while starry-eyed idealists strove vaingloriously to bring into politics niceties and delicate refinements that belonged elsewhere" (12). *Anthills of the Savannah* reiterates this predicament: "[b]ut it wasn't Authority that worried me; it never does. It was the thousands who laughed so blatantly at their own humiliation and murder." It is from the desensitized masses that the Nangas and their ilk recruit their political thugs, the vote swindlers, *et cetera*. Yet immediately the corrupt regime is overthrown, Odili narrates, in *Man of the People*

> [...] overnight everyone began to shake their heads at the excesses of the last regime, at its graft, oppression and corrupt government: newspapers, the radio, the hitherto silent intellectuals, and civil servants-everybody said what a terrible lot; and it became public opinion the next morning. And these were the same people that only the other day had owned a thousand names of adulation, whom praise-singers followed with song and talking-drum wherever they went (166).

This was Achebe's *quasi persona*, Odili in 1965. Some twenty-two years later, the writer's disenchantment remains, but a lot of the bitterness is gone, perhaps tempered by age and a sneaking sympathy and tenderness towards a people so ignorant that it possesses "this perverse kindliness towards oppression conducted with panache!" (*Anthills* 142). Evidently, the masses have not changed; rather, it is the artist who has matured and is willing to be tolerant because despite flaws, he perceives in the people "an artless integrity, a stubborn sense of community."

In his *The Trouble with Nigeria*, Achebe's sympathy for "the peasant scratching out a living in the deteriorating rural environment, the petty trader with all his wares on his head, the beggar under the bridge[...] - the wretched of the earth[...]largely silent and invisible" (21) is so manifest. Thus, it is into this community of urban and rural working class - the backbone of society - that Ikem, a more ideologically trained Odili and as ideologically oriented as the writer himself, desires entry. The kind of person Ikem is, his status as a member of the intellectual elite or what Du Bois aptly terms the "Talented Tenth" he can not help, so while remaining true to himself, to his knowledge and experience, he must yet find a way to use these talents to do some good.

Clearly, this envisioned brave, enlightened and humane leadership in Achebe's worldview can not come from the masses but must emerge from the top rank of leadership of which a shining example "will radiate powerful sensations of well-being and pride through every nerve and artery of national life" (*The Trouble with Nigeria* 17). Only a determined "renegade" from the rank of the elite can bring order and justice into the existing system, no matter how askew. In the *Anthills,* the stage is thus set to bring this about as events concatenate: Ikem is dismissed as editor of the *National Gazette*, six of the leaders of the Abazon delegation are arrested, including a mentor of sorts - the old storyteller whom Ikem calls "a holy man of the earth" (150).

With the descent of totalitarianism, Ikem's voice is unfettered; he acts swiftly and in these symbolic last acts, he achieves the kind of clear vision and concreteness of action that make him really and truly *A Man of the People* in the sense that neither Chief Nanga nor Odili Samalu of the same novel is. Also, in entering this community of the people of the earth, Ikem achieves with them the kind of rapport that Armah's nameless solitary hero of *The Beautyful Ones Are Not Yet Born* disdains to have. Thus refocused, vision sharpened, Ikem goes to deliver a lecture to the Students' Union of the University of Bassa.

Chapter Twelve of the *Anthills of the Savannah* is the novel's most ideological. From Ikem's address to the Kangan Students' Union crystallizes the artist's vision, and the momentum generated therefrom helps accelerate the eventual crumbling of Sam's corrupt regime. Ikem functions not only as the writer/conscience keeper of the nation, but also as the griot, the "Recalling-Is-Greatest" in action, who takes over and recalls the old Abazon griot's symbolic tale of the tortoise, who, moments before he is to be killed, requests a few minutes from the leopard "to prepare my mind" - a request that is granted. The tortoise, rather than stand still, begins to scratch the ground "with hands and feet throwing sand furiously in all directions." When the puzzled leopard inquires as to the reason for his curious action, the tortoise replies, "Because even after I am dead I would want anyone passing by this spot to say, yes, a fellow and his match struggled here" (128).

The moral seems to be that it is better to have fought and lost than to acquiesce in servile defeat. Not having the requisite strength to match the leopard's, the brainy tortoise uses his head. The signs of a struggle will be presumed from the scratched ground. Likewise, not having the guns to match the military dictator's, Ikem the ideologue/activist/ writer, uses his brains. He takes the people's case to the repository of ideas - the university students, whom he hopes to motivate into a positive and dynamic re-appraisal of the country's plight.

Several issues are entwined in Ikem's dynamic speech - the ideal political formula, the position of writers, who as "storytellers become a threat. They threaten all champions of control, they frighten usurpers of the right-to-freedom of the human spirit" (153). We have already seen that Ikem is by nature disposed to accommodate differing viewpoints to avoid "the mortal sin of righteousness and extremism" (154). In a personal interview with this critic, Achebe reiterates his personal belief that "None of the 'isms' - Capitalism, Marxism, *et cetera* can solve our problems[...] Belief in either radicalism or orthodoxy is too simplified a way of viewing things[...] I can understand one being attracted to these things - but one must grow out of them for the real life is more complex. Evil is never all evil; goodness on the other hand is often tainted with selfishness.[2]" Ikem then is echoing the more ideologically mature Achebe when he argues that even radicalism "must be clear-eyed enough to see beyond the present claptrap that will heap all our problems on the doorstep of capitalism and imperialism" (*Anthills* 158)

Essentially, the misdeeds of the imperialists can be classified as the remote causes responsible for our *malaise*. Nevertheless, Kangans (Nigerians/Africans) have had sufficient time to change a skewed order. Ikem's denunciation is blistering as he indicts the various middle-class unions who have worked towards the nation's doom - government workers, who he thinks are lazy, unproductive and parasitic, but who yet want the reins of government handed over to them in the name of revolution. Ikem declares he will not hand over to "a democratic dictatorship of parasites" (157) - parasites because they are guilty of absenteeism at their jobs, defrauding the nation by the practice of ghost workers, embarking on strikes when outmoded colonial privileges such as vehicle advances, subsidized houses, *et cetera* are threatened. Their national officers prefer being chauffeur-driven in Mercedes-Benz cars. The workers themselves who run the Kangan Electricity Corporation employ a chaotic billing system to deliberately cover their massive fraud. These are the same workers who ensure that the benefits of modern life will be denied the real victims of exploitation in the rural villages.

Next, Ikem tackles the students whom he labels the "cream of parasites" as tribalists, religious fanatics, electoral merchants who buy and sell votes, who disregard merit to agitate for lower admission requirements into institutions of higher learning. To such "a democratic dictatorship of mediocrity," Ikem refuses to hand over his life. In *The Trouble with Nigeria*, Achebe had pinpointed the causes of social injustice as first, ethnicity which sabotaged nationalism and then after independence, the cult of mediocrity and compromise used to replace merit: "I have tried to show that the denial of merit is a form of social injustice which can hurt not only the individuals directly concerned but ultimately the entire society" (20). Achebe re-emphasizes this concern "[...]the moment we decide to put merit aside and bring up whatever other considerations, the society is bound to be in trouble and I think that's one of the things that has happened to us. And the modern world has not been created on considerations aside of merit" (*Chinua Achebe Biography* 271). In other words, young Kangans

(Nigerians/Africans) including the "new intellectual" elite are challenged to live their radicalism rather than merely spouting and touting it.

As a demonstration of the shining exemplary act, Ikem teaches positive action by his simple lifestyle, by his role modeling; - he drives a battered car even though his girlfriend, Elewa is ashamed of it. He is engaged to this illiterate worker whose mother is a petty trader; he gets close to taxi drivers and mechanics. Therefore, Ojinmah notes, Ikem devoid of elitist ambitions, pledges his faith in a society not governed by class and status. It is this faith that at his death will galvanize not only his friend Chris, but also the student leaders to see beyond his death to his vision of tomorrow, in which "power is used rightly for the benefit of society" (*New Perspectives* 102). Critic Emenyonu adds that Ikem's and, later, Chris's "act of salvation is not a mass act; it comes through the vision of individuals who end up as victims of the society they wish to save" (*Studies on the Nigerian Novel* 112).

But what is Achebe's exact ideological viewpoint in the *Anthills* if indeed he is opposed to all the *isms*? Perhaps, one should look again at Ikem's declaration that "whatever you are is never enough; you must find a way to accept something however small from the other to make you whole and save you from the mortal sin of righteousness and extremism" (*Anthills* 154). Oladele Taiwo explains it this way, "The reader finds, almost invariably, that no one point of view is wholly acceptable, and that to reach a satisfying conclusion, several points of view have to be taken into consideration" (*Culture and the Nigerian Novel* 112). Earlier, Ikem has postulated that "the most one can do with a problematic psyche is to *re-form* it[...] to do more, to overthrow the psyche itself, would be to unleash insanity. No. We can only hope to rearrange some details in the periphery of the human personality" (*Anthills* 100). Continuing his commentary during the interview with me, Chinua Achebe himself restates his use of the word, *reform*. His social vision then would involve a sort of rightwing reformism since he is against extremism of any sort. To leave oneself enough room to accommodate other viewpoints and become whole, to live one's life truly to the best of one's ability, to be ready ultimately to lay down one's life for one's convictions as Ikem Osodi does, as Chris does; these seem to sum up his ideological bent. It is an eclectic, pragmatic yet idealistically accommodating kind of ideology. In a subsequent discussion with him on June 15, 1999, Achebe the mature ideologue counsels "patience." Nigeria's political troubles will be solved gradually. While some critics might term this characteristic of Achebe's "ideological ambiguity," Achebe's personal comment on this issue must however suffice.

Answering my question on the place of the Igbos in Nigeria's intractable political situation, he urges the Igbos "to play the role of the conscience, because of the suffering we endured. Oppression is wrong. Because we tried to rebel against oppression, whenever and wherever we see it, we must say 'no'. We must not say foolishly, it is not our business."[3] In the *Anthills*, he finds reprehensible this "I don't care - It is not my business attitude of society" that causes people to look on unconcerned at moral atrocities such as rape and murder: "a few women pleaded timorously. But *most of the men found it very funny*" (*Anthills* 215, my emphasis). Thus Achebe argues for conscious commitment on the part of any writer as well as the governed in the affairs of their society.

This view (to be treated in more depth later in this study) also finds echo in Soyinka, whose writings are firmly grounded in social relevance:

> when the writer in his own society can no longer function as conscience, he must recognize that his choice lies between denying himself totally or withdrawing to the position of chronicler and post mortem surgeon (*The Writer in a modern African state* 21).

A Re-orientation of the Governed

Fashioning out an ideological viewpoint may be the starting point of social reconstruction, but the crux of the matter remains how to communicate this vision to a people accustomed to misrule and who have grown cynical and collaborative as a result. To effect this change in the African polity, a re-orientation in the attitudes of the people is necessary. The masses that were the recipients of Odili's bristling indictment in *A Man of the People* quoted above have not changed. In *Anthills of the Savannah*, Ikem's road-encounter with the taxi driver restates the citizens' attitude. When the cab driver pays Ikem a visit, he voices his amazement at not recognizing Ikem's high status:

> [...] the thing wey confuse me properly well be that kind old car wey he come de drive. I never see such! Number one, the car too old; number two, you come again de drive am yourself. Wonderful! so how I fit know na such big man de for my front? I just think this I-go-drive-myself na some jagajaga person wey no fit bring out money to pay driver, and come block road for everybody (*Anthills* 138).

That an attempt at a modest lifestyle can earn Ikem a label as a miser whose simple act of driving himself rather than be driven denies employment to another unemployed citizen leaves Ikem sincerely struggling to comprehend the root cause of such wistful but misplaced "insistence by the oppressed that his oppression be performed in style." Elewa insistently berates Ikem, "this kind car wey you get de make person shame[...] Your own work different than other people? No be the same government work? Me I no understand am-o" (139).

It can then be assumed that the common Nigerian with his/her wrong-headed ambition hardly will be a recipient of the Biblical beatitude that promises "Happy are the poor in spirit[...]," for the ordinary Nigerian citizen is hardly poor in spirit as the exchange between the soldier and Chris's mechanic friend at the check-point illustrates. The mechanic, in an attempt to neutralize the suspicions of the soldier and divert attention from Chris observes to the soldier with seeming complicity:

> Make you no mind. No condition is permanent. [...] Even common bicycle I no get. But my mind strong that one day I go jump bicycle, jump machine and land inside motor car! And somebody go come open door for me and say yes sir! and I go carry my belle like woman we de begin to pregnant small and come sitdon for owner-corner, take cigarette put for mouth, no more kolanut, and say to driver comon move! I get strong mind for that (193).

Such wistful daydreaming of a life redolent of all the wrong values astounds because of the sincere credence given it by the dreamer. How else can a penniless worker scale such fiscal heights with all the health hazards implied in the daydream except by fraud. But modern nations of Africa run societies that exasperate even their wrong-headed citizens as seen in the seargent's exclamation of "This our country na waa![...]This Africa na waa!" A country where a bullying sergeant would drag a girl off at noontide to rape her behind a clump of bushes while bystanders watch, some laughing, some timorously pleading until Chris intervenes with his life.

Obviously, a deep empathy impels Ikem, the ideologue, to realize that even a radical dismantling of this society would never completely eradicate the ill, for the defect may not be in the system after all, but may be "a basic human failing that may only be alleviated by a good spread of general political experience" (139). In *The Trouble with Nigeria*, Achebe insists that "Nigerians are what they are because their leaders are not what they should be" (10). So, like most writers, Achebe believes that what is required is time, the enlightenment that time brings - that "one shining act of bold, selfless leadership at the top" - in order to effect any re-orientation on the part of the governed, and instill in them an awareness of their responsibility to the nation-state. This optimism is borne out in The *Trouble with Nigeria*, "Nigeria is not beyond redemption. Critical, yes, but not entirely hopeless" (10). Thus Achebe's satire in the *Anthills* is tinged with understanding compassion and the positive hope that time and enlightenment are the panacea for the ills of the nation.

This sympathy for the self-employed artisan, market-trader, shopkeeper, taxi-driver, *et al* - all who sweat to eke out a living seems to suggest additionally that in Ikem/Achebe's worldview, national salvation lies in honest self-industry. Ikem's death and the Government's refusal to give his body to his people for burial trigger a crisis which ends in the overthrow of the government. The *coup d'état* confirms the belief that change must emanate from the top not bottom. Chris, another idealist, gives his life in defense of an ideal. Shot by a trigger-mad sergeant, wasted by a man the *ndichie* of Umuofia (*Things Fall Apart*) would call an *efulefu*, Chris is able to live on eternally, his name untarnished and idolized. He would have been part of the new regime which turns out to be no better than its predecessors. Thus, Chris's promise of patriotism, humane and intellectual honesty, tainted but not entirely tarnished by lived experience, will then remain evergreen.

Tainted because earlier on, as Commissioner for Information, he had looked on with utter inertia, for the sake of recording a story, while Sam changed from a raw, programless President to a tyrannical manipulator, defrauder of public coffers and cold-blooded murderer. These experiences in the hands of Sam the President, "are a clear demonstration of the inherent danger in fraternizing with a wild beast, for some day, the beast may break loose and devour even its attendant" (*Anthills* 110). Perhaps, it is no accident that the trio - Sam, Chris and Ikem, formerly classmates and a sort of family - who, in between them, ran the affairs of Kangan, all die in the story.

Perhaps, a fresh start is clearly needed to wipe out what in *The Trouble with Nigeria* Achebe terms "a bankrupt and totally unuseable tradition of political maneuvering, tribal expediency and consummate selfishness" (60). The statement by Elewa's Uncle, "We have seen too much trouble in Kangan because those who make plans make plans for themselves only and their families" (*Anthills* 228) goes to reinforce Achebe's decided stand against elitist rule, military or otherwise, because "this world belongs to the people of the world not to any little caucus, no matter how talented" (104).

Ultimately, in *Anthills of the Savannah* as in *A Man of the People*, Achebe is concerned with the need for responsible governance - that people vested with power should exercise it with responsibility. The group assembled in the last chapter of the book can be read idyllically to portend a starting-ground for a new, equitable and gender-balanced beginning: Beatrice the intellectual, Elewa the illiterate worker and Agatha, the piteous religious-fanatic and maid, all represent women linked in an ideal friendship that transcends class, culture and religion; Braimoh and his taxi-driver friends and Aina, Elewa's petty-trader mother constitute the properly thinking, hard working class; Emmanuel represents the resocialized student leader /intellectual; Colonel Johnson Ossai is used to symbolize intelligent, benevolent military (his extended metaphor of the horse being both clever and aptly intriguing indicate a good intellect); Amaechina (usually a boy's name), is a properly androgynous name to symbolize the fusion of the male/female principles in harmonious balance; and Elewa's Uncle represents the wisdom and tolerance that come with age.

All classes are liberally represented, perhaps to accommodate all political opinions. Even the thorny problem of religion is summarily handled in a non-sectarian fashion by the old Uncle who maintains that the problem with Kangan (Nigeria) is not religious but one of leadership: "but we have no problem with Church people; we have no problem with mosque people. Their intentions are good, their mind on the right road. Only the mind fails to throw as straight as the eye sees" (228).

Beatrice from another ethnic group caps the accommodationism of this new age with a reconciliatory internal monologue as she joins in the singing and dancing: "Well, if a daughter of Allah could join his rival's daughter in a holy dance, what is to stop the priestess of the unknown god from shaking a leg" (224). Perhaps, it is fortuitous that it is a daughter of Ikem who is the reason for the unificatory dance - Ikem, whose motto accords with the author's that "whatever you are is never enough; you must find a way to accept something however small from the other to make you whole and save you from the mortal sin of righteousness and extremism" (154). Ikem's child is therefore, aptly named "Amaechina" - "May-the-path-never-close" - "The-remnant-shall-return" which like Sembene's *Vehi-Ciosane - White Genesis* - symbolizes regeneration, new hope, a promise of future order and progress. The "old masters" of a diseased tradition devoid of vigorous political thought at all costs must not be allowed "to block our vision of the present, or mortgage our children's chances of success in the twenty-first century" (*The Trouble with Nigeria* 60).

In the young lies regeneration, and the old uncle with wisdom born of aged living, "whose mind throws as far as the eye can see" more than any other present, has faith in the future, "I am laughing because in you young people, the world has met its match"(*Anthills* 227). The positively hopeful ending scene of *Anthills of the Savannah* counteracts the book's anguish and disillusionment.

The Role and Place of the Woman in the Structure of the Nation-State

Achebe's advocacy of the female principle is as profound a theme in *Anthills of the Savannah* as any of the already treated issues. Consummate pragmatist artist that he is, Achebe accepts the reality of change. The secret to his revisionist stance can be deduced from the central theme of his two tradition-based novels - *Things Fall Apart* and *Arrow of God*, namely that in a world of sweeping change, whoever is not flexible and adaptable enough will be swept aside. So, Achebe in contrast to his tragic epic hero, Okonkwo, and the inflexible Ezeulu, profiting from their mistakes, bows to the winds of change. An analogy can be made. In *Anthills of the Savannah*, he acknowledges that the malaise the African polity is experiencing is as a result of not including the other half of humanity - the women in the scheme of things.

Okonkwo fails in his singleminded quest for greatness because he lacks effective balance, having determinedly expunged from his consciousness the female principle present in his father Unoka and in his son, the gentle Nwoye. In Okonkwo's cosmic view, "to show affection was a sign of weakness; the only thing worth demonstrating was strength" (*Things Fall Apart* 30).

Now, through his persona Ikem, Achebe accepts that his former attitude towards women had been too respectful, too idealistic - in the best Negritudinal manner. Women had hitherto always been assigned "the role of a fire-brigade after the house has caught fire and been virtually consumed." Over the centuries, oppression of woman by man has worn many faces. For being the cause of the supposed fall of the first man, Adam, a scapegoat anima image had been ascribed to woman to justify whatever suffering man chose to heap on her (*Anthills* 97). The next phase in the history of man's conception of woman was the transfer of the Christian idealization of the virgin mother of God to the woman.

In Achebe's, summation, the traditional Igbos independently worked out a similar conception, only adding more local color to it by calling woman "Nneka" - "Mother is Supreme." In the manner of the Virgin mother of the Christ, woman is thus reverently put on a pedestal "where she will be just as irrelevant to the practical decisions of running the world as she was in the old days" (*Anthills of the Savannah* 98).

Henceforth, the traditional African in canonizing woman, is shielded from any guilt arising from his treatment of the species. Ikem ultimately confesses that he owes to Beatrice the gift of insight into the feminist problem. To remedy matters, Achebe now strives to affirm categorically the moral strength and intellectual integrity of African women (in his characterization of Beatrice), especially since the social (rural) conditions which had in the past kept Igbo women down are largely absent as urbanization and education have combined to broaden the social horizon. Now, rather than the obsession with tribal or communal welfare, the nation state and its survival become the focus of attention.

In *Anthills*, Beatrice, a Senior Assistant Secretary with a degree from Queen Mary College, University of London, is the medium of projecting Achebe's new vision of women's role in the "days ahead" and she helps to clarify Ikem's hazy thoughts on the issue. Beatrice is articulate, independent, self-actualized and able to hold her own. But the female principle has to be re-evaluated and upgraded; Beatrice does the re-evaluation. She has earlier indicted Ikem for his cavalier treatment of his girlfriends to whom he says little, not believing "they have enough brains." (65), The only category of women he seems to respect are "peasants, market women and intellectual women" (92). Beatrice therefore accuses Ikem of not having any clear ideological or political role for women:

> [...] the way I see it is that giving women today the same role which traditional society gave them of intervening only when everything else has failed is not enough, you know, like the women in the Sembene film who pick up the spears abandoned by their defeated menfolks. It is not enough that women should be the court of last resort because the last resort is a damn sight too far and too late! (*Anthills* 91-2).

But, a smart novelist must listen to his characters who, after all are created to wear the shoe and point out to writer and readers alike where it pinches. And modern African women are hollering that the shoe is pinching and are demanding a more egalitarian treatment. In like manner, African nations, in order to survive must show similar readiness to adapt to the new circumstances of a changing Africa, by invoking the female principle and not keep women in reserve "until the ultimate crisis arrives and the waist is broken and hung on the fire, and the palm bears its fruit at the tail of the leaf. Then as the world crashes around Man's ears, Woman in her supremacy will descend and sweep the shards together" (98).

However, Achebe's new envisaged woman's role is to be expounded, articulated and secured by woman, herself. Ikem therefore tells Beatrice: "I can't tell you what the new role for Woman will be. I don't know. I should never presume to know. You have to tell us,"(98) a prescription which accords with the feminist principle that a woman must be the agent of her own emancipation, must determine her own destiny.

Again, Achebe confessed during the 1996 telephone interview with me that in the character of Beatrice, he had subsumed a lot more of himself than people are aware of. The texture of her personality is of a deeply mystic, mythic essence. Daughter of Idemili, Beatrice could in ancient times have been priestess-diviner, intermediary between divinity and the world; at odd moments she is given to "prophesy when her divinity rides her" (105) like a Chielo in *Things Fall Apart*. Beatrice also gets to tell her own version of the events and in the process she participates both in the creation of the story and in wrapping it up.

Thus, it can be seen how the concept of *Nkolika*, a name given to female children - Recalling-Is-Greatest - also re-establishes the role of traditional woman as teller of stories to her children in her huts at night. In *Things Fall Apart*, it is the women who tell the stories: Nwoye's mother who regales him with tells of love and peace, Ekwefi who transmits to Ezinma the myths and legends of the quarrel between Earth and Sky, *et al*. The modern-day Beatrice at critical moments has a vague sense of this duality of being. Deeply conscious of her identity as a proud intelligent Black woman, she, like Aidoo's Sissie (*Our Sister Killjoy* 1981) cries for her Continent whose male leaders are such willing toys in the hands of neo-imperialist powers, leaders so easily flattered by the attentions of ordinary white women to the degree that they often belittle black womanhood. And so, Beatrice points out to Sam his lack of a proper consciousness of the dignity of his office as President, "If I went to America today, to Washington DC, would I, could I, walk into a White House private dinner and take the American President hostage, and his Defense Chief and his Director of CIA?" (81).

The role BB (Beatrice) is made to play in *Anthills*, though more substantial than women's roles in Achebe's earlier novels, still comes short of the desired one or even of the actual progress African women have made in the modern political arena. In "Of Goddesses and Stories" Elleke Boehmer points out that "the way in which Achebe privileges woman continues to bear familiar markings for gender for "[...]certain traditional gender-specific spheres of influence appear to remain in force" (108). There is still a twelve-man cabinet from which Beatrice is excluded despite her "walloping honors degree in English from London University" (*Anthills* 62).

By 1987, the date of *Anthills*'s publication, Nigeria, and indeed Africa, had produced several women of cabinet rank, professionals and corporate leaders. In fact, a woman, Oyibo Odinamadu had run in 1979 as the UPN Deputy Governorship candidate for Anambra State, Nigeria. Yet, it is Beatrice who attempts to reconcile Ikem and Chris in their childish bickering, who arranges to hide Chris, who looks after Ikem's pregnant fiancée Elewa bonding with the girl in the best feminist directive. BB is strong and, using her apartment as the operating center, orchestrates a gathering of the people and the naming of the new-born. Perhaps there is an implied wish by the author for bungling men to relinquish affairs to intelligent, capable women such as Beatrice - a reading that is lent credibility when, because Elewa's uncle comes late, Beatrice takes over and conducting the naming ceremony, assumes a spiritual leadership, perhaps, Ikem's "new and yet-to-be-imagined role as signifying new hope?"

Achebe seems to think so for Rutherford cites his conviction that Beatrice and her female entourage represent women in their place "in the forefront of history" (4). If having a woman eventually become ruler is the author's intention, it is only implied obliquely and not openly stated. BB's role therefore still smacks of that of the women in the Sembène movie that Ikem talks about. Ojinmah confesses that "Achebe also uses Beatrice to synthesize both Ikem's and Chris's dialectics and views about the nature of society" (104). When I confronted the novelist with the observation that Beatrice still functions as the comforter, the sounding board that helps the male characters clarify their different ideological positions, that holds things together, Achebe quips back:

> And who is to blame? You see, many people do not read fiction the way it should be read - as representing what is. They think it should show what "ought to be." Fiction is not a political argument. The book showed what there is. If I was Sam, I would have made Beatrice a member of the cabinet. I was not Sam. I am telling a story that illustrates that society had a huge flaw[...]. You see Beatrice has been coming in stages through all my work. In *A Man of the People*, she is called Eunice. All along, my vision of a woman's role has been developing, growing in intensity as the role of the Igbo woman has been growing in Igbo society.[3]

Since according to him, Achebe gives a portrait of women to reflect their growth within society, it is expected that his next novels will portray women in essential, self-determining, subject roles that give an accurate measure of their strengths and achievements in Nigerian (if not African) society. Perhaps, Chinua Achebe, who more than any other writer has fostered the growth of African literature (although he insists that, like the Owerri Mbari, African literature is a communal enterprise in creativity[4]), should be taken at his word - that they who have survived, Beatrice, Elewa, Amaechina - are the "anthills surviving to tell the new grass of the savannah about last year's brush fires" (*Anthills* 31).

The Creative Writer and Society

The artist/visionary, therefore, as the creator of the story becomes also the readers' guide. As Achebe conceptualizes it, the story - *Nkolika* owns and directs; in the best formalist manner, the story has a rich, complete life of its own:

> Recalling-Is-Greatest. Why? Because it is only the story that can continue beyond the war and the warrior. It is the story that outlives the sound of war-drums and the exploits of brave fighters. It is the story, not the others, that saves our progeny from blundering like blind beggars into the spikes of the cactus fence. The story is our escort; without it, we are blind[...]the story is everlasting (123-4).

In an interview with Chris Searle, Achebe reiterates the same ideas in other words:

> If you look at the things that are happening in the society: the struggle itself, the inspiration to struggle, the story of the struggle; when you put all these things together and ask what is the most important, then the choice falls upon the story. It is the story that conveys all our gains, all our failures, all we hold dear and all we condemn. To convey this to the next generation is the only way we can keep going and keep alive as people. Therefore, the story is like the genes that are transferred to create the new being. It is far more important than anything else (12-16).

The story which is literature not only revitalizes the living but teaches us to learn from our experiences so that we do not turn out to be like "a bunch of stage clowns who bump their heads into the same heavy obstacles again and again [...]" (*The Trouble with Nigeria* 54).

For Achebe, therefore, the craft of writing is a grave responsibility. Ikem expounds this belief in the seriousness of his craft, "I want to excite general enlightenment by forcing all the people to examine the condition of their lives because as the saying goes, the unexamined life is not worth living. As a writer, I aspire only to widen the scope of that self-examination" (*Anthills* 158). The writer is the observer and recorder of societal mores as well as the critic. This, Chris acknowledges, is his reason for lingering for so long in the dictator's corrupt cabinet, "I couldn't be writing this if I didn't hang around to observe it all" (2). Thus is underlined the functionality of writing. In the character of Ikem, Achebe acknowledges, that he put in a lot of himself. The artist is also the conscience of his people. For Ikem, it is the endorsement of the relevance of his writings, more than anything else that gives him the needed boost for activism. As the members of the Taxi Drivers Union tell him:

> The thing oga write too plenty. But na for we small people he de write every time. I no sabi book but I sabi say na for we this oga de fight, not for himself. He na big man. Nobody fit do fuckall to him. So he fit stay for him house, chop him oyibo chop, drink him cold beer put him air conditioner and forget we. But he no do like that. So, we come salute am (136).

For Ikem, it is heartening to know that the people will recognize and trust selfless leadership when they see it. Change therefore must emanate from the leadership, from the top, not from the masses. Consequently, for the writer the obligation to guide and direct becomes doubly necessary. For Achebe, Africans, African Americans, and indeed all groups under siege from a plethora of problems - ranging from foreign manipulation to endemic internal ills like hunger and underdevelopment - the theory of "art for art's sake" is an unaffordable luxury. Writer after writer reiterates Achebe's view that the artist in some peculiar milieux such as his can not afford to be on the fringe of, or hostile to society as happens in the West, but must be there at the forefront as "the sensitive point of his community"(*Morning Yet on Creation Day* 45).

The writer who must be a teacher and guide should not "expect to be excused from the task of re-education and regeneration that must be done". Part of this re-education is what Ikem declares as forcing his readers and audience "to think [...]to examine the condition of their lives." Achebe explains that a necessary part of this re-examination involves the primary exercise of looking back "to try and find out where we went wrong, where the rain began to beat us" (44); and in the best understanding of the meaning of the word "education," re-educate our societies not to accept the label of inferiority, to appreciate our cultures and make our weather, our landscape worthy subjects of poetry. By setting the example with his books, especially the traditionally-based ones, he thus is teaching his readers "that their past- - with all its imperfections - - was not one long night of savagery from which the first Europeans acting on God's behalf delivered them" (45).

In re-establishing the theory of functional writing, Achebe believes that education and aesthetics need not be mutually exclusive because a judicious balance can be struck. In this regard again, he appreciates the example of James Baldwin who bravely wrestled with the English language until he was able to sufficiently bend it to translate the burden of his Black heritage; or of Ralph Ellison, who with his finely textured writing and skillful characterization, understood fiction's potential for influencing change:

> [...] a novel could be fashioned as a raft of hope, perception and entertainment that might help keep us afloat as we tried to negotiate the snags and whirlpools that mark our nation's vacillating course towards and away from the democratic ideal (Introduction to the *Invisible Man* xx-xxii).

This dual goal of fidelity to the art of writing, yet simultaneously making its content functional, Achebe, for one, has successfully accomplished in his works, more so in *Things Fall Apart* and *Anthills of the Savannah* with African peoples as his primary audience. Using Ikem, Chris and Beatrice (*Anthills*) as examples, Achebe thus teaches his readers how to live in turbulent times and yet be true to one's self. In his view, "a writer is not a theorist. [Since] none of the "isms" - Capitalism, Marxism, *et cetera* can solve our problems, yet, "solutions can be found - in negotiating the tides of History - knowing where we came from. We must not allow History to be our masters. We must not become slaves to memory. We must use History and knowledge, and experience to negotiate the present."[5]

For Achebe, then, writing relates primarily to a people's survival and they who endure and learn from the mistakes of their historical past, they who learn how to use history, knowledge and experience to negotiate the present and ensure the future are the "anthills surviving to tell the new grass of the savannah about last year's brush fires" (*Anthills* 31). The story, everlasting in essence, remains the escort that helps us avoid the mistakes of the past. *Anthills of the Savannah*, thematically multiple-layered, skillfully crafted, socio-politically relevant yet entertainingly satirical is the concrete medium - *Nkolika - The Story is Greatest* - by which Kangan (Nigeria/Africa) can negotiate its thorny pathway to future greatness. Using the metaphor of Diop's young tree bent under its burden both external and internal, Africa like the young tree will yet survive and endure, but only if the lessons of the past are learnt and all - men, women and children - co-operate to sing *May-the-path-never-close*.

Notes

[1] *Anthills of the Savannah* will hereinafter be referred to as *Anthills*.

[2] Telephone Interview I held with Chinua Achebe on March 11, 1996.

[3] *Ibid.*

[4] *Ibid.*

[5] *Ibid.*

Works Cited

Achebe, Chinua. *Anthills of the Savannah*. Ibadan, Nigeria: Heinemann Educational Books, 1988.

--- *A Man of the People*. Nigeria: Heinemann, 1966.

--- *Morning Yet on Creation Day: Essays*. Nigeria: Heinemann, 1977.

--- *The Trouble with Nigeria*. Enugu: Fourth Dimension Publishers, 1983.

--- "African Literature as Restoration of Celebration." In *Chinua Achebe: A Celebration*. Kirsten Holst Peterson and Anna Rutherford, eds. Oxford: Heinemann Educational Books, 1991. 1-10.

Gordimer, Nadine. "A Tyranny of Clowns." *The New York Times Book Review* (Feb.21) 1988.

Emenyeonu, N. Ernest. *Studies on the Nigerian Novel*. Ibadan: Heinemann, 1991.

Ezenwa-Ohaeto. *Chinua Achebe: A Biography*. Indianapolis: Indiana University Press, 1997.

Farah, Nurrudin. "A Tale of Tyranny" in *West Africa*, 21 September 1987, pp. 1828-31.

The Humanities. vol.1. eds. Witt, Brown, Dunbar *et al*. 2 vols. Lexington, MA: D.C. Heath& Co. 1993.

Lindfors, Bernth and Bala Kothan Daram (eds), *South Asian Responses to Chinua Achebe* New Delhi: Prestige Books, 1993. pp. i-ii.

Moyers, Bill. "Interview with Achebe," in *A World of Ideas*. Ed. Betty Sue Flowers. New York: Doubleday, 1989.

Niane, D.T. *Sundiata : an epic of Mali*. transl. G.D. Pickett. London: Heinemann, 1993.

Ojinmah, Umelo. *Chinua Achebe: New Perspectives*. Nigeria: Spectrum Books Ltd., 1991.

Peterson, Kirsten Holst and Anna Rutherford, eds. *Chinua Achebe: A Celebration*. Oxford: Heinemann, 1990.

Rutherford, Anna. "Interview with Achebe." In *Kunapipi*, IX, 2 1987.

Soyinka, Wole. "The Writer in a Modern African State" in *The Writer in Modern Africa*. ed. Per Wastberg. N.Y.: Africana Publishing. 1969.

Searle, Chris. "Achebe and the Bruised Heart of Africa." In *Wasafiri*, 14. 1991, pp.12-16. Wastberg. N.Y.: Africana Publishing. 1969.

Taiwo, Oladele. *Culture and the Nigerian Novel*. New York: St. Martin's Press, 1976.

Achebe's Okonkwo and Hurston's Jody Starks: Twin Souls in Different Climes and Their Women

E uripides, most fair-minded of ancient dramatists, an iconoclast born ahead of his period, strove to strike a balance between Greek belief in humanistic capability and *"hubris."* For his empathetic literary depiction of women, he was derided and scorned and his plays did not, in his lifetime, receive the appreciation due them. Eventually, in 406 B.C. at the court of King Archelaus of Macedon, he was torn to death by hounds at the instigation of jealous rivals. Tainted with *hubris* like the ancient mysoginist Greeks are two fictional characters - Jody Starks and Okonkwo - separated by both temporal and spatial distance, and despite minor differences in their characters and their societies, kindred spirits nonetheless; both, ultimately are plagued by the repercussions of their public postures. Anna Lillios is not far wrong when she describes such characters as "narrow-minded, mean, jealous, judgmental men who beat their wives" (103).

In this chapter, an attempt is made to examine the similarities and contrasts in the cultures the characters Okonkwo and Starks lived in, their women and the attendant female reaction to the corresponding male *"hubris"* and finally, the narrative styles of Chinua Achebe and Zora Neale Hurston.

Hurston and Achebe: Objectives

Both Hurston and Achebe are pace-setters who inaugurated new literary trends – both writers have striven to present black folk art in its glory. Achebe goes on to become the patriarch of the literature of cultural nationalism while Hurston becomes the matriarch of African-American feminist literature. Both joyfully portray a love of the lore and mores of their ancestral past, promoting a racial health, "a sense of black people as complete, complex, *undiminished* human beings" (Henry Louis Gates, Jr. 190). Both writers in their books depict a well-defined societal structure, untainted by the intrusion of white manipulative presence. The societies in question - Umuofia (largely representing both Igbo and African civilizations of between 1850 and 1900) and Eatonville (in the early twentieth century) while not perfect, while in fact possessing some serious moral flaws, manage to celebrate black life as authentic ethos rather than as defensive reactions to white actions. One of Achebe's principal aims in writing *Things Fall Apart* as stated in his own words and earlier in this work is:

> [...]to help my society regain belief in itself and put away the complexes of the years of denigration and self-abasement[...]If I were God, I would regard as the very worst our acceptance - for whatever reason - of racial inferiority ("The Novelist as a Teacher" in *MYOCD* 44).

His book, *Things Fall Apart (TFA)* Achebe insists, is for him "an act of atonement with my past, the ritual return and homage of a prodigal son" (*MYOCD* 70). Hurston must have felt similarly though she does not confront social issues as directly as Achebe does. In their self-appointed tasks as apostles of cultural revalorization and pride of race, Hurston, from a gynocentric viewpoint and Achebe (totally patriarchal) can still be seen as twin souls united in the role of the writer as teacher/visionary, purposefully engaged in the task of re-education and regeneration. And so their fictional societies are exclusive ones. When white culture does intrude into Umuofia, for instance, it has a catalyst effect; the consequences are catastrophic and things really begin to fall apart. For Hurston who insists that she is "not tragically colored [and] does not belong to the school of sobbing negrohood," freedom was something internal. She states in *Moses, Man of the Mountain*, that the man himself must make his own emancipation. *Their Eyes Were Watching God* therefore marks a radical departure from the protest/realist tradition of the African-American novel.

Oblivious of the literary racial battle raging during the depression years, Hurston embarks on an original and independent course, putting on stage a female hero in quest of empowerment and self-actualization, to help Black women put away centuries of denigration and self-abasement. Simultaneously, she introduces a specific black vernacular tradition, thereby establishing a literary progeny: Toni Morrison's *Song of Solomon* and *Beloved*, Alice Walker's writings, the craft of Gloria Naylor, Toni Cade Bambara, *et cetera* trace a direct maternal literary ancestry to Hurston in their use of narrative strategies, vernacular framework, resonant imagery and figurative capacities. Ultimately, both Achebe and Hurston create vibrant fictional societies by upholding black myths, legends and lore. Henceforth, their literary progeny would be inspired by both writers to return as prodigal children in search of their ancestral folk roots.

Starks and Okonkwo: Their Societies

Eatonville is a rural community that settles down to a sedate, unhurried pace, peopled with folks rich in tall, ribald stories, side-splitting jokes and legends collected and polished with the anthropological skills only a Hurston possesses. But Eatonville is also a town in which the Jody Starks of this world have established a rigid gender bifurcation - the man to work, sport and office as mayor, and the woman restricted to the domestic realm and the porch in imitation of a ceremonial Southern belle, aping bourgeois values so dear to Nanny. And so man - whether a Starks or an Okonkwo - goes on happily to productively realize his destiny while the woman becomes trapped in the immanence of domestic chores and decorative irrelevance. Janie becomes a mere projection of Joe Starks' ambition with little substance or activity of her own: "How yuh lak bein' Mrs. Mayor?" he asks her. "You'se always off talkin' and fixin' things, and ah feels lak jus' markin' time" (*Their Eyes were Watching God* 43). But she feels she is in a rut.

Equally, Umuofia is a rural community with well-defined societal structures - political, social, cultural, religious, juridical - embodied in its war exploits, competitive wrestling matches, heart-throbbing ceremonial outings of the masked "egwugwu" - in all, an androcentric universe in which woman is defined and differentiated with reference to man and not he with reference to her; she is the inessential as opposed to the essential. He is the subject, he is the absolute; she is the "other."

Umuofia women remain on the fringes of their society merely as ciphers. If anything, that society exceeds Eatonville in rigidity, for it never would have occurred to any Umuofia man to call on any woman, as Eatonvillians ask of Janie, to make a speech while they "listen to uh few words of encouragement." Joe Starks' reply to this untoward proposition would have made Okonkwo proud: "[...]ma wife don't know nothin' 'bout no speech-making. Ah never married her for nothin' lak dat. She's uh woman and her place is in de home" (41). In both societies, man is subject, absolute; woman is the inessential, the object.

Starks and Okonkwo: Similar Character Traits

Both protagonists show remarkable similarities of character. They are, in fact, literary twin souls in their ambition to rank as *primus inter pares* in their respective societies. Hurston's Starks instantly cuts a swashbuckling figure as a dreamer, a citified, stylish dandy, hat set at a jaunty angle with the look that speaks to Janie of "far horizons" - representing infinite expectations:

> [...] hearin' 'bout them buildin' a new state[...] a town all out a colored folks, he knew he belonged for he wanted to buy in big[...] [and] be a big voice. (26-7).

Thus, Starks becomes part of the building up of a town and its culture - land, store, post-office, street-lighting, law-making and town incorporation. It is therefore both natural and reasonable that "de man that built things oughta boss it." Though not physically as imposing as Okonkwo, yet "the town bowed down to him" (47), accepting his material innovations but resenting his assertion of superiority.

On his part, physically imposing, right from the start, Okonkwo wants to be a lord of the land. With Unoka as a father, a flute playing wastrel, an "agbala" who dies shamefully and is thrown into the evil forest, Okonkwo had a disadvantaged beginning, inheriting neither yam barns, wives nor titles. Consequently, he is ruled by one passion, to hate everything that his father loved. The structure of the traditional society favors his meteoric rise; it is an achievement-oriented, egalitarian society in which a man's position is determined by the strength of his arm. How understandable therefore that he takes for his mentor, Nwakibie, the wealthy villager who has three huge yam barns, nine wives and thirty children - the status symbols of the era that will earn him entrance into the highest cults. Glowing iridescently in the horizon is the ultimate accolade:

> There were only four titles in the clan and only one or two men in any generation ever achieved the fourth and highest. When they did, they became the lords of the land (*Things Fall Apart* 123).

Okonkwo is determined to be a lord of the clan. The key to this signal achievement resided in a simple principle - relentless industry for "[...]among his people, achievement was revered." As the elders said, "if a child washed his hands, he could eat with kings" (8). So, he sets out to wash his hands and eat with kings, for is it not also said among these people that if a man says "yes", his *chi* will concur? Possessing an infinite capacity for hard work, he "worked daily on his farm from cock-crow until the chickens went to roost [...] he was a strong man and rarely felt fatigue" (13). "I am not afraid of hardwork," he reassures Nwakibie (21).

Naturally, the victims of his indefatigable energy are his wives and children, especially Nwoye, in whom Okonkwo perceives "signs of incipient laziness" (13). And soon, Okonkwo becomes famous. At eighteen, he throws Amalinze, the wily wrestler called "the cat," and becomes Umuofia's undisputed champion wrestler. Soon also, he becomes wealthy - two yam barns, two titles, three wives and as a tested warrior-hero, he also becomes the clan's proud emissary to Mbaino, and the eventual guardian of Ikemefuna, the fated symbol of Mbaino's capitulation to war-dominant Umuofia, a boy who will unwittingly expose Okonkwo's *Achilles heel* - fear of being thought weak. In the course of time, Okonkwo will become one of the juridical masquerades - *egwugwus*.

The omniscient narrator, generously concedes him his due: "If ever a man deserved his success, that man was Okonkwo[...]He said 'yes' very strongly[...]so not only his *chi* but his clan agreed" (27). Okonkwo's success is therefore not fortuitous, but earned.

Another clime, perhaps another era, Okonkwo reincarnates into Starks. Like his kindred spirit, Starks is a self-made man who "been workin' for white folks all his life until having saved up his three hundred dollars" (*Their Eyes* 27), he determines to be part of nation-building and of history. Endowed with uncanny business acumen, he decides to buy big - two hundred acres of land which he parcels out and sells at maximum profit. A born organizer of men, he excites the grudging admiration of the town folks, "Dat man talks like a section foreman," Coker comments:

> "He's mighty compellment [...] Ain't never seen no sich a colored man befo' in all ma bawn days. He's going tuh put up a store and git uh post office from de government [...]They bowed down to him rather, because he was all of these things, and then again he was all of these things because the town bowed down" (35-47).

Like Okonkwo, Starks announces hardwork as the secret of his "compellment:" "Ah means tuh put mah hands tuyh de plow heah and strain every nerve tuh make dis de metropolis of the state" (40). And he Does - incorporates the town, commissions street lamps, establishes a post office and is unanimously chosen the mayor of the new town. Like Okonkwo, Jody's success fuels his arrogance and condescension towards lesser mortals - a buccaneer, biting down on cigars, and swinging round on his chair – almost imposing his image on the people - for "he had a bow-down command in his face and every step he took made the thing more tangible" (44).

To him, the Eatonville folks are trash who "doesn't even own de house deh sleep in[...]They is jus' some puny humans playing' round in the toes of time'" (51), he tells Janie. Reciprocating, the envious folks backbite him: "He loves obedience out of everybody under de sound of his voice[...] You kin feel a switch in his hand when he's talkin' to you." Nevertheless, fair-minded Sam Watson concedes that Starks, like Okonkwo, has earned his success, "He can't help bein' sorta bossy [...] none o' all dis yuh see and you'se settin' on wasn't here neither, when he come. Give the devil his due" (46).

In Umuofia, Starks' "gum-grease trash" translates to "agbala", a derogatory appellation which the lordly Okonkwo calls the unsuccessful Osugo when he tells him, "this meeting is for men" (*Things Fall Apart* 26), prompting a swift reminder from an elder that "those whose palm kernels are cracked for them by a benevolent spirit should not forget to be humble " (27). To give the devil his due, for these twin souls of different climes, success does stem from the work of their strong hands and as Hurston herself acknowledges, "anyone who walks in the way of power and property is bound to meet with hate" (*Their Eyes* 45).

Their inflexibility

For our two protagonists, inflexibility is a further unifying trait. Eatonville folks typecast Starks as a man "dat changes everything, but nothin' don't change him" (46). To his wife's complaint that so much activity on his part "keeps us in some kind of strain" (43), he pays no heed. In attempting to change Janie, remaking her to reflect his image,

he excludes her from participation in communal activities. Janie later confronts him with the unpalatable truth that " You sho loves to tell me whut to do, but Ah can't tell you nothin'[...]you changes everything but nothin' don't change you - not even death" (46-82). And as a direct result of his inflexibility, Janie shames him to death. Rejecting both Janie's care and medical attention, Starks opts for death.

His twin soul, Okonkwo equally accepts no advice from any one, not even from his friend Obierika. Ogbuefi Ezeudu warns him not to take part in the killing of Ikemefuna because "the boy calls you father" (*Things Fall Apart* 57), a piece of sound advice Okonkwo flouts with grave consequences. He is inflexible towards accepting change for himself. He also does not want to see an alien religion come into his town. Umuofia's eventual betrayal of him would drive home Achebe's pertinent thesis that in a world where the principle of change is a constant, whatever cannot flow with the tide is always swept away. Inflexibility has its drawbacks.

To both men, tender emotions are never acknowledged openly; it is an acknowledgement of weakness. Thus Okonkwo glories in, and tries to bend Nwoye to glory in tales of violence and bloodshed to the total exclusion of feelings of love and any moderating female principle which would give his character balance. Having such abysmally low opinion of women, Ogbuefi Ndulue, who reportedly has a companionate, mutually respectful marriage with his wife, appears to him as a creature from outer space. To his puzzled comment, "I thought he was a strong man" comes the pertinent rejoinder, "He is" (68). The really very strong do not fear tender emotions - a reflection which would be lost on Okonkwo, of course; for he is not a reflecting man.

To complicate matters for Jody Starks, he is equally jealous of both Janie's youth and beauty which prompts his ordering Janie

[...] to tie up her hair around the store[...] She was there in the store for him to look at, not those others. But he never said things like that. It just wasn't him. (*Their Eyes* 52)

Starks and Okonkwo: The Violence of Temper

Twin souls, Starks and Okonkwo both have violent temper; to both, women are objects of domestic convenience and they demand instant obedience. Okonkwo, tense as a coiled spring, is introduced early in the story walking as if he is going to pounce on someone: "He had a slight stammer and whenever he was angry and could not get his words quickly enough, he would use his fists. Okonkwo is said to rule his household with a heavy hand. His wives, especially the youngest, live in fear of his fiery temper, and so do his little children" (8-16).

Just as Okonkwo batters Ojiugo for not getting his meal ready, so does Starks, down in Eatonville, slap Janie around "until she felt a ringing sound in her ears" because his dinner is not prepared the way he wants it: "He wanted her submission and he'd keep on fighting until he felt he had it" (*Their Eyes* 66). They both aim at total control of their wives, for as Stark starkly announces, "Somebody got to think for women and chillun' and chickens and cow [...]they sho don't think none theirselves" (67).

Their displays of temper do yield some unforgettable results. A savage beating would goad Okonkwo's son, Nwoye, never to return, into the welcoming embrace of that alien religion, the agent of the colonial power that will break down Okonkwo's society. Ekwefi gets a thorough beating for merely plucking a few leaves off a banana tree and for a muttered, dissenting comment, nearly gets her head blown off; "[t]he week of Peace" is desecrated as Ojiugo, his third wife, feels the fury of Okonkwo's fists for choosing to indulge her pleasure rather than his comfort. Janie utterly indicts Jody for his egocentric craving for instant obedience: "Thus too busy listening to your own big voice – [a]ll dis bowin' down, all dis obedience under yo' voice" (*Their Eyes* 82) will encompass the unuttered protest of Umuofia women.

Narrative Styles: the Metaphor of the Voice

Perhaps in no other area can a more distinctive analogy be made in the narrative styles of these two black writers as in their use of the "voice" as a metaphor for characterizing both men and women. I find that the metaphor of the voice is inextricably linked to the treatment of the women by both Starks, Okonkwo and their societies. Despite their successes, both Okonkwo and Starks are flawed heroes. Regarding Starks, the metaphor of the "big voice" mediates the history of his rise and fall. He exercises his voice to put up a big show, be it lighting the street lamps, buying the mule off Matt Bonner, or even burying the mule.

Paradoxically, as he exercises his voice, Jody denies Janie the use of hers. Like the mule, Janie is his prized possession - symbol of his grand success. But, if truth be told, right from the beginning, he has made no bones of his intent. Appreciating Janie's beauty, he tells her quite early in the story that:

> A pretty doll-baby lak you is made to sit on de front porch and rock and fan yo'self and eat p'taters dat other folks plant just special for you (28).

He would later express his outrage at her lack of appreciation,

> She wasn't even appreciative of his efforts and she had plenty cause to be. Here he was just pouring honors all over her; building a high chair for her so sit in and overlook the world and she here pouting all over it! [...]. He ought to box her jaws[...]. He wanted her to use her privileges. That was the rock she was battered against (*Their Eyes* 51).

 And he boxes and batters her often enough. When Janie, uncaring of his middle class values, therefore realizes their incompatibility, she holds back speech and commences an interior existence. Thus, she discovers that "she had a host of thoughts [...] and numerous emotions she had never expressed to him." Clearly, Hurston demonstrates with the figure of Starks her uneasiness with the conventional male hero "who asserts himself through his powerful voice" (xii). Endowed with special insight by so much interior living, Janie sums up her husband's life as

well as her community's, "talkin' don't amount tuh uh hill uh beans when yuh can't do nothin' else." "[...]and how surprised y'all is goin' tuh be if you ever find out you don't know half as much 'bout us as you think you do" (71).

Evidently, orality which excludes inner growth but is only based on a learning experience has obvious limitations. For, living with Starks has taught Janie to appreciate the virtue of limited speech: "and no matter what Jody did, she said nothing. She had learned how to talk some and leave some"; which makes it poignant as "she thought back and forth about what happened in the making of a voice out of a man" (71-83).

Nevertheless, Hurston is preoccupied with the need to empower her female hero through the medium of "voice," *judiciously* used: "*how to talk some and leave some.*" Hurston herself always remembered the bedside scene of her dying mother, then incapable of voicing her wishes, "[b]ut she looked at me, or so I felt, to speak for her. She depended on me for a voice". So, Zora has to speak for women of all time by giving Janie as well as her mother a voice, to be used as an instrument of empowerment, friendship and change. Phoebe will attest after hearing Janie's story, "Ah done growed ten feet higher from jus' listenin' tuh you, Janie. Ah ain't satisfied wid mahself no mo" (284). Thereafter, women such as Phoeby will try to change things in their homes and take steps towards self-definition and affirmation. Thus, Janie's (Hurston's) represents women's collective voice for a new world order.

In contradistinction, while Hurston struggles to give women a voice through Janie, a contemporary, Richard Wright in *Blackboy* rather identifies with Achebe's Okonkwo by begging his dying mother to be "quiet. That night, I ceased to react to my mother. My feelings were frozen." For such as these two, *voice* becomes a metaphor of suppression. It is remembered that Wright's negative critique of *Their Eyes* translates to an attempt to suppress the book and deny Hurston a voice. But today, feminists and Hurston addicts insist that contrary to Richard Wright's 1937 critique, *Their Eyes* does carry multiple themes, messages and thoughts. For these agree with Hurston that men's talking - be it Starks' or Okonkwo's - is a method of exerting power. Hurston therefore exploits Janie's voice to revise and redefine a hitherto male-dominated canon.

The character of Janie, articulate and self-reliant, as the folks of Eatonville would say, is one of "compellment." Goaded into revolt, just as the oppressed mule rears up and rushes to attack its tormentor,

Lum (53), Janie finds her voice and uses it. Countering Jody's jealous denigration of her attractions, she reaffirms confidently,

> "Ah'm uh woman every inch of me, and ah know it[...]You big bellies round here and put out a lot of brag, but 'tain't nothin' to it but your big voice[...]when you pull down yo' britches, you look lak' de change of life"(75).

Contrastingly, while Achebe depicts Okonkwo's treatment of his wives with complacency, Hurston's Janie protests the putting down of women of all time; she revises the *statusquo* - be seen and not be heard. Janie is now both seen and heard:

> Then, Joe Starks realized all the meanings and his vanity bled like a flood. Janie had robbed him of his illusion of irresistible maleness that all men cherish[...]There was nothing to life anymore. Ambition was useless" (75-6).

Hurston's is reductive technique *par excellence*. Gazer, Jody now becomes the object of gaze. Ousmane's Sembène's El Hadji (*Xala*) can empathize with him as he stands there in full gaze of the wretched of the earth, to be mocked, spat at. Nwapa's Amarajeme (*Idu*), unable to withstand public derisive gaze hangs himself. Jody equally can not take it for,

> [...] what excuse can a man give in the eyes of other men for lack of strength? Raggedy-behind squirts of sixteen and seventeen would be giving him their merciless pity out of their eyes[...]Ambition was useless (*Their Eyes* 76).

And so, sobbing with frustration, Jody Starks dies a failure: "For the thing which I greatly feared is come upon me and that which I was afraid of is come unto me" (*Job* 3:25). Here, Starks' character differs from that of Okonkwo, who would not have waited to be so thoroughly humiliated before calling any of his wives to order. The offending wife would have long before then been thoroughly beaten and deprived of the opportunity to get as far as Janie does, even at the risk of killing whoever it is. Jody Starks, in temper, is weaker than Okonkwo. Chapter Seven of *Their Eyes* is a scant two pages, but it makes a crucial and definitive statement in the history of African American fictional writing. Here the style of the two writers further contrasts more starkly.

Achebe in an expository narrative, presents the repressive treatment of women of Umuofia without apology. Traditional Igbo (African) society was a man's world in which the power of patriarchy was total. In *Things Fall Apart*, the female viewpoint is so subdued that the omniscient narrator ends up talking for them. Umuofia women's "voices" lack the resonant vigor and authority of those of the men, even when they are injured. When beaten, Ekwefi and her only daughter weep a tearful "voice" and the other wives dare not interfere "beyond an occasional and tentative 'it's' enough Okonkwo' pleaded from a reasonable distance" (39). But for the authoritative voice of Uchendu, "Leave that boy alone! are you mad?" Nwoye could have been killed for attending a Christian meeting, as the women stood "screaming outside, afraid to go in" (141).

Men's voices are depicted to carry the weight of authority and domination. To an innocent question from his first wife, he, Okonkwo *thunders* "Do what you are told woman, when did you become one of the *Ndichie* of Umuofia?" (18) and his first wife subsides into acquiescent invisibility. Starks would say to his wife, "you gettin' too moufy, Janie." (*Their Eyes* 71) The "voices" of the male *Egwugwu* masquerade, ancestral spirits and judges sound "guttural and awesome" (*Things Fall Apart* 84) inspiring mystical fear.

The only female "voices" capable of matching the men's in vigor and resonant authority are those of females when they assume the mystical mantle of divinity like Chielo, the priestess of the Oracle of the Hills and the Caves; or the awesome and inescapable *Ani*, the earth goddess, who determines fertility - biological and agricultural – and disdains the burial on her soil, of people who die ignominiously like Unoka or Okonkwo. This deity has Ezeani, a man to serve her as priest. And the men of Umuofia, including Okonkwo live in awe of her retributive propensities and are quick to pacify her.

It has been my postulation that Umuofia's shabby and degrading treatment of women (wives) stems from their unconscious fear of, rather than reverence of the ubiquitous and capricious Earth goddess, Ani or Ala - who wreaks such havoc on their lives. To the men of Umuofia, she must have seemed like the embodiment of the two-faced Greek furies, Scylla and Charybdis joined together - capricious, vengeful, unavoidable and incomprehensible. In the words of Ezeani, the priest of Ani to Okonkwo, the goddess when offended was capable of wiping out "the whole clan[...]the earth goddess, whom you have insulted may refuse to give us her increase and we shall all perish" (*Things Fall Apart* 32).

In mortal dread of a fearsome female principle before whom they are helpless, lacking the voice to reprimand her, they therefore descend heavily indeed on their mortal wives whose lives they can control. The men therefore deny some Umuofia women their voice, individually or collectively.

"The Violence of Fear"

Both – Okonkwo, literally and Stark, figuratively - are masquerades; they both wear masks, for crouched beneath the façade of violent temper, ready fists and swaggering ambition lies a living, lurking fear, buried deep in the subconscious. For Okonkwo, "it was the fear of himself lest he be found to resemble his father" (*Things Fall Apart* 17). For Starks, it was a mix of fears - lest he be found to be less than other men, fear of losing his voice; lowering the value of the possession secured through his relentless ambition and industry. A concatenation of events occasion his downfall. Firstly, his prized possession, Janie, symbol of his success as "Mrs. Mayor Starks" (*Their Eyes* 50), pedestalized out of any meaningful contribution to productive living, stages an unanticipated rebellion and decamps from the "throne on the porch" where he had made her an object of gaze. Employing the technique of reductive characterization, a style so reminiscent of Buchi Emecheta's derisive description of the ridiculous Nnaife, NnuEgo's husband in *The Joys of Motherhood*, Hurston shows Jody Starks up through Janie's mercilessly critical gaze:

> [...] no longer young with something dead about him[...]He squatted over his ankles when he walked[...]His prosperous-looking belly that used to thrust out so pugnaciously to intimidate folks, sagged like a load suspended from him... (*Their Eyes* 73). ...Then Janie strikes him where it hurts most, his pride of manhood, with her mortal put-down - "when you pull down yo' britches, you look lak de change uh life." Henceforth, good-for-nothings will look with envy at the things he owns but will laugh at the man when he parades his possessions: "she had cast down his empty armor before men (75-6).

In any culture, impotence will always reduce a man to a cipher. In African literature, examples abound - Ousmane Sembene's El Hadji

Kaber (*Xala*), Nwapa's Amarajeme (*Idu*), Raymond S. Easmon's Francis Briwa (*The Burnt-out Marriage*) are risible castrates. Ultimately, impotence entails a kind of role reversal, making *man* not *woman* the object of derision and dictating death as a final way-out. Janie's final revolt receives Hurston's formal signature of approval when she tears off the "head-rag" (symbol of confinement and repressed womanhood), shakes down her plentiful hair and in ultimate narcissism, glories in its length and weight. This is her assertion of her right to her beauty and to personal identity.

Similarly with Okonkwo, "fear[...]is the deciphering key that unlocks all his subconscious feelings of violence" (Mezu, "Violence of Fear" 7) culminating in the dastardly murder of Ikemefuna. With telling swiftness, calamities descend on Okonkwo - he commits an accidental *ochu*, gets exiled, returns to a position of reduced stature in Umuofia, confronts the encroaching alien religion, kills the court messenger and since his pride will not let him be taken alive, kills himself: "That which I most feared has come upon me and what I dread befalls me" (*Job* 3:25). His grand life, based on a reactionary principle against his father Unoka ends as an exercise in futile living since he dies a comparable ignoble death, ending up in the same "evil bush." Thus his whole life is submerged in violence, engendered by his own internal fears. Clearly, Okonkwo and Starks, twin souls in different climes are classic examples of men who as the Igbos would say, could not rise above their personal *chi*.

Conclusion

Achebe and Hurston, therefore use Okonkwo and Jody Starks to ultimately highlight their respective literary philosophies. With Hurston, Jody and her other two husbands serve as foil and catalysts to Janie's transition first from subject to object and final emergence into transcendence as a pioneering female subject hero in African American fictional history. With Killicks, she ferociously resists a broken life in the muledom of an exploited existence; with Starks, she spiritedly combats an enshrined reification as a prized showcase item of possession. While, it is true that with TeaCake, the son of the evening sun, the bee to her pollen, she finally experiences a flourishing of her capacities, yet she is still defined by him, for he is still the quintessential master; he makes all the decisions, robbing her of autonomy (the quality of his decision-making ability becomes

160

debatable when it is remembered that it is through his lackadaisical attitude that they stay too long in the muck and get caught up in the storm); and when his dominance is in doubt, he restates it by slapping her around.

Perhaps, it can be surmised that both Hurston consciously and Janie subconsciously find themselves unable to forgive that beating meted out by a being so trusted and loved that TeaCake is, to echo Morrison, "rebuked" as thoroughly as Sethe is by the unforgiving Beloved. He, Tea Cake, is bestialized as a mad dog. What is then the final message? That all female barterers are rabid dogs? The outcome is the final message. With the death of both Starks and TeaCake, she arrives at the end of her quest for identity. Janie at last becomes truly autonomous, self-determining, self-contained - free to pull in her horizon and out of its "fish-net of memories," choose the ones to drape over her shoulder for a lifetime of restful contemplation. *She is free to choose. It is an autonomous decision.*

This is Hurston's message - that freedom is both personal and internal; that like man, a woman must make her own emancipation. And Achebe, some fifty years after Hurston, will proclaim through Ikem, a male character: "I can't tell you what the new role for Woman will be. I don't know. I should never have presumed to know. *You have to tell us*" (*Anthills of the Savannah* 90). Both black writers are in agreement about this. For the women of Umuofia, their voices are collectively subdued, fearful but simmering with discontent. Eatonville is a more permissive society and so Janie can rebuke Joe for his "big voice." And so, Hurston extols a judicious use of the female voice as an instrument of injury, of love and friendship and finally of the realization of personhood, empowerment and transcendence.

Finally, Hurston's Jody and Achebe's Okonkwo, two men, twin souls in different climes, different eras, meet their downfall because of their "hubris" as they, out of a lurking fear of being seen as weak or as a failure, seek to dominate their women and their societies as symbols of ambition, success, power and repression. Euripedes' warning issued so long still rings true in these times. Starks and Okonkwo provide the appropriate platform for woman's emergence to a self-defining existence - Janie in her lifetime, the women of Umuofia in the succeeding generations. Hurston in a work whose language resonates high poetry and lyricism puts it thus:

> [...] two things everybody's got tuh do fuh themselves. They got tuh go tuh god and they got tuh find out about living fuh themselves (*Their Eyes* 183).

Even TeaCake, like the other men in Janie's life, feels the need to control and dominate her. TeaCake has to fade out to allow Janie to come into herself and find out about living. With Achebe, it will take him nearly thirty years from the publication of *Things Fall Apart* (1957) to confess in *Anthills of the Savannah* that "women are[...]the biggest single group of oppressed people in the world" (98), to concede graciously to woman the right to self-determining existence, as subjects not objects, as partners in progress. For ultimately, salvation is an individual experience and the human soul knows no gender as both Okonkwo and Jody Starks, *twin souls in different climes* (both consumed by their *hubris),* do ultimately find out for themselves.

Notes

¹ *Their Eyes Were Watching God* will hereinafter be referred to as *Their Eyes.*

Works Cited

Achebe, Chinua. *Things Fall Apart.* New York: Fawcett Crest. 1991.

--- *Anthills of the Savannah.* London: Heinemann, 1988.

--- *Morning Yet on Creation Day.* London: Heinemann, 1977.

Collins Liturgical Publications. *The Holy Bible.* London. 1971.

Gates, Henry Louis, Jr. "A Negro Way of Saying." *The New York Times Book Review,* April 21, 1985, 1, 43, 45. Reprinted as Afterword in Harper Perennial editions of Zora Neale Hurston works. *Their Eyes Were Watching God.* New York: Harper and Row, 1990.

Hurston, Zora Neale. *Their Eyes Were Watching God.* New York: Harper and Row, 1990.

--- *Dust Tracks on a Road.* Second Edition. Urbana: University of Illinois Press, 1984.

Job. In *The Holy Bible*. RSV Catholic Edition for Africa. 468-500.

Lillios, Anna. "Zora Neale Hurston's Eatonville." *MAWA* Vol.7, No.2, 102-106.

Mezu, Rose Ure. "*Things Fall Apart* and The Violence of Fear." In *The Leader*. Owerri, Nigeria: Assumpta Press, 1974.

7

Achebe's Writings as Authentication of the Igbo Culture of Equiano's 1789 *Narrative*[1]

1. Achebe [...] reflectively and unobtrusively has modified the traditions of fiction, derived forms which are distinctively his own for the purposes of envisaging and conveying experience which is deeply convincing. Deceptive profundity, discriminating insight, mental and moral fastidiousness, elegance and lucidity, these are the hallmarks of Achebe's art [...] **Words** *are an epitome of the man. They show the spiritual and moral qualities that reveal themselves in his writing* [...] . *There is nothing ostentatious in his manner. And why should there be: the power is in the* **Word**.

(G.D.Killam, *'A Personal Note'* in *Chinua Achebe: A Celebration* 162; my emphasis)

2. The African writer cannot therefore be unaware of, or indifferent to, the monumental injustice which his people suffer. Among the very earliest African writers in English was an ex-slave, Olaudah Equiano who called himself Gustavus Vassa, the African [...] *One of his primary concerns was to do battle against those fundamental assumptions of which I speak.*[...] *It must have taken a lot of courage to fight that lonely battle in London in 1789*[...]. *I might add with pride and no chauvinism, I hope, that Olaudah Equiano was born* [...] *in that part of West Africa called Biafra today.*

("The African Writer and the Biafran Cause." In *Morning Yet On Creation Day*[2] *79-80)*

3. Who are we looking for, who are we looking for?
  It's Equiano we're looking for.
  Has he gone to the stream? Let him come back.
  Has he gone to the farm? Let him return.
  It's Equiano we're looking for.
(Chant about the disappearance of an African boy, Equiano).

T he sentiments about Chinua Achebe contained in first epigraph apply aptly and equally to Equiano (1745-1797). Olaudah Equiano's *The Interesting Narrative of the Life of Olaudah Equiano or Gustavus Vassa, the African Written by Himself* (self-published by subscription) establishes black literary heritage as well as serves as connection to the interrupted continuum of African diasporan cultural and the linguistic heritage lost through the institution of slavery. Equiano, the forefather of all black writers uses his *Narrative* to re-establish Africa's cultural heritage. And using *Things Fall Apart* and other writings, Achebe provides a historical, literary reconstruction of a lost civilization [...] and helps to restore that vital something taken away by the institution of slavery (Rose Ure Mezu, *Africa and the Diaspora* 22-3).

A careful reading of Equiano's *Narrative* (especially the first three chapters) reveals to any Igbo reader that Equiano is indeed what he says he is, an "Eboe from Essaka". Contrary to charges leveled by his detractors, anthropological and linguistic issues validate that Equiano is what he ays he is, an "Eboe." This can be seen, for instance, in his naming of people and agricultural products which today are still in use such as plaintain, *ede, et cetera*. In a 1975 essay, Achebe becomes one of the earliest Africans to corroborate this claim when he states that "Equiano was an Ibo, I believe, from the village of Iseke in the Orlu division of Eastern Nigeria" ("The African Writer and the English Writer" In *MYOCD* 59).

In fact, Equiano maintains the phonological essence of the E in Eboe as a native speaker of today would spell and pronounce it rather than the I in Ibo (pronounced "Eye-bo" by non-native speakers). *Ibo* is an anglicized version of **Igbo** pronounced **Egbo**. The altered version Ibo was coined by colonial rulers for their own ease of pronunciation. Even though the recollected memories of a young boy published in middle age in 1789, much of Equiano's portrait of the "Eboe" still rang true in 1958 - a hundred and sixty-nine years later when Achebe's *TFA* was published - and rings true even today. Achebe uses Umuofia as a fictional setting to describe in detail his mature first hand knowledge [and recollections of the life of his maternal great-grandfather, Udo Osinye, and what his mother and elder sisters told him[3]] of the real, indigenous Igbo who are his people and, of the culture in which he grew up. Consequently, this chapter examines *Things Fall Apart* and other writings in their careful presentation of those aspects of the life of the fictional Umuofians or Umuaro Igbo and compares and contrasts them with the details of Igbo culture as found in Equiano's *Narrative*.

I argue that Achebe's writings indeed provide an authentication of Equiano's remembered accounts of his Essaka "Eboe" nation with its structured socio-cultural, political, judicial and religious organizations. This chapter further posits that Equiano's own character - in its wiliness, pragmatic adaptability, resilience, love of adventure and acumen in commerce is actually typical of that of the average modern Igbo man. Finally, *The Narrative* inaugurated Black Autobiography and Slave Narrative/Abolitionist genres. Achebe's literary corroboration authenticates Equiano's claims and serves as powerful defense against the many detractors – past, present and future - of Equiano's remarkable work.

The Igbo Culture according to Equiano and Achebe - The white man appears

In the first chapters of the *Narrative*, Equiano describes the customs and religious and other cosmological beliefs of his society. The Eboes lived in the "interior part of the country [...] unexplored by any traveler." Born in 1745, Equiano describes his native village situated in a charming, fruitful vale and names it Essaka[4] or Isseke as sociological findings now show. He continues, "the distance of this province from the capital of Benin and the sea coast must be very considerable, for **I had never heard of white men, or Europeans, nor of the sea** (*The Narrative* in *Humanities in the Modern World* 196; my emphasis).

Comparatively, in the first part of Achebe's *Things Fall Apart* (*TFA*), it is also evident that Umuofians - children of the forest, as the name indicates - are part of the life of the real Igbo heartland which as Equiano had attested back in 1789, is situated far from the sea coast. The natives of Umuofia do not have much commerce with white people since the first part of the drama is deliberately crafted to make few references to Europeans.

Throughout the first part of *TFA*, there is no mention of white people -- a narrative strategy designed to underline the holistic structure of the mythic Umuofia society. The nearest apprehension of the *Otherness* of Europeans is through the peoples' dread of the white disease – leprosy. When Obierika speaks of "white men who they say are white like this piece of chalk[...] and these white men they say have no toes," his friend Machi recalls seeing one of them called Amadi pass by frequently, and the two friends laugh. The omniscient narrator explains that Amadi "was a leper and the polite name for leprosy was 'the white skin'" (*TFA* 74). Another mode of apprehension of white presence is through the term, "albino." "During the last planting season a white man had appeared in their clan," Obierika informs the exiled Okonkwo who then tries to understand, "an albino?" Obierika replies, "He was not an albino. He was quite different" (*TFA* 138).

In the essay "Onitsha, Gift of the Niger," Achebe sums up what must have been the first impressions on Umuofia / Igboland of the appearance of the first Europeans, "[...] strange-looking toeless harbingers of white rule [beheld] at first by an amused and indulgent black population that assembled in their hundreds to enjoy the alien spectacle [...] the occult no-man's land between river-spirits and mundane humans" (In *MYOCD* 91). It should be remembered that Equiano's feelings on beholding white men for the first time are one of "terror," believing that he "had gotten into a world of bad spirits." He thinks they are going to kill him, so different did they look with "their long hair, and the language they spoke." His feelings go from panic terror to actual fear for his life at which he faints:

> When I looked round the ship, and saw a large furnace of copper boiling, and a multitude of all description chained together, every one of their countenances expressing dejection and sorrow, I no longer doubted my fate; and quite overpowered with horror and anguish, I fell motionless on the deck and fainted. When I recovered a little[...] I asked them if they were not to be eaten by those white men with horrible look, red faces and long hair (*The Narrative* 206).

The fear remains with him for quite sometime, for later in Chapter 3, he repeats, "I did not know what to think of these white people, I very much feared they would kill and eat me" (*Narrative* 211).

These passages speak volumes for the *otherness* of cultural perspectives. Equiano, the African thinks the white men are cannibals and would eat him. But Africans have all along been dubbed "cannibals," or "savages" by the Western world that sees no merit whatsoever in anything African. Westerners were encouraged in this by what Achebe in "Colonialist Criticism" calls "the sedate prose of the district-officer-government-anthropologist" (*MYOCD* 5) of yesteryears.

Achebe continues to indict the rumors and reports of "those worthy men [who] saw little good around them, only grotesque and childlike distortions [speaking of African art]" (*MYOCD* 17). But now, here's a native-born son of Africa, fresh from his "Eboe" village who thinks the Europeans are not only cannibals but attributes to their nature unqualified proclivity for cruelty, the kind of which he has never seen in his homeland: "the white people looked and acted, as I taught, in so savage a manner; for I had never seen among any people such instances of brutal cruelty" (*The Narrative* 207).

And Achebe, reading European writers' discourses such as those of the District Commissioner in *TFA*, would in *Arrow of God* parodize Winterbottom's colonialist discourse about "cruelty of a kind which Africa alone produced. It was this elemental cruelty in the psychological make-up of the native that the starry-eyed European found so difficult to understand" (*Arrow of God* 58). Not surprisingly, Christopher Miller regards Winterbottom's "starry-eyed" tirade as an example of an "Africanist discourse" made up of "ideas received from always anterior sources, which cannot be located; hearsay from 'one who has witnessed'" (*Blank Darkness* 8). This "Africanist discourse" is part of Western effort to forge an "African Personality;" but in Henry Louis Gates, Jr.'s opinion, it is a discourse which contains "the irreducible element of cultural difference that shall always separate the white voice from the black" ("James Gronniosaw and the Trope of the Talking Book" 25).

The Socio-Cultural World of the Igbo

When Olaudah Equiano proclaims, [w]e are almost a nation of dancers, musicians and poets. Thus, every great event such as a triumphant return from battle or other cause of public rejoicing, is celebrated in public dances, which are accompanied with songs and music most suited to the occasion (*Equiano's Travels* 3), the reader recognizes the accuracy of this assertion throughout Achebe's novels.

Achebe's narratives show the integrated nature of music, poetry and performative dance so necessary to the meaning of the lives of the Igbos. Music, poetry and dance are used in wrestling, masquerade appearances, marriage, burial and Coming-of-Age ceremonies as well as New Yam and other festivals. In fact, the father of the principal hero

Okonkwo (*TFA*), despite all his physical weakness and lack of fiscal largess, is a master musician, "very good on his flute;" he has a band operating in conjunction with a "dancing *egwugwu*" group and they would be hired seasonally to teach new tunes to other villages. Unoka is a poet who loves the Harmattan season, who will watch with pleasure the magical return of the first kites with the dry season or, a kite "sailing leisurely against the blue sky" (*TFA* 3). He appreciates the poetry and rhythm of nature.

Chapter Six of *Things Fall Apart* recounts a memorable wrestling match, with the whole village – men, women and children – turned out in the *ilo* (outside)– playground – and the drummers warming up the crowd:

> There were seven drums **and they were arranged according to their sizes** in a long wooden basket. Three men beat them with sticks, working feverishly from one drum to another. They were possessed by the spirit of the drums (*TFA* 47; my emphasis).

Whenever the prowess of the youthful wrestlers reaches fever-pitch, the crowd would clap and roar, drowning out, says the omniscient narrator, "the frenzied drums" (47). As a musical instrument, the drum is very significant in the African cultural context. To Africanists like Du Bois, "the drum is a living and speaking thing [...] rich in rhythm [...] syncopation [...] and polyphony [through which] the black man achieves the independence of human voice." (In Winberg's *W.E.B.Du Bois: A Reader* 380). It is to emphasize the foreignness of the Europeans, and the differences in cultural aesthetics that what thrills one group represents to the alien *Other* unspeakable heathen rites in the heartbeat of the African darkness. For instance, in *Arrow of God*, Captain Winterbottom is terrified one night that wherever he lay awake at night in Nigeria, the **beating of the drum** would come with the same constancy. And so to debunk and spoof the scientific or factual claims of the discourse of "knowledge" of Winterbottom, the "hardened coaster," the man on the spot "who knew his African," the omniscient narrator poses the ironic rhetorical question, "Could it be that the throbbing came from his own heart-stricken brain?" (30).

But to the Igbo (African), music has different functions, and many varieties suitable for different occasions and seasons. To this fact, Equiano attests masterfully in the now memorable words: "we are almost a nation of dancers, musicians and poets." To the Igbo, the drum presents no terror, no nightmare and Equiano himself testifies to its variety, "we have many musical instruments, particularly drums of different kinds, a piece of music which resembles a guitar, and another much like a stickado." The Essaka dance ritual is choreographed to depict or represent either a great achievement, domestic employment, a pathetic story, or "some rural sport and as the subject is generally founded on some recent event, it is therefore ever new "(*The Narrative* 197). This in fact, confirms the origin and practice of dance and recitative poetry in songs not just among the Igbo but in many parts of Africa, and used during ceremonies such as hunting, harvesting, festival, marriage, birth and funeral. The efficacy of the musical rendition depends on voice performance which derives its meaning, strength and scope at the linguistic level. In fact, Kofi Awoonor divides African oral music poetry into four groups: occupational, social, cult and drum (*The Breast of the Earth* 81-2). Ijala poetry serves as the best illustration of occupational poetry; Ifo or divinitive group serves for cult, while the social encompasses the dirge (used in funeral ceremonies), praise, love and cradle / children songs. Everyone participates. As Equiano has explained and Achebe illustrates in his writings, often these songs, are composed extemporaneously, stanza by stanza. This view is further expanded in S. Okechukwu Mezu' s "Poetry and Revolution in Modern Africa," an introduction to his book of poems, *The Tropical Dawn*:

> In the villages of Africa, dances are held periodically and most of the tunes are made up of poetic verses. In the evening when children gather to listen to stories, yarns and fairy tales from their grandparents, they listen to pieces interspersed with rhymes, lyrics and choruses. Everyone takes part in the recitation….Often these are composed extemporaneously, stanza by stanza. Everyone participates. When an individual feels that he has created a verse, a stanza or even a line that fits into the dirge, he simply takes to the floor and sings his new verse. The new stanza if good is adopted and becomes part of the repertoire (9).

Relating to the African diaspora, slavocracy forcibly stripped away much of the personhood of Africans who survived the horrific Middle Passage through the Atlantic but, just like Equiano, their remembrances of their Mother Country's *oral tradition* of musical forms, rhythms and idioms kept intact some measure of their *humanness*. Civil Rights activist and Senior Pastor of Canaan Baptist Church of Christ in Harlem, Wyatt Tee Walker underscores the importance of music in the life of indigenous Africans -- past and present -- when he records that

> African history has been preserved in its music. Troubadours, storytellers and griots (official village historians) have been the history keepers. Within the context of the holistic theological systems of Africa, all life is manifestly religious. The events of life -- birth, death, puberty, fertility, harvest, famine, marriage, tragedy -- have religious rites that give expression to that event. In the absence of any prescribed formula as to what is done and when, the music and the companion ceremony have been the key to the orchestration of events and the primary preservative ingredient of tradition. ("Roots – Musically Speaking;" In Mezu, *Religion and Society* 18).

Thus, this Civil Rights activist Pastor who worked and marched alongside Martin Luther King, Jr. corroborates Equiano's testimony about traditional Africa. Exploring the survival of Africa's cultural legacy in the diaspora, Walker asserts that "if one listens to what Black people are singing religiously, it is a clue to what is happening to them sociologically" (Mezu, *Religion and Society* 18). This is made manifest in the prodigious talents of diasporan Black youth whose rap lyrics constitute a social critique of their urban, spatial displacement. Thus, they are keeping alive this heritage of music, dance and rhythm which came out of Africa.

Therefore, marriage ceremonies featuring love and dance songs would also fall into the Awooner-defined category of social poetry Here again, Equiano is our guide in this odyssey of self-affirming cultural remembrances of things past. He explains the marriage customs of the Issaka. Couples are betrothed while young. The betrothal represents one of those great events of public rejoicing of which he speaks, and which involves communities of relations and friends in celebration. Later, the bride is brought to her husband's home. Relations of both parties are invited, and in their presence, they are married

> [...] accompanied with a number of blessings, [...] dowry, which generally consists of portions of land, slaves, and cattle, household goods and implements of husbandry[...] besides which the parents of

the bridegroom present gifts to those of the bride, whose property she is looked upon before marriage; but after it she is esteemed the sole property of her husband. The ceremony being now ended, the festival begins [...] celebrated with [...] acclamations of joy, accompanied with music and dancing (*The Narrative* 197).

Equally, Chinua Achebe underlines the importance of communal bonds even as he authenticates Equiano's account of marriage ceremonies. Chapter Twelve of *TFA* opens with the "entire neighborhood" wearing a festive air because Okonkwo's friend, Obierika is celebrating his daughter's *uri*. Her suitor would bring palm-wine not only to her parents and immediate relatives but to the wide and extensive group of kinsmen called *umunna* (111).

Men, women and children are invited with the bride and the women as central figures. In its details, Achebe's description of the festive proceedings matches Equiano's. The suitor's people bring altogether fifty pots of palm-wine, and then sit in a half-moon, thus completing a circle with their hosts, with the bride, her mother and women relatives going round welcoming their visitors. The married women wear the best attire. The young girls wear waist-beads and anklets of brass. Equiano's account would present to readers the bride, tying "around her waist a cotton string of the thickness of a goose-quill" (*The Narrative* 196).

The festivities in Obierika's compound reach their apogee with songs in a call-and response format amidst general merriment; lords of the clan offer **libation**, and there are "huge bowls of foo-foo and steaming pots of soup[...] It was a great feast" (*TFA* 119). The festivity is climaxed with the dance of the maidens, followed by the bride who now appears. She holds in her right hand a cock which she presents to the musicians, while still dancing, her brass anklets rattling, while the "musicians with their wood, clay and metal instruments went from song to song. And they were all gay [happy]" (*TFA* 118).

Libation as a Ritual of Accommodation

Equally, Equiano accurately describes **libation** as a ritualistic custom in which celebrants are seen "pouring out a small quantity of the drink on the floor[...] for the spirits of departed relatives, which the natives suppose to preside over their conduct and guard them from evil" (*Narrative..*197). In another section, he explains the African

172

religious belief in Re-incarnation which represents another reason for the complex ritual of libation:

> Those spirits, which are not transmigrated, such as our dear friends or relations, they [Essaka] believe always attend them, and guard them from the bad spirits or their foes. For this reason they always before eating, as I have observed, put some small portion of the meat, and **pour some of their drink, on the ground for them** (*Narrative* 199; my emphasis).

This account by Equiano, Achebe's *TFA* authenticates in its description of an Umuofia ceremony in which both wine and the kola nut (a peace symbol) are usually toasted, ancestors are remembered, and libation wishes for well-being offered in communal unison:

> We shall all live. We pray for life, children, a good harvest and happiness. You will have what is good for you and I will have what is good for me. Let the kite perch and let the eagle perch too. If one says no to the other, let his wing break (*TFA* 19).

This is virtually a transliteration of the Igbo proverb: "*egbe bere, ugo bere; nke si ibe ya ebela, nku kwa ya.*" As to what people of Essaka in Igboland drink, Equiano remembers palm-wine as the principal beverage, explaining that it is "got from a tree of that name, by tapping at the top and fastening a large gourd to it; and sometimes, one tree will yield three or four gourds in the night." The accuracy of his remembrances puts to rest any doubt as to his Igbo origin, for what African will not agree with Equiano that "when drawn, it [palmwine] is of a most delicious sweetness; but in a few days, it acquires a tarish and more spirituous flavor[...] . The same tree also produces nuts and oil" (197).

The multiple utility and versatility of the palm-tree are very well-stated by Equiano. Equally, Achebe's account of betrothal and other ceremonies in *Things Fall Apart* and *Arrow of God* replicate the symbolic palm wine in countless rituals of **libation** as described earlier. Thus, both writers' accounts of Igbo socio-cultural practices complement each other with Equiano's fragmentary remembrances being given detailed and dramatic completion in Achebe's fictional narratives, and in his essays. Some of the symbolism and metaphor of myth and poetry lacking in Equiano's autobiographical slave narrative find completion in Achebe as he fully recounts details of Igbo mythopoeia in form of proverbs, proper names, rituals and festivals, coupled with tape-recorded interviews with old people whose way of life is being depicted.

The traditional Igbo were very accommodating of other people. In a cosmological sense, they must have felt that in allowing the missionaries to stay they were paying due reverence to other gods unknown to the Igbos – a gesture comparable to that of the Athenians who dedicated an altar to "an unknown god" (*Acts of the Apostles* 17: 22-3), which the apostle Paul exploits as a vehicle to introduce Jesus Christ as God and man. The Igbo tolerance for the message brought by these alien missionaries carries a postmodernist lesson about accepting the authentic strangeness of others in both racial and religious sense. But, the cultural subtext in Equiano's and Achebe's narratives underpins the holistic structure of pre-slavery, pre-colonial African communities. While Achebe is in touch with his roots, having suffered no spatial or emotional displacement, the displaced Equiano determinedly imprints indelibly in his memory this knowledge of a beloved homeland now lost to him forever. Writing as an act of memory recovery simultaneously represents the acquisition of both a voice and an identity.

The Igbo Politico-judicial Organization

In both Essaka and Umuofia, aspects of the political structure collapse into the judicial system. Equiano says that a council of elders called Embrenche settles matters affecting the community in addition to adjudicating disputes between warring parties: "Those *Embrenche*, or chief men decided disputes and punished crimes, for which purpose they always assembled[...] . In most cases, the law of retaliation prevailed" (Jackson, *Humanities in the Modern World: An Africana Emphasis*, 196). A case against a kidnapper is settled by asking him to make recompense by providing a man or woman slave.

In *TFA*, Achebe confirms that the elders or *ndichie* decide important community issues. A case in point is that of the woman of Umuofia, the wife of Ogbuofi Udo on her way to the market who is killed by people from Mbaino. Umuofia sends Okonkwo as an emissary to present Mbaino with an ultimatum to recompense Umuofia or go to war. Mbaino wisely sends Okonkwo home with a virgin girl to Udo as replacement for his murdered wife, and fifteen year old Ikemefuna whom Umuofia entrusts to Okonkwo as hostage.

The boy becomes a surrogate son. His cowardly killing by Okonkwo is a transgression against natural and moral law, and has karmic consequences. When Okonkwo insists that the earth cannot punish him for obeying her messenger, Obierika remonstrates with him, "That is true. But if the Oracle said that my son should be killed I would neither dispute it nor be the one to do it" (*TFA* 67). Prior to this dialogue, Ogbuefi Ezeudu had come to warn Okonkwo not to have a hand in the killing of Ikemefuna even though the Oracle called for it, because the boy "calls you father." As in the epic struggle between King Creon and the eponymous Antigone, there is a higher moral law that transcends even a socially-constructed, judicial plane. It is Ezeudu's young grandson that Okonkwo kills accidentally, necessitating his exile, with a resulting loss in prestige. And from thereon, Okonkwo's strength literally runs out, thus fulfilling the symbolical meaning of the name *Ikemefuna* -– May my strength not run out!

From among the Ndichie, members are selected to belong to the judicial body called *Egwugwu* which also performs as a masquerade cult. And in *TFA*, their judgment is seen to be just, fair and swift. Says Equiano of the Embrenche in assembly, "the proceedings are generally short" (*Narrative* 197).

Achebe authenticates this fact by presenting a judicial case between the warring families: the Odukwe brothers who go to their in-law's house, beat him up, take away his wife (their sister) and her children and refuse to return the bride-price. Uzowulu, the husband complains to the Egwugwu who, led by the masked Evil forest, give swift judgment. To Uzowulu, they say, "Go to your in-laws with a pot of wine and beg your wife to return to you. It is not bravery when a man fights with a woman" (*TFA* 93). Thus, as can be seen, like Embrenches, the Ndichie as Egwugwu settle disputes. They also punish crimes as occurs when the over-zealous Christian, Enoch unmasks a masquerade, symbolically killing "an ancestral spirit [at which] Umuofia was thrown into confusion" (186). The enormity of the abominable offense is described in somber tones:

> That night the Mother of the Spirits walked the length and breadth of the clan. It was a terrible night. Not even the oldest man in Umuofia had ever heard such a strange and fearful sound, and it was never to

be heard again. It seemed as if the very soul of the tribe wept for a great evil that was coming—its own death (187).

Thus, Achebe is able to provide more details from the perspective of a mature "insider" who has the first hand knowledge to corroborate and situate cultural descriptions provided by Olaudah Equiano.

Communalism as a Socio-Economic Mode of Living in the African Village: The Perspective of Equiano and Achebe

Equiano presents the "Eboe" society as an egalitarian system in which people rise through the ranks according to their prowess; and, regardless of the ordinariness of their birth, they have a voice in the decision-making process. The society is open to all but the slaves. Strong kinship ties and other communal rituals made this society complex. More than two centuries following Equiano's birth, Chinua Achebe authenticates a lot of what Equiano's *Narrative* presents as a valid social system, fluid and egalitarian in which a man determines his own *locus* in society regardless of the ignominy of one's ancestry, as Okonkwo's personal story illustrates.

Achebe's *Ndichie* and Equiano's *Embrenche* form a mobile, fluid group - both desiring as members only people of the highest social, physical and economic distinction: warriors, wrestlers, farmers, hunters, men of eloquence, *et cetera*. In both societies, the accent is on personal worth and merit. When *Things Fall Apart* opens, Okonkwo is already a renowned wrestler at eighteen. His father's poverty rather than be a disadvantage brings into bold relief his ambitions, resilience and skills. And at thirty-eight, he is made ambassador plenipotentiary and embarks on a mission to Mbaino to negotiate on behalf of Umuofia. Even the boy, Ikemefuna -- a ward of Umuofia – is entrusted to him. And with two yam barns, three wives, two titles, he joins the Ndichie, and becomes a lord of the clan as is Ogbuefi Ezeudu, or Nwakibie who has the highest but one title in the land, three huge barns, nine wives and thirty children.

To give a start to the trusted Okonkwo, Nwakibie even lends him eight hundred yam seedlings instead of the four hundred that Okonkwo requests. This is a clear evidence of **Communalism** – a coherent, integrated socio-economic system in which the wellbeing of the community is paramount and people are their brothers' keepers, affording abundant opportunities to whomsoever has the strength, initiative and willingness to work hard. Privileging Okonkwo's well-known indomitable energy and drive so as to emphasize that hardwork is the overriding principle of **Communalism** in Igbo society, Achebe, through this fictional illustration, corroborates Equiano's assertion that "we are habituated to labor from our earliest years. Everyone contributes something to the common stalk and we are unacquainted with idleness. We have no beggars. The benefits of such a mode of living are obvious" (*Narrative* 198).

Next, W.E.B. Du Bois validates Equiano's statement by expatiating on the integrated, functional holism of the African communal system in which there is "no monopoly, no poverty, no prostitution, and the only privilege was the definite, regulated, and usually limited privilege of the chief and headmen, given in return for public service, and revocable for failure" This primal village life, Du Bois laments, crumbled before colonial onslaught, but not before it had "played its part in the world as a rare contribution to civilization" (In Weinberg, 378).

In Achebe's writings, these assertions about the Igbo / African lifestyle make the society come alive as a throbbing community of living beings – a dramatized picture that supports Du Bois's thesis that the world owes to Africa the debt of a holistic social system made up of "Beginnings, the village unit, and art in sculpture and music [for] [...] in the African village were bred religion, industry, government, education, art, and these were bred as integral interrelated things" (What is Civilization? Africa's Answer" 376). As already seen in Achebe, and as emphasized by Du Bois, the African village thoroughly socialized the individual by privileging communal wellbeing over the personal without stifling or obliterating one's distinctive individualism.

It must be pointed out that when Karl Marx formulated his vision of Communism, he did this in a cultural / economic landscape which had known not a communalist ethos but an individualist one that would culminate in a capitalist system with its characteristic "winner-take-all" implying a struggle for the survival of the fittest. It should be remembered that historically, Europe's economy from its earliest days had been based on feudalism – a hierarchical system in which people of the lower order worked and served their overlords on the upper echelon starting from the peasantry up to the king or the papacy.

Marx's Communist ideology is obviously foreign to Europe. Marx indeed owes an obvious debt to the African Communalist[5] system - "in its limited way, a perfect human being" (Du Bois 376) - on which he based his *Communist Manifesto*.

Gender Relations

In both narratives, women occupy a marginal position full of inequities. Equiano presents a polygamous society in which punishment for adultery was decidedly lopsided and biased against the woman. In his society, adultery is a crime whose punishment is either slavery or death, "so sacred among them is the honor of the marriage bed, and so jealous are they of the fidelity of their wives" (*The Narrative* 196).

Equiano cites the case of an adulterous wife condemned to death but who is spared because she is nursing a baby. But he is quick to point out the gender-biased injustice of it all since "the men, however, do not preserve the same constancy to their wives which they expect from them, for they indulge in plurality" (196). Centuries later, Achebe confirms both the systemic plurality of wives and the fact that women of Umuofia, and by extension, traditional women largely existed on the "fringes" of the social fabric, for during some festive events, "it was clear from the way the crowd stood or sat that the ceremony was for men. There were women, but they looked on from the fringe like outsiders" (*TFA* 87).

Achebe also confirms the patriarchal obsession with female chastity that was an ethos of Igbo traditional life. In *Arrow of God*, for instance, Obika's wife passes the test and her parents will be sent gifts as proof that she is virginal before marriage. Even Buchi Emecheta sees the need to highlight the issue in both *The Joys of Motherhood* and *Double Yoke*. Equiano equally restates Essaka society's expectations of chastity for its women, when he observes, "nor do I remember to have heard of an instance of incontinence amongst them before marriage" (*Narrative [...]* 198). But the discerning reader sees that Equiano has another motive in coming to the defense of the African female, stereotyped in Western literature as lacking in virtue, as sensuous and a seducer of the plantation master whose very libidinous proclivities have caused mulatto babies to be littered on the plantation.

Also, a closer reading of both Equiano and the Achebe texts reveals an important phenomenon - a salient undertone of an unspoken female solidarity. Just as the wives of Okonkwo provide solidarity to one another, covering for Ojiugo when she decides to go plait her hair rather than cook Okonkwo's dinner, the women of Essaka, in an unspoken act of female conspiracy, provide support for the condemned woman, for the text reports that throughout the land "no woman being prevailed upon to perform the part of a nurse, she was spared on account of the child" (*The Narrative* 196). Since agreeing to play wet-nurse to the child would mean giving the go-ahead to a death sentence, it stands to reason that no woman would be found. And thus, these traditional Igbo women silently and effectively make a collective act of protest and defiance at an unjust feature of traditional society. Thus, both Equiano and Achebe objectively present their society, unvarnished and with attendant imperfections.

Again, Equiano underscores his people's idealistic treatment of women when he asserts that "our women, too, were in my eye at least, uncommonly graceful, alert and modest to a degree of bashfulness" (*The Narrative*. In *Humanities in the Modern World* 198). In *TFA*, the figure of Nneka – mother is supreme – surfaces as a metaphor of comfort and shelter for suffering, exiled man whose mother and her people are always there providing balm to the bruised male psyche. But a slight difference in attitude has Equiano presenting specific and peculiar situations in which the androgynous make-up of Essaka women can be exploited – as in time of war when "all are taught the use of weapons –even our women are warriors and march boldly out to fight along with the men" (*The Narrative* 199).

Even in matters of religious worship, Equiano who confesses to being "very fond of my mother, and almost constantly with her," accompanies her as she makes oblations at her mother's tomb, which was a kind of small solitary thatched house. I sometimes attended her. There she made her libations, and spent most of the night in cries and lamentations" (*The Narrative* 200). His mother is strong enough to accomplish by herself these solitary rituals of worship which Equiano often finds extremely terrifying. In *TFA*, Ekwefi's character (although not fully developed) also comes across as strong and fearless, for she follows the priestess Chielo, making her rounds of the village with her only child, Ezinma. Both authors therefore show empathy for women, even though their mode of narrative remains presentational rather than prescriptive.

Agriculture as Traditional Igbo Society's lifeline -- Food and Economic Crops

But before Achebe's narratives, there was Equiano proclaiming agriculture as the economic mainstay of Essaka society: "I was trained up from my earliest years in the arts of agriculture [...] . Agriculture is our chief employment, " for:

> [o]ur land is uncommonly rich and fruitful, and produces all kinds of vegetables in great abundance. We have plenty of Indian corn, and vast quantities of cotton and tobacco. Our pineapples grow without culture; they are about the size of the largest sugar-loaf, and finely flavoured. We have also spices of different kinds, particularly pepper; and a variety of delicious fruits which I have never seen in Europe; together with gums of various kinds, and honey in abundance. All our industry is exerted to improve those blessings of nature [...] Our tillage is exercised in **a large plain** or **common**, some hours walk from our dwellings, and all the neighbors resort thither in a body. They use no beasts of husbandry; and their only instruments are hoes, axes, shovels, and beaks, -or pointed iron to dig with (*The Narrative* [...] 198).

Since the "common" is often a site of war, the people go out to till their land in a body, generally taking their arms with them for fear of a surprise attack. In addition to agriculture, animal husbandry – bullocks, goats and poultry -- "constitutes the principal wealth of the country, and the chief part of the food . .. " (*The Narrative* 197-9). Equiano takes this opportunity to counter the charge of primitivism by insisting that the flesh of these animals and birds is stewed in a pan and made savory with pepper and other spices. His peoples' cleanliness, he insists, is proverbial with washing of hands as an indispensable ceremony.

Equally, Achebe's tradition-based narratives present agriculture as the center of novelistic drama. In *Things Fall Apart*, the agricultural process is given a pride of place. The drive and stamina needed to become an "*ezeji* – king of yams" with multiple yam barns underline the competitive spirit that defines masculinity. A man's harvest is good according to "the strength of his arm." Lacking this strength earns a man the pejorative name of "*agbala* – woman" (*TFA* 17) – a source of mortification for Okonkwo determined not to be anything like his father, Unoka whose gentleness, Okonkwo believes, is synonymous with idleness (*TFA* 13).

Yam remains the king of crops and an "exacting king" as opposed to vegetables and cocoyams – dubbed **female crops**. An entire section in Chapter Four of *TFA* is a panegyric on yam as the "king of crops" – its cultivation, tending, and harvesting. It is a crop on which is based a man's hierarchical status for it empowers him to take titles and to belong to the lofty class of elders – *Ndichie*. In *Arrow of God*, the delay in harvesting the yam which in turn occasions a delay in the planting season produces chaos in the internal structure of Umuaro. In fact, it leads to the ostracism of the chief priest, Ezeulu and facilitates the decamping of the citizenry to the Christian religion, with its more benevolent worship rituals.

Equiano further states that "every one, even the children and women, are engaged in it. Thus we are all habituated to labor from our earliest years. Everyone contributes something to the common stock; and as we are unacquainted with idleness, we have no beggars" (*Narrative[...]* 198). One is forced to remember Okonkwo whom Achebe describes as a very strong man who during the planting season works "daily on his farms from cock-crow until the chicken went to roost;" and because he rules "his household with a heavy hand" expects his wives and children to work as hard. Okonkwo worries at the incipient laziness of his first son, twelve year-old Nwoye whom he seeks to correct with constant nagging and beating" (*TFA* 13-4). When forced into idleness like during the Week of Peace, Okonkwo generally gets into trouble as seen in the instances when he has transgressed the laws of the land by beating, or shooting at his wives. One remembers also how Ezeulu insists on Oduche joining the rest of the family to finish work on Obika's compound before the arrival of the latter's bride:

> I did not send you so that you might leave your duty in my household. Do you hear me? Go and tell the people who chose you to go to Okperi that I said no. Tell them that tomorrow is the day on which my sons and my wives and my son's wife work for me (*Arrow of God* 13).

And so, Equiano admiringly states that the Igbo ethics of physical hard work confer on the people great benefits in form of general healthiness of the people, their vigor and comeliness, for deformity is unknown among them. It must be remembered that even though

Okonkwo's heavy-handedness is an aberration rather than the rule, yet other prosperous households including Ogbuefi Ezeudu, Nwakibie and Obierika follow the same work ethic.

We also know that neither Umuofia nor Umuaro (*Arrow of God*) has ever reported a case of a beggar. Even the lazy, improvident Unoka is a musician and dancer. And thus Achebe authenticates Equiano's testimony regarding the Igbo people, who because they are industrious were fair game to the Europeans as preferred plantation workers: "the West India planters prefer the slaves of Benin or Eboe to those of any other part of Guinea, for their hardiness, intelligence, integrity, and zeal" (*Narrative* 198).

Equiano discusses other aspects of food cultivation. With careful attention to detail, Equiano recounts the blighting of crops caused by invading locusts since they **devour every green** thing in sight. The locusts, he says, "come in large clouds, so as to darken the air, and destroy our harvest. This however happens rarely, but when it does, a famine is produced by it" (*The Narrative* 198). In Chapter Seven of *TFA*, Achebe, using similar words, describes the invasion of these edible insects:

> quite suddenly a shadow fell on the world and sun seemed hidden behind a thick cloud[...] [locusts] appearing on the horizon like a boundless sheet of black cloud moving towards Umuofia. Soon it covered half the sky, and the solid mass was now broken by tiny eyes of light like shining star dust. It was a tremendous sight, full of power and beauty" (*TFA* 56).

Umuofia natives have not seen the locusts "for many, many years, and only the old people have seen them before" (56-7). However, Achebe presents a more favorable view of the utility of these voracious visitors. Because locusts are good to eat, the people are happy; men, women and children shout with joy, "locusts are descending!" as the edible insects settle on roofs, leaves, weighing down tree branches and eventually falling down wingless, and being gathered into baskets.

Achebe supplies all the local flavor with his portraits of natives roasting locusts in clay pots, spreading them out to dry in the sun until brittle, to be eaten later with palm-oil. These examples of a rich cultural heritage are supplied by an adult "insider." But Equiano remains the pioneer literary archivist/griot despite his humble apology for any incompleteness in his recalling of fact: "such is the imperfect sketch my memory has furnished me with of the manners and customs of a people among whom I first drew my breath" (*Narrative . . 198*)..

Architecture - The *Obi* as Hearthstone of Cultural Life

Remarkably, Equiano provides an architectural prototype of the Igbo compound, while Achebe again delineates the significant symbolism of the structure. In terms of building, Equiano admits that Essaka Igbo go for functionalism rather than ornamentation: "**Each compound is fenced with a wall made of red mud which [when] tempered** is as hard as rock." The principal building belongs to the *paterfamilias* for his sole use and is divided into two apartments: "in one of which he sits in the day with his family, the other is left apart for the reception of his friends." There are houses for his sons, wives and, "for his slaves and their families distributed throughout the rest of the enclosure" (*The Narrative* 197).

As he was a titled *"embrenche*," Equiano's father's compound must have resembled somewhat the prosperous compound of Okonkwo. In architectural style, the descriptions are nearly similar. Okonkwo's "**large compound is enclosed by a thick wall of red mud**[...] . His own hut, or *obi*, stood immediately behind the only gate in the red wall. Each of the three wives had her own hut, which together formed a half moon behind the *obi*." *Obi* is a word that signifies the architectural centrality of an Igbo compound, but it also stands for the "hearth." *Obi* (though pronounced differently) also means the "heart." ***Obi*** becomes a metaphor for virile masculine headship since to enter a man's compound and attack its members, one practically has to go through the *obi* and figuratively through the man himself. For the priestess Chielo to get to Ekwefi's hut and take Ezinma, she actually had to walk through Okonkwo's *Obi* (*TFA* 101).

Differences in African and Western Slave Systems

Slavery and, subsequently, colonialism were twin plagues that devastated Africa. Just as the enslaved Africans in the diaspora groaned under its physical, mental and spiritual scourge, Africans in the mainland suffered the pains of colonialism, for both systems entailed a radical and fundamental restructuring of the continent and of the humanity of its African victims. The writings of Chinua Achebe deal with both issues, especially colonialism. In *Arrow of God*, Nweke Ukpaka of the Otakagu age group of Umuaro working *gratis* on Mr.

Wright's road project articulates succinctly and poignantly the relationship between Europe and Africa by outlining the list of possible provocations that can validate acts of aggression such as the ones perpetrated by the West against African nations:

> Umuaro was here before the white man came from his land to seek us out. We did not ask him to visit us. He is neither our kinsman nor our in-law. We did not steal his goat or his fowl; we did not take his land or his wife. In no way whatsoever have we done him wrong. And yet he has come to make trouble for us. [...] All we know is that Our *ofo* is held high between us and him. The stranger will not kill the host with his visit; and when he goes may he not go with a swollen back. I know that the white man does not wish Umuaro well (*Arrow of God* 85-6).

And Moses Unachukwu, a pioneer Umuaro Christian, tries to prepare the youthful Otakagu (Obika's) age-grade members for the inevitable presence of the European in Africa, "there is no escape from the white man. He is here to stay. When suffering knocks at your door and you say there is no seat left for him, he tells you not to worry because he has brought his won seat" (85). Europe's objective was for evangelization and civilization, and as Achebe's Unachukwu points out to Umuaro youth, "the white man, the new religion, the soldiers, the new road – they are all part of the same thing" (85). With Church and Colonial authorities allied together, the results were disastrously divisive and deadly. But Colonialism was during Achebe's age, long after the eleven year-old Igbo boy, Equiano was captured along with his sister and sold to slave traders.

Equiano highlights the distinctive differences between African and Western slave systems. His father owns "many slaves," who live with them, and sometimes marry with the freeborn. Slaves are obtained through battles or kidnapping and he indicts the "avarice" of native chiefs who organize raids such as the one in which Equiano and his sister are kidnapped. In his various trajectories to the Atlantic coast, he remains relatively well-treated in many of the homes. In beautifully scenic Tinmah, a wealthy widow who owns many other slaves buys Equiano as companion for her son, "a young gentleman about my age and size." He is treated humanely eating and drinking with the son. He even begins to believe that he has been "adopted into the family" (*Narrative* 205).

As a way of comparison, Equiano points out that slavery as operated in traditional Africa lacks the inhuman cruelty of its Western version. Achebe provides another example: Ikemefuna as a hostage from Mbaino lives in Okonkwo's household, and in time, "begins to feel like a member of Okonkwo's household[...] He and Nwoye become deeply attached to each other." With his rich stock of folk stories, and good work ethics, Ikemefuna serves as an excellent role model for the "effeminate" Nwoye (*TFA* 34). Also, Equiano's narrative presents the first written account of the horrors of the Middle Passage (Chapters 2-3) with such unprecedented torture and bestialization that he is compelled to exclaim, "I had never seen among my people such instances of brutal cruelty[...] the shrieks of the women, and the groans of the dying rendered the whole a scene of horror almost inconceivable" (207-8). Some Africans jumped into the sea preferring death to slavery.

A corollary of slavery is the fragmentation of families, for as Equiano testifies, "without scruples, are relations and friends separated, most of them never to see each other again. I remember in the vessel in which I was brought over[...]there were several brothers who, in the sale, were sold in different lots; and it was very moving on this occasion, to see and hear their cries in parting" (209). A case in point is the poignant separation from his sister - "the dear partner of all my childish sports" (205). After a brief and accidental reunion, Equiano and his sister are parted never to see each other again. Such was the impact of the system of slavery on African family lives.

Igbo Religious Thought

On the issue of religion and its implications, Equiano and Achebe again agree. Missiological anthropology has acknowledged that Western missionaries operated in Africa despite their limited knowledge of African cultures, and by extension, African spirituality. Joseph Conrad's *Heart of Darkness* (1898) is considered a classic example of an "outsider" account using dominant stereotypes to make Africa intelligible and more manageable to European administrators working in concert with Christian missionaries. And Achebe claims the eagle prize as one of the earliest to fictionally capture and freeze in time aspects of native culture hitherto considered "impenetratable" and which were fast crumbling under the fierce onslaught of a putative European civilization.

His is an Africa described by an African not as "a scenario for an exploration of the black side of the European soul but as a place where people live normal, unfrenzied lives" (David Carroll 23). Achebe's fictional portraits of authentic Africans have helped generations of young Africans penetrate this impenetrable [cosmo-theological] forest. And African religion would receive a substantive theological treatment in *Things Fall Apart*. Long before Achebe, Equiano's discourse unequivocally asserts the Igbo's belief in one Creator God, omnipotent, omnipresent, omniscient:

> **As to religion, the natives believe that there is one Creator of all things**, and that he lives in the sun [...] They believe he governs events, especially our deaths or captivity; but, as for the doctrine of eternity; I do not remember to have ever heard of it: some however believe in **the transmigration of souls** in a certain degree. Those spirits, which are not transmigrated, such as our dear friends or relations, they believe always attend them, and guard them from the bad spirits or their foes. For this reason they always before eating, as I have observed, put some small portion of the meat, and pour some of their drink, on the ground for them; and they often make oblations of the blood of beasts or fowls at their graves (*The Narrative* 199; my emphases).

Thus, with this passage, he introduces the Essaka Igbo's belief in Re-incarnation - **the transmigration of souls**. Equiano's fragmentary recollections of Igbo spiritual beliefs receive full exegetical treatment in Achebe's writings. In Chapter Twenty-One of *Things Fall Apart*, Mr. Brown, the missionary and *Ndichie* Akunna, one of the great Umuofia men debate the merits of their respective religions. Akunna can be seen as an amalgam of the characters of both Udo Osinyi, Achebe's maternal great-grandfather, and Ezeulu of fictional Umuaro. Udo Osinyi, described as "republican and egalitarian" had brought the first missionaries to operate in his compound. He thought the new religion would add luster to his compound despite its "crazy theology." He only sent the missionaries packing when he thought their singing was "too sad to come from a man's house. My neighbors might think it was my funeral dirge" ("Named for Victoria, Queen of England" 66).

Osinyi is seen by Achebe as the very embodiment of tolerance. Like *Ndichie* Akunna who despite calling the new religion "lunatic," had allowed "one of his sons to be taught the white man's knowledge in Mr. Brown's school," Udo Osinyi had also allowed his grandson to join the missionaries. Thus, the real-life Osinyi and the fictional Akunna show the same pragmatism as Ezeulu who uses his son Oduche so as to have a representative in the Christian camp. One can discern in each of these men's self-interested decision, an awareness of the inevitable social change encroaching from the horizon.

Akunna, just as Mr. Brown does for the West, claims, for Igbo Traditional Religion the same belief in one supreme God who made heaven and earth: "We also believe in Him and call him Chukwu. He made all the world and other gods." To Mr. Brown's rejoinder that "Chukwu is the only God" and all others are false, being made of wood like Akunna's **ikenga**. Akunna agrees, but points out that "it is indeed a piece of wood. The tree from which it came was made by Chukwu, as indeed all minor gods were. But He made them for His messengers so that we could approach Him through them" (TFA 179). Because Chukwu is held in such reverence by the Umuofia people, the smaller gods help him because

> We approach a great man through his servants. But when his servants fail to help us, then we go to the last source of hope. **We appear to pay greater attention to the smaller gods but that is not so.** We worry them more because we are afraid to worry their Master. Our fathers knew that Chukwu was the overlord and that is why many of them gave their children the name of Chukwuka – "God is Supreme" - (*TFA* 180).

And when Mr. Brown explains to Akunna that the Christian Chukwu is a loving God who need not be feared by those who do His will, *Ndichie* Akunna gives an enigmatic rejoinder, "And who is to tell His will? It is too great to be known" (181). This is the same kind of rhetorical question that Pilate asks Christ, "And what is the Truth?" In this fashion, the wise Mr. Brown gets to learn a lot about Igbo religion and concludes that a frontal attack would fail. To the native Umuofia / Igbo, the messengers of Chukwu compare easily with the Christian saints and guardian angels of the Latin-rite Christology in their roles as intercessors and intermediaries between God and humans. And so, to explain the African's later Christian religious enthusiasm, Lamin Sanneh points to the "African factor" as key to why Christianity is thriving in West Africa, for traditional African religion is seen to have some kinship with the New Testament thought of Jesus Christ.

But there are differences. Even though Equiano asserts that there were priests, and magicians, wise men and diviners, he also states that African Traditional Religion had no formal places of public worship unlike the Christian church. Achebe's writings authenticate this statement that there is no central place of public worship. In *TFA*, Okonkwo's shrine or "medicine house" is located near his yam barn, and the shrine contains wooden symbols of his ancestral spirits, and his personal god. These he worships "with sacrifices of kola nut, food and palm wine;" and there also, he offers "prayers on behalf of himself, his three wives and children" (*TFA* 14).

A violation of this shrine or of his personal god translates to an abomination, a desecration of a man's spiritual personhood. The consequences of such a violation can be dire as is dramatized in *Arrow of God* where a battle ensues between Okperi and Umuaro because the Umuaro Emissary Akukalia rushes to the *obi* of Ebo, and seizing his *ikenga*, splits it into two. Thereafter, the violated Ebo "reached for his gun and blew the fellow's head off" (*Arrow of God* 37). Both communities concede that Akukalia's desecration of Ebo's ikenga is an extreme provocation. Even Umuaro are forced to agree that their clansman has done "an unforgivable thing" (*Arrow of God* 23-4). Mr. Winterbottom demonstrates an understanding of the issue's underlying mystical and occult signification when he explains to Mr. Clarke that the

> *ikenga* is the most important fetish in the Ibo man's arsenal[...] It represents his ancestor to whom he must make daily sacrifice. When he dies, it must be split in two; one half is buried with him, the other half is thrown away. In splitting his host's fetish[...] this was, of course, a great sacrilege (37).

This emphasizes that in traditional Igbo religious thought, the symbols of spiritual beliefs denote a man's vulnerability to his *chi* – a concept examined in the next section.

The Importance of "Chi" in Igbo Cosmo-theological Thought

Chinua Achebe's essay, "*Chi* in Igbo Cosmology" gives central focus to this indispensable component of Igbo religious beliefs. Akunna of *TFA* explains to Mr. Brown that the Supreme deity is **Chukwu** (*Chi ukwu*) - Great **Chi,** or, its alternative name, **Chineke** – God who creates. Thus, **chi** becomes crucial to Igbo philosophical /

religious thought because **chi** as *spirit being* is said to complement one's terrestrial *human being*. Achebe hazards an explanation analogous to the Christian dogma: that chi, by partaking of the nature of the Supreme God, can reasonably be interpreted to be "an infinitesimal manifestation of Chukwu's infinite essence given to each of us separately and uniquely" ("Chi in Igbo Cosmology" 100). Chi's all pervasive significance is reflected in Igbo names such as "*Chinyere* – God has given;" "*Chika* - God is supreme;" "*Chukwuma* – only God knows," "*Lewachi* - look to God," "*Chiekezie* – God who creates rightly," "*Okechukwu* – God's own portion (gift)," and many other such names. Because traditional African religion is highly transcendental, the Christian prayer is manifestly true in the Igbo / African context – "in **Him** we live and move and have our being" - for *Chukwu* – Supreme God / Creator – is the central reference point of the African's cosmological life.

A person's **chi** is supposed to be ever vigilant and watchful over the person's welfare; therefore no matter the supernatural forces plotting one's ruin, if the person's **chi** is not in agreement, the machinations will come to nothing. But the Igbo psyche abhors such complete power over one's destiny, hence another proverb - "**onye kwe, chi ya ekwe**"-- if a person agrees, the *chi* agrees also." The functions of this personal involvement is to limit such an absolutist use of power, vesting it rather on the human being. This effort to take back the initiative in determining one's destiny explains somewhat the Igbo's great unyielding spirit, hard work, and pragmatism.

The early success of Okonkwo, the young, hardworking lord of the clan epitomizes this belief. Just as names of children tell the story of how life has treated someone - joys, sorrows, fears, hopes, accomplishments, complaints, resignation - a hardworking or good person may yet come to have a bad **chi** - one that is intransigent and unvigilant as made evident by the tragic fate of Okonkwo or Ezeulu. Thus, **chi** is exclusively concerned with success or failure in life while the arbitration over morality rests with **Ala** or **Ani** - the earth goddess, a powerful female deity who dispenses moral sanction, fertility, and the like. Personal fortunes are controlled more or less by one's **chi** who has close communion with Chukwu. Events in *TFA* brilliantly illustrate these arguments.

Re-incarnation

This concept of **"chi"** totally permeates the Igbo's psychology in an intricate fashion and yet it is so enigmatic as to elude complete interpretation. Because **chi** as a concept carries with it the notion of duality, nothing is absolute for as Achebe puts it, "where Something stands, Something else will stand beside it" (*"Chi* in Igbo Cosmology" 94). The world and everything in it is believed to have a double and a counterpart in the spirit world. The traditional Igbo, as Equiano explains, believed in re-incarnation. The Igbo view of life is **holistic** - a community of the living, the dead and the unborn and which has a sensibility to the delicate balance between human society and natural forces in the universe - sometimes visible, sometimes, invisible. In other words, they believed in a spirit world where the dead recreate a life analogous to the terrestrial, a world parallel and contiguous, **with an endless coming and going between the two through birth, death and rebirth – or re-incarnation.**

Therein resides the great importance of the **masks**, representing the spirit of the ancestors. During ceremonies - births, funerals, festivals, initiation and cult rituals, these masked spirits who grace the occasions with their presence, represent visitors from the underworld and thus, they inspire fear and awe in the uninitiated. The ancestral spirit may thus be represented by the masquerade. But beyond all concepts is the One Supreme God – *Chukwu* or *Chineke*. It is not surprising that African theologian John Mbiti, clearly establishes in *Bible and Theology in African Christianity* that West Africans were devotees of monotheism as early as 500 A.D., pointing to the disposition of the African Traditional Religion as the key.

Inculturation as the Fruit of Equiano and Achebean Igbo Cosmo-theological Thoughts

Missionaries had met with more resistance in other ancient civilizations such as in Asia. Yet it would be simplistic to explain the African religious enthusiasm by pointing to an imperialistic cultural imposition. The "African factor" in the Continent's reception of Christianity is a key motif in Lamin Sanneh's 1983 historical *West African Christianity: The Religious Impact*. Also, African theologian John Mbiti has pointed to the disposition of the African Traditional Religion as a key factor in Africa's warm reception of Christianity in Africa. He insists, "Western missionaries did not introduce God to Africa - rather, it was God who brought them to Africa[...] . African religion had already done the ground work of making people receptive to the gospel of Jesus Christ" (Qtd. in *Religion and Society* 50).

The current project that recognizes African cultural and spiritual thought is called *Inculturation*. It is aimed at encouraging the growth and flourishing of the Christian church experience on the native soil. Inculturation as a *transforming dialogue* between Christianity and the faith of traditional African cultures is aimed at *bridging the gap between faith and life*. This process represents the about-turn made by the Latin-rite Christian Catholic Church which reached its apogee, during the pontificate of the well-traveled Pope John Paul II with the 1994 "African Synod." The synod -- a meeting of bishops with the Pope John Paul II - is designed to bring Africa into the heart of the Church. The Synod had as themes: proclamation, dialogue, justice and peace, social communications, along with inculturation. One of the recommendations of *Ecclesia in Africa* synod was to set up commissions

> [...] for matters concerning marriage, veneration of ancestors, and the spirit world, in order to examine in depth all the cultural aspects of problems from the theological, sacramental, liturgical and canonical points of view (Qtd. by Mezu in *African Renaissance* 116).

As Rev. Ezewudu observes, it was pointed out during the Synod that terms which depicted aspects of African traditional life and religion, such as polygamy, paganism, heathenism, fetishism, animism, idolatry, and which were negatively interpreted as primitive, were not only misnomers but inaccurate representations of realities that were incomprehensible to the foreign missionary. It can be demonstrated that even "Western bourgeois Christianity" with its exclusive claims on history, the bible, the crucifix and the Sacraments, is not immune from the use of symbols, for it was through these symbols that European Christianity is able to hold on to its own "fetishes."

Pope John Paul II, therefore, apologized on behalf of the Christian Church for abuses, violations and ignorant misperceptions by Western missionaries of Africa's artifacts, shrines, peoples, and Africans' cultural/religious beliefs. He continues, "the adherents of African traditional religions should be treated with great respect and esteem and all inaccurate and disrespectful language should be avoided" (Qtd. in *Pope John Paul II and Africa*, 51). Consequently, during his trip to Nigeria to beatify the Sub-Saharan African, Cyprian Michael Iwene Tansi – an Igbo - (March 21-23, 1998), the Pope challenged Catholic bishops to **move quickly to inculturate** the church in the face of very stiff competition and threat posed by the Pentecostal assemblies:

> Do all that you can [...] so that your people will feel more and more at home in the Church, and the Church more and more at home among your people. Necessary here will be research into traditional African religion and culture (Qtd. by Ezewudo in *Religion and Society* 57).

And this inculturation job, African Bishops insist, must be done by African theologians and missionaries who are "insiders." As a first step, the Pope encouraged the African ecclesiastics to encourage the assimilation of positive traditional values that proclaim belief in One Supreme Being who is Eternal, Creator, Provident and Just Judge: values which are readily harmonized with the content of the Christian faith. He exhorted the African Christian Church to draw up their own martyrology to honor people we know who are saints – proclaimed or not. As can be seen, the "African soul" is still intact since Africa's lost reverences are gradually being recovered owing to the resilience and authenticity of African cultural and spiritual heritage.

That Africans should now be encouraged to revisit the honor given to their dead -- the veneration of ancestors - is a vindication of the pristine value of the spirituality and faith of the Africans' ancestors discredited through Western missionary superciliousness and ignorance. These modern developments are the fruits of the Cosmo-theological thoughts propagated by (among others), Achebe (in essays and fictional works) and Equiano – the earliest, important, literary and cultural ancestor of all peoples of African descent.

Significance of names, religious symbols and Eco-system in the works of Equiano and Achebe

In the history of slavery, naming can be a metaphor for denial or for validation of humanity. In "Named for Victroria, Queen of England," the free-born and un-enslaved writer knows his name: "I was baptized Albert Chinualumogu." He has a last name "Achebe." He says he "dropped the tribute to Victorian England when I went to the university" (In *MYOCD* 67). Achebe knows his mother's and his father's people. He knows his locale: "I was born in Ogidi in Eastern Nigeria of devout Christian parents"(65).

Trained in the British educational system, his keen intellect empowered him sufficiently that he realized that Colonialism was a disservice to him and his people. And so the "appalling novels" he read impelled him towards a vindication of African civilization just as Western negative stereotyping of Africans would also inform Olaudah Equiano's creative vision. Achebe speaks for both of them when he states: "the story we had to tell could not be told for us by anyone else no matter how gifted or well-intentioned" (In *MYOCD* 70). Their "insider" status is an empowering trope for the cultural validation of personhood as well as for the reclamation of personal liberty.

If naming is a trope of personhood, of physical and psychological liberation, Frederick Douglass's life is a classic example in its stark contrast to the lives of Equiano and Achebe. Douglass laments in his *Narrative* that he has no certain name and identity. Ignorance of these things was a source of concern to Frederick Douglass. As he strives to reconstruct his identity, he laments with poignancy the lack of a real name, and a date of birth: "I have no accurate knowledge of my age[...] I do not remember to have ever met a slave who tell of his birthday; [...] a want of information concerning my own was a source of unhappiness to me even during childhood (*Narrative of the Life of Frederick Douglass, an American slave, Written by Himself* 39).

The process by which Douglass comes to acquire his definitive names is a lesson on the importance of naming as a trope for the definition of humanity. First called "Frederick Douglass Washington Bailey," he quickly dispenses with the two middle names, being known only as "Frederick Bailey." In Baltimore, he takes the name of "Stanley," and in New York, he becomes "Frederick Johnson." Finally, in Bedford, well over twenty-seven years old, he chooses a lasting name "Frederick Douglass" by which posterity would come to know him.

Older than both Douglass and Achebe, Equiano knew both worlds. Like Achebe, he had known a certain cultural space and identity and like Douglass, he knew a loss of his freedom and personhood. But Equiano had imprinted indelibly on his eleven year-old mind those unforgettable memories of his land of birth: "I was born in the year 1745 [...] in a charming, fruitful vale named Essaka." He knows his town's location, geographical surroundings, and above all he knows details of his life in Africa. He is the favorite of his mother and his father is "an Embrenche, a term, as I remember, importing the highest distinction and signifying in our language a *mark* of grandeur" (*The Narrative* 198). Son of a chief, or an elder, Embrenche - which equates Umuofia's rank of *Ndichie* – lords of the clan. Embrenche can be read to mean *Mgburuichi*, made up of a combination of two words *Igbu ichi* – an Igbo cultural practice that means an act of scarification. Thus *Mgburichi* (Embrenche), Catherine Acholonu explains, is the term used for the generality of men who bear the scarification (*The Igbo Roots of Olaudah Equiano* 12). Equiano's father and brother had their skin cut "across at the top of the forehead, and drawing it down to the eyebrows[...] [until] it shrinks up into a thick *weal* across the lower top of the forehead[...] I was also *destined* to receive it by my parents" (*The Narrative* 196).

Equiano continues on the significant import of naming as a cultural trope of individuation: "Like them [Jews]also, our children were named from some event; some circumstance, or fancied foreboding at the time of their birth" (*The Narrative* 200). And Achebe corroborates this in detail using his fictional works as well as his essay, "Chi in Igbo Cosmology." Equiano continues with no ambiguity, "I was named *Olaudah*, which in our language signifies vicissitudes, or fortunate; also, one favored, and having a loud voice, and well-spoken" (200).

Lacking freedom, just like Frederick Douglass, naming becomes problematic for him. He is first called **Jacob**; then aboard the *African Snow* he is named **Michael**, and on purchasing him, Lieutenant Michael Henry Pascal gives him the name of **Gustavus Vassa**, after the Swedish patriot – king who led his people to victory. The name seems aptly suitable for him to accept, but once he secures his freedom, he promptly changes his name back to what gives him most confidence as to his true African identity – Olaudah Equiano. Made up of two words – *Ola* - (ornamental jewel), and – *udah* - (resounding sounds).

The symbolic potency of his naming is noted by critic Ure L. Mezu who likens Olaudah to *"flute-voice"* - the flute whose lyrical singing resounds through the ages (*Religion and Society* 158), because Equiano's *Narrative* is not only pre-eminent as the first authentic scripted (not oral) documentation of African communal life as lived by an African, but it also defends and validates African civilization; it indicts the barbarism of the slave institution; it upsets racial and class hierarchies by proving that intelligence is not race-dependent. It is so very germane to apply Killam's eulogy of Achebe to his progenitor Equiano: "*Words* are an epitome of the man. They show the spiritual and moral qualities that reveal themselves in his writing [...] . There is nothing ostentatious in his manner. And why should there be: the power is in the *Word* (In *Chinua Achebe: A Celebration* 162). Thus, Equiano and Achebe remain the clearest examples of the will to power as the will to write. One should add that "Equiano" probably comes from the Igbo words – *Ekwuo* (when you speak), *Anu* (he listens and understands). *Ekwuoanu* (Equiano) lived up to his name. He listened very well, observed very well, absorbed very well and documented accurately what he saw and heard during the very first eleven or twelve years of his life.

Priests, Naming and Igbo Linguistics in the Writings of Equiano and Achebe

Arising from traditional African religious beliefs, Equiano underscores the function and importance of "priests and magicians, or wise men" revered not just as interpreters of the will of the gods (see *Agbala*'s priestess Chielo, and *Ani*'s Ezeani in *TFA*), but because "they calculated our time, and foretold event," and so were called "Ah-affoe-way-cah, or calculators or yearly men" (*The Narrative* 200). The Essaka call their year "Ah-affoe" (Igbo *Afo*) which they compute "from the day on which the sun crosses the line, and on its setting that evening there is a general shout throughout the land" (200). Acholonu opines that Equiano had more problems with Ah-ffoe, *Ah-ffoe-way-cah*, and his own names Equiano and Olaudah, *et cetera*: "When I first came across the word Ah-*ffoe*, I was convinced it was made up of two names *Afo* and *Aho*" (*Igbo Roots* 11*)*.

Equiano was writing in a pre-linguistic era, and adopting the English letter "e" found in the names Essaka, Oye-Eboe, Eboe, Embrenche, the phonetic symbol should be "i" as will be discussed later in the next paragraphs. Suffice it to say that given that most African languages were unwritten during Equiano's time, and despite the imperfect recollections of an eleven year-old, the phonetic similarities are remarkable. Still the modern Igbos call their year "Afo" with their calendar consisting of "the four-day 'small' week and the eight day 'great' week (Chi in Igbo Cosmology 100). Certainly, any Igbo would agree with Catherine Acholonu's linguistic interpretation of the real meaning of the names Equiano remembers:

> Today, Equiano would have written *Ibo* (or *Igbo*), *Isseke*, and *Igbu* (*r*) *ichi* [for **Embrenche**]. Equiano also sometimes used the name of the English letter –a- to describe the almost identical Igbo sound /e/ or /E/. Thus we have *Essaka* rather than *Isseke* [...] We also notice a similar dilemma in his rendering of the word *Eboe*. He opted for –oe, knowing that most English words that end with an –o- are pronounced /oa/ or /ou/. And the closest similarity to this sound a the end of the words can be seen in such words as *foe, woe, toe* ---(*The Igbo Roots of Olaudah Equiano* 11).

The African Medicine-Man in the Works of Equiano and Achebe

These magicians function as doctors or physicians, practicing "bleeding by cupping; and were very successful in healing wounds and expelling poisons. They had likewise some extraordinary method of discovering jealousy, theft, and poisoning; the success of which no doubt they derived from their unbounded influence over the credulity and superstition of the people" (*The Narrative 200*). Such a priest or medicine man, Okagbue Uyanwa, is seen in action in *Things Fall Apart* guiding Okonkwo's favorite child round the compound to uncover where she buried her *Iyi-uwa*, the symbol of a former life-cycle. Ezinma is suspected to be an *ogbanje* - (the equivalent of the Yoruba *abiku*) - the evil child that constantly dies and gets reborn to plague its parents. When the *Iyi-uwa* -a small pebble wrapped in a dirty rag – is dug up, women shout with joy because it is believed that Ezinma, the only surviving of Ekwefi's nine children, will now live, her link with the spirit world being broken.

Equiano also talks about the "unbounded influence" the magicians have over the credulity and superstition of the people. Certainly, these medicine men must have been quite clever, able to work their psychology on the psyche of the natives to have been so successful. Achebe paints a successful and vivid portrait of Equiano's medicine-man as a strange occult figure, with his "goatskin bag" in his "underwear" and "a long and thin strip of cloth wound round the waist like a belt and passed between the legs to be fastened to the belt" (*TFA* 83). It is in fact Elechi Amadi who in *The Concubine* gives a memorable drawing of the finesse and wizardry of a medicine man called Agwoturumbe.

Transplanting the African Medicine-man to the Diaspora

W. E. B. Du Bois would effect the diasporan connection to Africa by immortalizing the African medicine man – the medium of connection with the invisible - who would in a different spatial-temporal horizon transform and transmute into both the preacher with the multiple roles of healer, and shepherd of the displaced and uprooted Africans. Du Bois describes the African medicine-man functioning in the community as "the healer of the sick, the interpreter of the unknown, the comforter of the sorrowing, the supernatural avenger of wrong and the one who rudely but picturesquely expressed the longing, disappointment and resentment of a stolen and oppressed people" (*The Souls of Black Folk* 123).

It is from these multiple functions of the African Medicine-man as bard, physician, judge and priest that the Negro preacher emerged to lead the first Afro-American institution, the Negro Church. But Equiano's *The Narrative* also provides the first historical recorded foundation. Achebe and other writers would in time see themselves as novelists, visionaries, healers of wounds, guides and conscience of the people. Calling for the best possible education, these writers would embark on a self-appointed task of "re-education and regeneration" in which they as well as others would be the sensitive point of the community, and would "march right in front" to restore Africa's past, a past which, "with all its imperfections--was not [seen as] one long night of savagery from which the first European acting on God's behalf delivered us." ("The Novelist as a Teacher." In *MYOCD* 45).

The Eco-system -- Africa and the West

Another vindication of Africa's cosmological thought is the present global call to respect Nature. In Western countries, respect for Nature comes with slogans urging people to preserve the ecosystem, to show respect for Mother Earth. There is also the Greenpeace movement which can be viewed as some sort of eco-spirituality. This is a strange reversal of attitudes of the erstwhile Western colonials and missionaries who denigrated the supposed naïveté of African transcendentalism – which was dubbed **"animism," "paganism," heathenism,"** and **"polytheism."**

Thus, the African ancestors would see God – Chineke's presence in nature – trees and rivers, hills, landscapes and earth's creatures, seasons and festivals; they would likely build an altar near some rise of earth close to a lagoon or body of water sensing that when the wind blew, it would make a special sound as an emanation of Chukwu's spiritual energy. Umuofia has a practice of dedicating a whole week to the formidable earth deity – *ala / ani* – during which time people rest from work, and the community observe peace among its members. Therefore, Nature dominated the worldview. Stiff penalty is imposed for offenses against the land (*nso-ala* or *-ani*). An infraction such as Okonkwo's beating of his wife at this time, would bring out Ezeani, **male** priest of the Earth goddess Ani. Speaking sternly to Okonkwo, Ezeani brings down his staff on the floor to emphasize the seriousness of his point:

> Listen to me! You are not a stranger to Umuofia. You know as well as I do that our forefathers ordained that before we plant any crops in the earth we should observe a week in which a man does not say a harsh word to his neighbor. We live in peace with our fellows to honor our great goddess without whose blessing our crops will not grow. You have committed a great evil. Your wife was at fault, but even if you came to your obi and found her lover on top of her, you would still have committed a great evil to beat her[...]. The evil you have done can ruin a whole clan. The earth goddess whom you have insulted may refuse to give us her increase and we shall all perish (*TFA* 30; my emphases).

The same principle informs Umuaro's Festival of the Pumpkin Leaves which symbolizes sacrifice, renewal, veneration of the earth, and which re-unites the people as well. (Chapter 7, *Arrow of God*).

Python as a Sacred symbol

Even certain animals such as pythons were considered sacred, possessing spiritual energy. Olaudah Equiano mentions sacred serpents, "esteemed ominous" that come into their houses, and these (each of which is as thick as a calf's leg) he says, "we never molest." Some would creep into

> **my mother's night house, where I would lay with her, and coiled themselves into folds,** and each time they crowed like a cock. I was desired by some of our wise men to touch these that I might be interested in the good omens, which I did, for **they were harmless,**

and would suffer themselves to be handled., and then they would be put into a large earthen pan and set on the side of the road (*Narrative [...]* 201; my emphases).

Certainly, the Chiefs priests of Ulu and Ezidemili respectively would testify to the supreme signification of the sacred python which Ezeulu's son Oduche desecrates because his missionary teacher dares them to do so. The event provides the priest of Ezidemili a providential excuse to dig into Ezeulu and exacerbate hostilities between the two communities. Using strikingly similar descriptions, the narrator of *Arrow of God* describes the two pythons "which lived almost entirely in "Oduche's **mother's hut**, on top of the wall which carried the roof. **They did no harm** and kept the rats away" (*Arrow of God* 50; my emphases). Oduche succeeds in imprisoning the python in his school box, and the ensuing scandal rocks the villages of Umuaro.

That Ezeulu, seeking to keep pace with a "changing world" sends his son to the Christian school, and that Oduche desecrates the symbolic python are acts that would accelerate the fall of the Umuaro Chief Priest. It is worth noting that in *Things Fall Apart*, a python assumes a mystical signification beyond all proportions. An *osu* Christian convert follows the fiery missionary fervor of Mr. Kiaga and kills the royal python which is revered throughout Mbanta and the surrounding clans. The people address it as "'Our Father.' As in Equiano's case, Achebe narrates that "**it was allowed to go wherever it chose, even into peoples beds**. It ate rats in the house and swallowed hens' eggs." (*TFA* 157; my emphasis). Even accidentally killing it will require rituals of sacrifices and cleansing, but nobody believes such an abomination can happen until Okoli, the *osu* kills it. Since Okoli promptly dies by nightfall of that day, the people attribute his death to vindication by their God, and serious conflict is averted. But the hot-headed Enoch, son of the python-priest would bring traditional religion and the Christian church into direct confrontation.

But under Western Christianity, the Umuofia traditional belief symbols such as the *Evil forest* lose their sacred aura, and moral control agency. To the Christians, it becomes "fetish" to fear and reverence them. Those who persevere are labeled *animists*, heathens and superstitious pagans. But now with the current jargons, *animism* seems back in style with a vengeance, because people are belatedly realizing that human beings must preserve Nature's balance, or face Nature's wrath. In the confrontation with the traditional religions, Christian missionaries and their over- zealous followers occasionally engaged in destroying religious symbols and village shrines, burning down their wooded sanctuaries and killing totem animals just to prove that they worshiped a superior God. Could this curious "back-to-nature" phenomenon now be seen as a vindication of the discredited faith and religion of the African ancestors?

Kinship System - Affinity with the Jews

Much has been made about the Igbo affinity with the Jews. Interestingly enough, by 1789, Equiano believed this issue to be an important discussion topic. Drawing attention to the relatively "light" complexion (compared to other Sub-Saharan African groups) of the Igbo, he lauds the "comeliness" of his own people, citing as examples, the "Eboe" in London noted for their "complexion" -- ideas of beauty "being wholly relative. I remember while in Africa to have seen three negro children, who were tawny, and another quite white, who were universally regarded by myself, and the natives in general, as far as related to their complexions" (*The Narrative* 198). In *Arrow of God*, Winterbottom appropriates authorial voice to hazard a viewpoint as to the origin of the Igbo who, he concedes, lack a central kinship authority. He describes Ezeulu as

> a most impressive figure of a man[...] very light in complexion, almost red. One finds people like that now and again among the Ibos. I have a theory that the Ibos in a distant past assimilated a non-negroid tribe of the same complexion as the Red Indians (37-8).

Or, could it be that in the distant past a group of Igbo left the ancestral homeland, and journeyed northward, and assimilated into other groups to become ancient Hebrews?[6] Equiano remembers that his people practice circumcision like the Jews, and "made offerings and feasts on that occasion in the same manner as they did. Like them also, our children were named from some event; some circumstance, or fancied foreboding at the time of their birth." He recounts other cultural practices similar to those of the Jews who "never polluted the name of the object of our adoration; on the contrary, it was always mentioned with the greatest reverence" (*The Narrative* 199).

In *Arrow of God*, Akukalia's desecration of Ebo's *ikenga* and Enoch's unmasking of an Umuofia masquerade (*TFA*) are contextually illustrative. Also, as among the Jews, Equiano points out, swearing and cursing are not encouraged, nor are "all those terms of abuse and reproach which find their way so readily and copiously into the languages of more civilized people" (*The Narrative* 200). Thus, Essaka "Eboe" religious observances resemble those of the Jews, as seen in the "many purifications and washings; indeed almost as many, and used on the same occasions, if my recollection does not fail me, as the Jews." To this day, the cleansing, purification rituals are still being practised by those Igbo who, as Equiano documents, have "touched the dead at any time. [They] were obliged to wash and purify themselves before they could enter a dwelling-house" (200).

Treatment of women present a common usage, for like the ancient Hebrews who out of gender discrimination consider menstruating women unclean, Equiano offers a comparable Essaka cultural ritual:

> Every woman too, at certain times, was forbidden to come into a dwelling-house, or touch any person, or any thing we ate. I was so fond of my mother I could not keep from her, or avoid touching her at some of those periods, in consequence of which I was obliged to be kept out with her, in a little house made for that purpose, till offering was made, and then we were purified (*The Narrative* 200).

Equiano appears struck by other striking similarities in customs: the old Jewish patriarchs and judges are the equivalent of Igbo heads of families, elders and wise men. Before the onset of Jewish kings, the Jews had an egalitarian system of elders and judges just like the democratic Igbo. Then, there is the similar principle of retaliation in both their legal systems. Also from ancient times, the two societies practiced circumcision of the male, and many other such rituals of sacrifice and purifications.

To support his arguments, Equiano cites commentaries on Christian religion by Dr. John Clarke, former Dean of Sarum, and Dr. Gill's commentary on Genesis which "deduces the pedigree of the Africans from Afer and Afra, the descendants of Abraham by Keturah his wife and concubine (for both these titles are applied to her). These and the similarities listed above compel Equiano to conclude that the Igbo / Africans descended from the Jews. It must be mentioned again that the Igbo of today believe it is the other way around.

Equiano attributes the difference in color between the "Eboan Africans and the modern Jews" to Africans having to live under the torrid zone, citing sources such as Reverend Mr. T.Clarkson's Essay on the *Slavery and Commerce of the Human Species*. Equiano's introduction to the politics of color provides the background to his thoughts on the issue of color. At Guernsey, with his friend Dick, Equiano stays with a shipmate's family. The family treats him very well and teaches him, but Equinao notices that when washed, their young daughter's

> face looked very rosy, but when she washed mine I did not look so. I therefore tried oftentimes myself if I could not by washing make my face of the same color as my little play-mate, Mary, but it was in vain. **And I now began to be mortified at the difference in our complexion** (*The Narrative* 213).

The goal of all his arguments being to fight prejudice, therefore to study and expose the reasons for color differences may "tend to remove the prejudice that some conceive against natives of Africa on account of their color" (*The Narrative* 201). Allowances must be made for the young impressionable Equiano as he was being socialized into a Eurocentric world. *The Narrative* is the work of a mature, self-confident man who has reasoned things out, and is at peace with himself. But, not having known slavery, yet Achebe is also introduced to the politics of colorism and racism through Western colonial education. Through writing, these shackles are thrown off by both writers.

Rationale for Writing - Equiano and Achebe

In their creative vision, Equiano and Achebe are motivated by the same reasons, one of which is to authenticate their claims of an anterior African civilization. Noticeably, in both works, every word, line, or incident is designed to counter a specific charge. Achebe acknowledges Equiano's *Narrative* as "an attempt to counteract the lies and slander invented by some Europeans to justify slave trade" ("The African Writer and the English Language." In *MYOCD* 59). Equiano appears to indicate a definite political motive for his writing:

> If it affords any satisfaction to my numerous friends, at whose request it has been written, or in the smallest degree promotes **the interest of humanity**, the ends for which it was undertaken will be fully attained, and every wish of my heart gratified (*The Narrative* 195).

The thrust is to indict slavery as a practice against "the interest of humanity" (*The Narrative* 195). It is exposed by one who, despite handicaps, and irrespective of a non-scriptive background, is as good a writer as any European, then and now. Equally, Equiano wishes to counter the widespread myth that Africans were either not fully human, or, belonged to a not-so-developed branch of the human race. Achebe recalls Albert Schweitzer's arrogant words that *"the African indeed is my brother, but my junior brother"* (In *MYOCD* 3). Thus, the aims and aspirations of both writers (Equiano and Achebe) coincide. Neither is ready to accept the label of inferiority; and it is to challenge this that the act of writing constitutes an effort in Black self- and communal representation. To paraphrase Achebe, their validation of African civilization symbolizes the homage and ritual return of a prodigal son. Achebe's own creative goal is well-stated:

> to help my society regain belief in itself and put away the complexes of the years of denigration and self-abasement [...]I would be quite satisfied if my novels (especially the ones I set in the past) did no more than teach my readers that their past--with all its imperfections--was not one long night of savagery from which the first European acting on God's behalf delivered us ("The Novelist as a Teacher." - (In *MYOCD* 45).

Achebe makes it a capital sin for Africans to "ignore the presence and role of racism in African history or that somehow it was all the black man's fault" ("Colonialist Criticism, 11.") Thus, says Achebe, "If I were God I would regard as the very worst our acceptance—for whatever reason—of racial inferiority [...] For no thinking African can escape the pain of the wound in our soul" ("The Novelist as a Teacher," 44). And it is to heal those "soul" wounds that Equiano declares from the start that his motive for writing is to promote "the interests of humanity" (*The Narrative* 195). Every chapter is filled with commentaries of denunciation, reprimands, exhortation or explanation – all designed to encourage his "countrymen" or to denounce the cruel inhumanity and hypocrisy of the so-called "polished and haughty Europeans whose ancestors were once [...] uncivilized and even barbarous." Thus, he categorically denounces Western Christian hypocrisy: "O, ye nominal Christians! Might not an African ask you---- Learned you this from God?" (*The Narrative* 201; 209). Equiano credits the rationale for slavery to the "**avarice**" of Westerners. Consequently, both writers have utilized every opportunity to disprove the barbarity and lack of culture usually attributed to Africans.

Adventures at Sea and in Writing - an Odyssey

Equiano's multifaceted character, in its wiliness, pragmatic adaptability, business acumen, and intelligence, typifies the character of the modern Igbo. Through his travels, Equiano provides a model for the modern Igbo entrepreneur/ creative intellectual who like the industrious Jews are to be seen in far-flung corners of the globe. The Igbo (especially the Orlu people of which "Esseke" or Isseke is a part) are renowned for their entrepreneurial skills. Equiano engaged in petty trading, earning and saving money. He had numerous maritime adventures, from Africa to Barbados to Virginia and then to England, Holland and North America. His ship engaged in rambunctious naval battles during the Seven Years' War. Through Richard Baker (Dick), a young shipmate, Equiano learnt to read and write. He perfected the learning process in England. Despite his kindness, Michael Henry Pascal of the Royal Navy sold Equiano in 1763 to Captain James Doran who took him to the West Indies. He suffered a cruel human betrayal, yet the intellectual, highly resilient Equiano in 1766, was able to raise the sum of forty pounds (the sum used to purchase him) to buy back his **physical** freedom - "manumission" - from his then owner, Philadelphia Quaker Robert King.

The emphasis is on physical freedom because reading is a trope which he has used long before then to liberate himself **mentally**. To avoid harassment and recapture, he settled in England, working for Dr. Charles Irving, a scientist experimenting with salt-water purification. He also studied opera and architecture. The adventurous Equiano made further travels to Italy, Turkey, Portugal, Canada during General Wolfe's campaign. Still enamored of the seafaring and adventuring life, Equiano traveled to the Mediterranean working as a ship's steward, and as a gunpowder carrier. He served under several commanders and Caribbean traders, and then sailed on to America and the West Indies and, even to the Arctic with the 1772 Phipps Expedition. His sense of enterprise made possible the publication of his *Narrative* by subscription. He also got such important personalities as the Prince of Wales and about eight dukes to contribute in advance for his book. Then world traveler that he is, he embarked on a book promotional tour, giving lectures in England, Scotland, Ireland and Wales. He worked co-operatively with local abolition committees. Thus, he was able to generate a lot of publicity and in the process publicized his ideas about the abolition of slavery.

In 1786, he received appointment as Commissary of Provisions and Stores to oversee the resettling of freed slaves in Sierra Leone, a position he resigned because of a disagreement. Finally he settled in England, and became the foremost champion of the Abolition movement and a cornerstone of the antislavery movement. In 1792, Equiano married Susanna Cullen, but died shortly after in March 1797 survived by just one living daughter. Brycchan remarks that it would be "a full ten years before the slave trade was abolished in British ships, forty years before slavery was abolished in British colonies, and 68 years before slavery was ended in the United States," concluding that although Equiano did not live to see slavery and its atrocities abolished, "his narrative played an important part in bringing them about" (Brycchan, "Olaudah Equiano: A Critical Biography" 4). These details of an eventful, achievement-filled life evidently belie his own statement, "I believe there are few events in my life which have not happened to many" (*The Narrative* 195), but rather confirm indeed that he, is "a ***particular favorite of heaven*** (*The Narrative* 195; Equiano's emphasis).

Achebe's Pride in Equiano as a Compatriot and Literary Ancestor

Finally, the contributions of Equiano's *Narrative* to *Les belles letters* lie in its history-making uniqueness in inaugurating literary genres such as Black Autobiography, Slave Narrative and Abolitionist literature. From the feelings condensed in the second opening epigraph of this essay, Achebe admires the courage Equiano needed "to fight that lonely battle in London in 1789;" and Achebe himself confesses his pride in having Equiano as a compatriot: "and no chauvinism, I hope, that Olaudah Equiano was born [...] in that part of West Africa called Biafra today" ("The African Writer and the Biafran Cause," 80). Although Biafra as a political entity did not survive, it still survives in the hearts of all Igbo as an ideal of the quest for justice and equal human dignity that must have inspired Equiano's and Achebe's desire to right socio-cultural inequities through the medium of writing.

The third opening epigraph is a prototype of an oral village chant for the whereabouts of a missing son, "Who are we looking for, who are we looking for? [...] It is Equiano we are looking for." Definitely, Africa found her son, alright; and peoples' of African descent found Equiano – their link to their African homeland – in his literary legacy to all his progeny. Equally, Achebe discovered Equiano through his writing, sufficiently admired him as a model on which to construct his own artistic legacy. Equiano is unforgettable. And because of him, the history of slavery will never be forgotten, for it is today the foundation of Black and African studies, history, sociology, literary studies, anthropology, linguistics, *et cetera*. It is because of Equiano that Ama Ata Aidoo can also exclaim with wonder:

> I don't know how people react when they leave Africa and go to places outside where there are concentrations of other Black people; for me it was incredible. I just couldn't believe it that I could cross the whole of the Atlantic and find all of these people who are like people at home..But definitely this is the reason I keep coming back to this because I think it is part of what is eating us up. **You can't cover up history[...]. It is time we faced the question of what happened** that so many of us are in Harlem and so many in the West Indies[...]You see, grief accepted is grief overcome. -- (Wilentz, Gay. *Binding Cultures* 39; my emphasis)

Conclusion

Certainly, Equiano's *Narrative* successfully uncovered history. Through the unsurpassed intellectual achievements of both Olaudah Equiano and Chinua Achebe, the enslaved, or colonized Africans and their free, indigenous or hybrid progeny have uncovered enough records of African cultural history and civilization to achieve undiminished wholeness. What Achebe's writings have accomplished for African and Diasporan blacks owe their impetus to Equiano's 1789 two-volume *The Interesting Narrative of the Life of Olaudah Equiano, or Gustavus Vassa, the African, Written by Himself* which is an early, global model for the celebration of African history, culture, and autobiography. Both their legacies testify to the enduring hardiness, creative talent and the indomitable, democratic spirit of survival of the Igbo, and by extension, of peoples of African descent despite travails and generations of dehumanization.

Finally, the courage and genius shown by both authors underscore the need for every life to count for something and for somebody, for human life to be continually under vigilant review in its growth process. The two narratives emphasize the necessity of deploying individual talents for the good and the well-being of not just the self but of the many. Thus, where it should count maximally, the personal must become the public. Ultimately, Chinua Achebe corroborates and authenticates Equiano's fragmentary but accurate memories of the socio-cultural, juridical, economic, religious, and other facets of the lifestyle and thoughts of the ancient Eboe. Chinua Achebe's scriptive authentification remains the best sociological and historical defense against any detractors of Equiano who may charge his narrative with falsifications, or a lack of authenticity.

Notes

[1] Achebe's *Things Fall Apart* will hereinafter be referred to as *TFA* and Equiano's *The Interesting Narrative of the Life of Olaudah Equiano or Gustavus Vassa, the African Written by Himself* will hereinafter be referred to as *The Narrative*. The chant that forms the third epigraph is from "The African Slave Trade and the Middle Passage," Narrative 4 [featuring commentary by Chinua Achebe], Africans in America, Part 1: The Terrible Transformation (PBS Online, 1999): <http://www.pbs.org/wgbh/aia/part1/-1narr4.html>

[2] *Morning Yet On Creation Day* will hereinafter be known as *MYOCD*.

[3] See "Named for Victoria, Queen of England." In *MYOCD*.

[4] Dr. Catherine Acholonu in *The Igbo Roots of Olaudah Equiano* (Owerri: Afa Publications, 1989) claims to have traced Equiano's ancestry to the village of Isseke in Orlu, an Igbo town in what is now Imo State.

[5] See S. Okechukwu Mezu's *Communalist Manifesto*. Washington, D.C.: Nigerian Students Voice, 1966.

[6] For a discussion on Igbo affinity with the Jews, see "The Mezus Visit with the Achebes," the last chapter of this work.

Works Cited

Achebe, Chinua. *Things Fall Apart*. Revised edition. New York: Anchor Books, Doubleday, 1994.

--- *Arrow of God*. Revised edition. New York: Random House, 1974.

--- "The African Writer and the English Language." In *Morning Yet On Creation Day.*London: Heinemann, 1975. 55-62.

--- "The African Writer and the Biafran Cause." In *Morning Yet On Creation Day.* London: Heinemann, 1975. 78-84.

--- "Named for Victoria, Queen of England." In *Morning Yet On Creation Day.* London: Heinemann, 1975. 65-70.

--- "The Novelist as a Teacher." In *Morning Yet On Creation Day.* London: Heinemann, 1975. 42-45.

Acholonu, Catherine. *The Igbo Roots of Olaudah Equiano.* Owerri, Nigeria: Afa Publications, 1989.

Andrews, William L. *African American Autobiography: A Collection of Critical Essays.* New Jersey: Prentice Hall, 1993.

Awoonor, Kofi. *The Breast of the Earth.* Nigeria: Nok Publishers, 1975.

Brycchan, Carey. "Olaudah Equiano: A Critical Biography" 2000-2003. <http://www.brycchancare-y.com/equiano/biog.htm>.

Carroll, David. *Chinua Achebe,* N.Y.: Twayne Publishers, Inc., 1970.

Douglass, Frederick. *Narrative of the Life of Frederick Douglass, an American slave, Written by Himself.* Ed. David W. Blight. N.Y.: Bedford Books, 1993.

Du Bois, W.E.B. "What is Civilization? Africa's Answer." In *W.E.B. Du Bois: A Reader.* Ed.Meyer Weinberg. New York: Harper and Row, 1970. 374-382.

Edwards, Paul, ed. *Equiano's Travels.* London: Heinemann, 1967.

Equiano, Olaudah. *The Narrative of the Life of Olaudah Equiano or Gustavus Vassa, the African Written by Himself.* In *Humanities in the Modern World: An Africana Emphasis.* Ed. Jackson, Wendell, et al. Boston, Ma: Pearson Custom Publishing, 2001.

Ezewudo, Gabriel. "Christianity, African Traditional Religion and Colonialism: Were Africans pawns or players in the Cultural Encounter?" In *Religion and Society.* Ed. Rose Ure Mezu. MD: Black Academy Press, 1998. 43-61.

Gates, Henry Louis, Jr. "James Gronniosaw and the Trope of the Talking Book." In *African American Autobiography: A Collection of Critical Essays*. New Jersey: Prentice Hall, Ltd. 1993. 8-25.

Mbiti, John. *Bible and Theology in African Christianity*. Nairobi: O.U.P., 1986.

Mezu, S. Okechukwu . *Communalist Manifesto*. Washington, DC: Nigerian Students Voice, 1966.

--- *The Tropical Dawn*. Buffalo, NY: Black Academy Press, 1970.

Mezu, Rose Ure. ed. *Africa and the Diaspora: the Black Scholar and Society*. Black Academy Press: MD, 2000.

--- "The Omnipresent Papacy: Pope John Paul II on Feminism, the Youth, and Africa." In *African Renaissance*. London: (May/June) 2005. 111-125.

Mezu, S. O and Rose Ure Mezu, eds. *Pope John Paul II and Africa*. Baltimore, MD: Black Academy Press, 2005.

Mezu, Ure L. The Odyssey and Legend of Olaudah Equiano. In *Leadership, Culture and Racism*." Eds. Mezu, Rose Ure and Burney J. Hollis. Black Academy Press: MD, 1998.

Miller, Christopher L. *Blank Darkness: Africanist Discourse in French*. Chicago: University of Chicago, 1985.

Pope John Paul II. *Ecclesia in Africa*. (A post-Synnodal Apostolic Letter issued September 14, 1995, and later signed in Yaounde, Cameroun.

Sanneh, Lamin. *West African Christianity: The Religious Impact*. London: Christopher Hurst Publishers, 1983.

Walker, Wyatt Tee. "Roots – Musically Speaking;" In Mezu, *Religion and Society*. Ed. Rose Ure Mezu. MD: Black Academy Press, 1998.

Wa Thiong'O, Ngugi. *Decolonizing the Mind: The Politics of Language in African Literature*. London: James Curry Ltd., 1986.

8

Women in Achebe's World: A Womanist Critique

When literary activities marking the sixtieth birthday of Chinua Achebe reached fever-pitch in 1990, the greatest accolade given him was summed up in one metaphor: the eagle on the iroko. Now, anybody familiar with the African landscape knows that the iroko is the tallest, strongest tree-king of trees in the African rain forest, and that the eagle is, of course, the king of the birds. It is not an easy feat to scale the tree; that is why the Igbo proverb insists: "One does not climb the iroko twice." Having succeeded in climbing the iroko, the climber should appropriate all that s/he finds there, for [s]he may not be able to do so again.

The eagle, however, can both scale and soar above the tree over and over. In this metaphor, the iroko-tree king represents the field of African literature, and the eagle, Chinua Achebe. Achebe has, of course, literarily climbed and soared above the iroko several times. More than those of any other African writer, his writings have helped to develop what is known as African literature today. And the single book which has helped him to launch his "revolution" is the slim, classic volume called *Things Fall Apart* (1958). Having been the first, so to speak, to scale the top of the iroko, this eagle, Achebe, and other male eaglets after him, arguably have appropriated all that they have found there. This chapter will explore what is left for female eagles.

The focus of this chapter includes: (1) Achebe's portraiture of women in his fictional universe, the existing socio-cultural situation of the period he is depicting, and the factors within the society that condition male attitudes towards women; (2) the consequences of the absence of a moderating female principle in Achebe's fictions; (3)

Achebe's progressively changing attitude towards women's roles; and (4) feminist prospects for African women. In the context of this study, the Igbo people whom Achebe describes will represent the rest of Nigeria -- and a great many of the nations of Africa.

Sociocultural Background

Were traditional Nigeria and Africa oppressively masculinist? The answer is, "Yes." Ghana was known to have some matrilineal societies such as the Akans, but Nigeria's traditional culture, Muslim as well as non-Muslim, had been masculine-based even before the advent of the white man. The source, nature, and extent of female subordination and oppression have been a vexed problem in African literary debates. Writers such as Ama Ata Aidoo of Ghana and the late Flora Nwapa of Nigeria have insisted that the image of the helpless, dependent, unproductive African woman was one ushered in by European imperialists whose women lived that way. On the other hand, the Nigerian-born, expatriate writer Buchi Emecheta, along with other critics, maintains that African women were traditionally subordinated to sexist cultural mores. I ally myself to the latter camp. I believe that, in creating a masculine-based society, Achebe was merely putting literature to mimetic use, reflecting existing traditional mores. Colonial rule merely aggravated the situation by introducing a lopsided system in which African men received a well-rounded education while, like their European counterparts before the mid-nineteenth century, African women received only utilitarian, cosmetic skills in Domestic Science Centers -- the kinds of skills that could only prepare them to be useful and decorative helpmates of educated, pioneer nationalists and professionals such as the late Nnamdi Azikiwe, Nigeria's first President, and the late Obafemi Awolowo, the Yoruba leader of Western Nigeria.

Things Fall Apart remains significant because it began the vogue of African novels of cultural contact and conflict. It has been translated into over twenty major world languages. Commensurate with its popularity, images of women receive a great deal of attention. In a style that is expository rather than prescriptive, Achebe's novel mirrors the socio-cultural organization existing in the Africa of the era he describes. Like Zora Neale Hurston's Janie Mae Crawford (when married to Jody Starks), Achebe's women are voiceless. But where even Janie is highly visible, women within the patriarchal culture in

Things Fall Apart are virtually inconsequential. In *Of Woman Born* (1977), Adrienne Rich unwittingly captures all the nuances of the African traditional social milieu when she describes patriarchy as:

> the power of the fathers: a familial, social, ideological, and political system in which, by direct pressure -- or through tradition, law and language, customs, etiquette, education, and division of labor -- men determine what parts women shall or shall not play, and the female is everywhere subsumed by the male (57-58).

The world in *Things Fall Apart* is one in which patriarchy intrudes oppressively into every sphere of existence. It is an androcentric world where the man is everything and the woman nothing. In domestic terms, women are quantified as part of men's acquisitions. As wives, women come in multiple numbers, sandwiched between yam barns and titles. These three leitmotifs -- wives, yam barns, social titles -- are the highest accolades for the successful farmer, warrior, and man of worth. These determine a man's social status, as illustrated by Nwakibie who has three huge barns, nine wives and thirty children, and the highest but one title which a man can take in the clan (21).

The society that Achebe is describing (1850-1900) is an agrarian one in which the crop - the yam -- is synonymous with virility. Achebe explains that this all-important crop stands for manliness, and he who can feed his family on yams from one harvest to another is indeed a very great man: "Yam, the king of crops, [is] a very exacting king" (34-35). Consequently, to produce an abundant harvest, the traditional farmer needs a good workforce. Women constitute (and still do) the core of the rural workforce -- farming, tending animals, nurturing children, among other activities.

To echo the Nigerian critic Juliet Okonkwo, Achebe's cultural universe is one in which women are to be seen not heard, coming and going, with mounds of foofoo, pots of water, market baskets, fetching kola, being scolded and beaten before they disappear behind the huts of their compound (36). It would not be out of place to ally the existence of such women to that of other black women in the Diaspora described by Zora Neale Hurston's metaphor in *Their Eyes Were Watching God*," mule[s] uh de world" (14). Indeed, Zora's Janie is robbed of her voice by her own husband Jody, who, like Okonkwo, chauvinistically believes that women's place is in the home (41), lumps together "women and chillun and chickens and cows (67), and wants to be a big voice" (27) in the affairs of the community.

A similar near-invisibility of women in *Things Fall Apart* is acknowledged by the story's omniscient narrator. Describing a communal ceremony, the narrator confesses, "It was clear from the way the crowd stood or sat that the ceremony was for men. There were many women, but they looked on from the fringe like outsiders" (85). For centuries, African women languished on the fringe of their universe - neglected, exploited, denigrated - and indeed made to feel like outsiders. Women were not invited to stay when men were engaged in any discussion; they were not included in councils of war; nor, did they form part of the masquerades representing the judiciary and ancestral spirits.

Evidently, Achebe's sexist attitude is unabashed and without apology. Unoka, Okonkwo's father, is considered an untitled man, and thus called "agbala" denoting femininity (20), whereas Achebe intends Unoka's "artistic powers" to signify the medium the Igbo have evolved to counter excess power and masculinism. Coco-yam, of smaller size and lesser value than other yams, is regarded as female. Osugo has taken no title; and so, in a gathering of his peers, Okonkwo unkindly tells him, "This meeting is for men" (28). Guilt-ridden after murdering Ikemefuna, his surrogate son, Okonkwo sternly reprimands himself not to "become like a shivering old woman" (72) -- this he considers the ultimate insult. Forced to flee after the accidental shooting of Ogbuefi Ezeudu's young son – its accidental nature making it a female crime - Okonkwo has no other refuge than his mother's town, which, of course, has to be called Mbanta -- "small town" -- which I read as being contrasted in Okonkwo's thinking to the rugged, wild, violent, strong, masculine connotations of his town, Umuofia (literally meaning "children of the forest"). Such gender-stereotyping is not peculiarly limited to *Things Fall Apart*, for in *Arrow of God*, Obika, having seen a spirit, is frightened, his teeth knocking together and Ezeulu scolds his beloved second son, "hold yourself together. You are not a woman" (8).

Such excessive emphases on virility, sex-role stereotyping, gender discrimination (including a one-sided emphasis on brides being virgins before marriage), and violence as virtue, create an imbalance, and a resultant denigration of the female principle. And it is just such denigration that brings Okonkwo to ruin just as much as it presages the demise of his society's way of life. Okonkwo largely embodies "all the virtues and some of the excesses of this society [...] . [for] around [him are] heard the rhythmic beats of Umuofia's heart" (Awoonor, 253). The novel leaves the reader with the impression of a stranglehold on individuals, especially on the weak, the untitled - considered as *efulefu* or "worthless," the outcast as well as the embittered mothers of twins. This group of the weak and down-trodden would eventually seek refuge in the welcoming arms of Christianity. This alien religion will steal quietly into the clan and gather adherents from the ranks of those oppressed by Umuofia's rigid insistence on allegiance to gods, certain customs and inflexible laws.

The Absence of a Moderating Female Principle

Consequently, the novel, *Things Fall Apart* is redolent of violent conflicts occasioned by the utter lack of a moderating female influence. One example of this absence can be found in Achebe's employment of the folktale narrating the conflict between Earth, representing fertility or the female principle, and Sky, representing the male principle. It can convincingly be argued that the initial quarrel [contained in the folktale] between Earth and Sky represents the struggle between masculine and female powers and principles. They assert that Okonkwo, who occasionally but reluctantly yields his tender emotions most often expressed perversely towards Ikemefuna and Nwoye, is a paradigm for Sky – the male - who withholds rain but releases it reluctantly and perversely, since rain [falls] as it [has] never fallen before, preventing vulture, who represents the female principle, from returning to deliver his message, just as Nwoye, with his effeminate nature, [does] not return to Okonkwo's compound (20-21).

In the manner of the tragic hero, Okonkwo's consequent despair and fall represents the despair and break-up of the Igbo clan before the inexorable, invincible forces of the white man's religion and political organizations; and all these catastrophes occur because of the absence of the female principle which could have maintained balance and sanity. This view is echoed by Chikwenye Okonjo Ogunyemi's postulation that present-day Nigeria finds itself in the same quagmire as Umuofia of old because of a similar degree of machismo. Is it any wonder, she wonders in "Women and Nigerian Literature" that the country is in shambles "when it has failed to solicit the help of its better half [women] [...] for pacific pursuits, for the betterment of the country?" (60). In fact, women such as Ekwefu or Ojiugo who because of their spirited behavior had the potential of becoming dynamic and essentialist were lamentably left as undeveloped characters. Consequently, Achebe's female characters are visibly stunted individuals such as the women in *Things Fall Apart*; or they are idealized as mothers in the manner of such Negritude writings as Camara Laye's *The African Child*. Equally, the maternal valorization in *Things Fall Apart* is indicated by the meaning of Nneka -- "mother is supreme" -- as provided by Okonkwo's uncle Uchendu:

> It is true that a child belongs to its father. But when a father beats his child, it seeks sympathy in its mother's hut. A man belongs to his fatherland when things are good and life is sweet. But when there is sorrow and bitterness, he finds refuge in his motherland. Your mother is there to protect you (*TFA* 124).

The only women respected in Umuofia are women such as Chielo, the priestess of the Oracle of the Hills and Caves, who is removed from the pale of normalcy. Clothed in the mystic mantle of the divinity she serves, Chielo transforms from the ordinary as she wields power even over men. She can reprimand Okonkwo and even screams curses at him: "Beware of exchanging words with Agbala [the name of the Oracle of the Hills and Caves]. Does a man speak when a God speaks? Beware!" (95). Yet, if Okonkwo is powerless before a goddess's priestess, he can, at least, control his own women in his own home. So, when Nwoye's mother asks if Ikemefuna will be staying long with them, Okonkwo bellows to her: "Do what you are told woman. When did you become one of the ndichie [clan elders]?" (18).

Thus, it can be argued that, perhaps, Umuofia's shabby and degrading treatment of women and wives stems from an unconscious fear of, rather than reverence for, the ubiquitous and capricious Earth goddess Ani or Ala, who, when offended, wreaks such havoc on the townspeople's lives. Ani has boundless powers. She is the goddess of fertility. She also gives or withholds children; she spurns twin children who must be thrown away; she prohibits anyone inflicted with shameful diseases from burial in her soil. To the men of Umuofia, she must seem the embodiment of the two-faced Greek furies and Scylla and Charybdis joined together -- vengeful, unavoidable, and incomprehensible.

Umuofia men can be compared to the ancient mysogynist Greeks who were noted for similar cruel images of women such as Pandora, who let loose evil in the world, Circe, the witch whose magic wand bestializes men, Medea, who to spite her cheating husband Jason, kills her own two sons out of spite, and Clytemnestra, who wreaks murderous vengeance on Agamemnon, the commander king of the Greek army. And so, in helpless, mortal dread of a fearsome divine female principle, Ani, men of Umuofia such as Okonkwo, come down heavily indeed on ordinary women whose lives they can control as they deem fit.

The Issue of Chastity/virginity in *Things Fall Apart* and *Arrow of God*

This is a vexed issue in the cultural societies of Africa. It is part of the idealization of women that because women are the mothers, African societies therefore expect girls as brides to be virginal and married women to be chaste while not expecting the same of the bridegroom and the married men. In Buchi Emecheta's works, the issue receives continuous attention. In *The Joys of Motherhood*, Nwokocha Agbadi, the patriarch is happy that Amatokwu and his people have brought him six "full kegs of palm wine" to show their pleasure that his daughter Nnu Ego "has been found an unspoiled virgin." Says this paterfamilias, exuding smug wisdom, "There is nothing that makes a man prouder than to hear that his daughter is virtuous[...] When a woman is virtuous, it is easy for her to conceive. You shall soon see her children coming here to play" (*The Joys of Motherhood* 31) and this, from a man with multiple wives, slave women and whose concubine Ona, mother of Nnu Ego, refused to even marry him, thus making Nnu Ego a love child.

Needless to say, Nnu Ego remains childless with Amatokwu and in due course, that marriage fails for she is sent back to Agbadi in disgrace for being barren. But it is in *Double Yoke* that Emecheta brings the full weight of irony to bear on the issue of virginity / chastity. Nko, the virginal lover of Ete Kamba, scorned by him for precisely having given in to him, will turn around to make a fool of him, conceiving a child and having Ete at the end of the novel be sufficiently resocialized into a more tolerant African male. This makes him humane enough to recognize the lopsided, double-faced nature of virginity / chastity as a gender-structured feature of morality practiced in the African social *milieux*.

But in Achebe's two tradition-based novels – *Things Fall Apart* and *Arrow of God*: the issue receives full andro-cultural treatment. At a wedding ceremony, Obierika gives full assurance to his in-laws that his virginal daughter Akueke will bear "you nine sons like the mother of our town" (*Things Fall Apart,* 117). At Mbanta, Okonkwo's place of exile, the youngest of his Uncle Uchendu's sons, Amikwu was marrying a new wife. Men and women (umuada - daughters of the soil) sat in a circle with the bride in the center holding a hen while Uchendu sat beside her holding the ancestral staff of the family. The honor of his family is at stake. His eldest daughter, Ndide questions the unnamed bride, "How many men have you lain with since my brother first expressed the desire to marry you?" "None" came the answer. Amikwu is not questioned, but to prove her truthfulness, the bride must swear, says Uchendu, the paterfamilias, "on the staff of my fathers." Thereafter, the hen (a gendered motif), sheds its sacrificial blood by having its throat slit and its "blood *allowed* to fall on his ancestral staff" (131-2).

Olaudah Equiano, in his *Narrative*, had much earlier (1789) protested the inequities of gendered morality in his native Essaka where the men are so "jealous of the fidelity of their wives" that a woman who was convicted of adultery was given, as custom demanded, "to her husband to be punished." Conversely, the men "do not preserve the same constancy to their wives which they expect from them: for they indulge in plurality[...] (*Humanities in the Modern World,* 196).

In *Arrow of God,* Okuata, finely cut, tall (from a race of giants), is nicknamed *Oyilidie* because in beauty she resembles her handsome husband, Obika, and has been certified by a diviner that she will bear "nine sons." And Obika wonders anxiously if "when he took his wife to his hut, would he find her at home – as the saying goes – or would he learn with angry humiliation that another had broken in and gone off with *his prize*? (my emphasis). Thus women, in men's thinking, remain man's property and his spoils of love whose pristine virtue must be intact. And Obika, the drunken rake, has an enormous goat ready should his wife prove to be a virgin, but if otherwise, he did not know what he would do. But he need not worry, for everyone "who knew her witnessed Okuata's good behavior" (118).

And thus Okuata emerges from her husband's hut greatly relieved that her childhood's escapades with Obiora on moonlit nights have done no damage, for "every girl knew of Ogbanje Omenyi whose husband was said to have sent her parents for a matchet to cut the bush on either side of the highway which she carried between her thighs" (123). Any wonder that Judith Kegan Gardiner explains cynically in "Gender, Values, and Lessing's Cats" that, socialized from childhood to be preoccupied with her beauty, a woman's position as an object of observation is quite different from that of the male since the latter is the observer, and that:

> Sexual desirability to men defines women's beauty, and sexual fidelity to men defines women's truth. When not assured of possessing women's truth, men have believed women deceitful, changeable, and unreliable. Similarly, women's goodness fits a narrow box. A good man can possess many virtues, but a good woman must be sexually faithful and altruistically giving, an idealized wife and mother. Thus for women sexual fidelity and maternal nurture collapse the categories of truth, honor, and goodness into one another (*Feminist Issues in Literary Scholarship* 112; my emphases).

Achebe's Progressive Vision of Women

A cursory look at the place of women in Achebe's other works will confirm a diachronic development. In *No Longer at Ease* (1963), there is a discernible change in the style of Achebe's female portraiture. At the end of the novel, Obi Okonkwo yields to the implacable force of traditional ethos when choosing between his mother (representing traditionalism), who threatens to kill herself if he marries an outcast or *osu*, and the outcast protagonist Clara (representing the modern female). The pregnant Clara gets an abortion and fades out of the story. But, at least, she is cast as an educated, financially independent woman. She has the makings of a spirited, independent character, by virtue of her overseas education and profession as a nurse. She can afford to do without Obi Okonkwo.

In *A Man of the People* (1966), there are images of women playing traditional roles such as singers and dancers, or women adoring rich politicians like Chief the Honorable M.A. Nanga. Mrs. Eleanor John, a tough party woman and board member -- rich, independent, assertive -- lamentably is cast as a semi-illiterate businesswoman with no noteworthy role. We see Chief Nanga's wife, a beneficiary of the colonial, utilitarian education, dissatisfied with her husband's extramarital relationship and impending marriage to the young Edna. Mrs. Nanga complains to Odili, but when the latter sets out to unseat her husband, she reverts to her traditional role of helpmate fighting to retain her precarious social and economic position. Consequently, Mrs. Nanga remains a dependent, peripheral figure, deriving validity as a human being only from her husband, the essential, activist, autonomous character.

A somewhat strong characterization in *Man of the People* is Eunice, the lawyer. She is the fiancée of Odili's schoolmate Max, and founder of the Common People's Convention that opposes corrupt Chief Nanga and his ilk. When Max is shot by the thugs of a political adversary, Eunice takes decisive, retaliatory action: "[S]he opens her handbag as if to take out a handkerchief, [takes] out a pistol instead and [fires] two bullets into Chief Koko's chest" (160).

Following this strong portrait, Achebe adds pointedly, watering down the woman's individualism: "Only then [does] she fall down on Max's body and *begin to weep like a woman* [...] *A very strange girl*, people said" (my emphasis, 160). It begs the question, why, in a novel that deals with the total breakdown of law and order in which looting, arson and political killings constitute the order of the day, a single act of retaliation by an injured girl is considered "strange."

Yet, the inexorable winds of change did cause Achebe, a consummate pragmatist, to make a volte-face. The secret of his revisionist stance can be deduced from one of the central themes of his two tradition-based novels, *Things Fall Apart* (1958) and *Arrow of God* (1964): In a world of change, whoever is not flexible enough will be swept aside. Therefore, profiting from the mistakes of his tragic heroes, the inflexible Okonkwo and Ezeulu, Achebe becomes flexible -- a change that is most obvious in his last novel.

In *Anthills of the Savannah* (1987), speaking through his alter ego, Ikem, a journalist and writer, Achebe acknowledges that the malaise the African party is experiencing results from its exclusion of women from the scheme of things. Beatrice of the *Anthills*, who has an Honors degree from Queen Mary College, University of London, projects

Achebe's new vision of women's roles and clarifies Ikem's hazy thoughts on the issue. Ikem accepts that his former attitude towards women has been too respectful, too idealistic. In the best Negritudinal manner, he had reverently put every woman on a pedestal as an Nneka, where she is just as irrelevant to the practical decisions of running the world as she was in the old days (98). Beatrice gives Ikem insights into a feminist concept of womanhood. She is articulate, independent, and self-realized, and she re-evaluates women's position, asserting, "[I]t is not enough that women should be the court of last resort because the last resort is a damn sight too far and too late!" (91-92).

In Beatrice, Achebe now strives to affirm the moral strength and intellectual integrity of African women, especially since the social conditions which have kept women down in the past are now largely absent. Urbanization and education have combined to broaden women's horizons. Therefore, Ikem confesses to Beatrice, "I can't tell you what the new role for Woman will be. I don't know. I should never presume to know. You have to tell us" (98). A revisionist reading of this new attitude is that Achebe's newly envisioned female roles can only be expounded, articulated, and secured by woman herself. Since then, modern African women have been busy creating a literary and cultural space of their own.

However, *Arrow of God* escapes this upward revision of women's societal role, for the novel is even more masculinist than in *Things Fall Apart*. The women still exist on the fringes of society. While the wives of Okonkwo experience a kind of unity amongst them, shielding each other, for Okonkwo is characteristically hard on all equally, the wives and children of Ezeulu come out in shouting and swinging matches because of a perceived partiality to one wife and to some children. And therefore, quarrels and animosity are the characteristic features of Ezeulu's household, thus undermining his strength as paterfamilias. Matefi and Ugoye quarrel incessantly - the latter's youthful attractiveness, enhanced by her "new ivory bracelets" earning her "envy and hostility from her husband's other wife, Matefi" (68). Ezeulu's daughter Akueke takes sides with Ugoye against Matefi, the senior wife, and as she gossiped to Ugoye, "In all the time I have come across bad people, I have not yet met anyone like her. Her own badness whistles" (69).

But Matef herself indicts her husband for favoring Ugoye. Ojiugo openly fights with Oduche as she narrates the gossip about the python imprisoned in Oduche's box to Okuata, Obika's new bride, thus triggering a quarrel between their mothers. What comes across is a dysfunctional household with a resented authoritarian head gradually losing grip of the peace in his home. Treatment of women in *Arrow of God* remains therefore, tradition-based for the men of Umuaro and Okperi - just like the ancient Greeks and Romans - frolic in their masquerade sports, fight in battles, dispute, settle quarrels, and lay down policies / laws in concourse, to the exclusion of the women whose sphere is exclusively home-bound and ornamental.

Feminism, Womanism, and Modern African Women

It is insufficient that Achebe, the literary icon, merely acknowledges the injustice of his earlier treatments of women. Feminist ideology veritably lays the task of self-actualization on women themselves. Like Ngugi wa Thiong'o's female characters Wanja (*Petals of Blood*) and Wariinga (*Devil on The Cross*), African women are playing active roles in their nations' histories by resisting "being pushed or tempted into accepting subservient or degrading or decorative roles" (Evans 134). They are developing what I have termed "the will to change" in *Women in Chains[...]* (Mezu 217).

In 1966, Flora Nwapa published *Efuru*. Significant in African feminist scholarship, the novel signals a long-awaited departure from the stereotypical female portraiture in male-authored African literature. The eponymous *Efuru* chooses her own husband and marries without her husband paying any dowry. She decisively deals with conflicts, radically departing from the script of the traditional African woman "in the peripheral, tangential role of a passive victim of a masculine-based cultural universe" (Mezu 27-28). But Efuru is plagued by infertility, polygyny, infidelity, and abandonment by two undistinguished husbands. She decides that she has finally had enough and abjures marriage, opting for meaningful singlehood as priestess of the goddess of the river, Uhamiri, vindicator of victimized womanhood.

Again, in *Idu* (1970), Nwapa embarks on a revisionist course, now making a man responsible for infertility. Though in a similar vein, the Ghanaian writer Ama Ata Aidoo published a play, *Dilemma of a Ghost* (1965), Nwapa was for a long time the lone African female novelist voice lamenting patriarchy. Then, prolific Buchi Emecheta joined the fray with *The Joys of Motherhood* (1980). As the female Nigerian critic, Chikwenye Okonjo Ogunyemi, writes, "If Nwapa is the challenger, Buchi Emecheta is the fighter[...] For the first time, female readers through female characters are aware of their subjugation by their fathers, uncles, husbands, brothers and sons"(62). All of Emecheta's novels expound the theme of female oppression, and the slave girl becomes her leitmotif -- the archetypal African woman buried alive under the heavy yoke of traditional mores and customs. This list of African feminist novelists, dramatists, poets, and literary critics is growing. African women feature equally in publishing -- Nwapa with her Tana Press and Emecheta with Ogwugwu Afor Press.

Women Liberation in Africa: The Achebe Factor

Home after a faculty lecture that elicited a lively debate, I kept on ruminating on a number of issues and questions raised during the "question and answer" session. One questioner, a fellow Nigerian, complimented me on an effective presentation and for being a "worthy, intellectual ambassador of the Igbos, of Nigeria and of Africa." He then went on to wonder if a society that could produce such as I could be said to be *"that bad."* Then it appeared to me that my paper, notwithstanding my moderate Womanist position, had indeed hurt sensibilities. The compatriot is an Igboman. Despite the fact that the whole exercise was kept at an academic level, the resentment is still there: the hurt feelings that an entire culture could be laid bare to the critical scrutiny and occasional derisive amusement of listening foreigners. But then, like Achebe, I believe there should be no apology for denouncing the excessive chauvinism of either the men of the patriarchal societies under study or the ideological aberrations of the modern Okonkwos of Africa or the world. Left to them, neither I nor any modern woman - whether radical feminist, conservative or accommodationist - would have seen the four walls of a school. We would, all the budding female Achebes, have been stifled by strangulating cultural mores and values and relegated into a sub-category existence like the hypothetical Judith Shakespeare of Virginia Woolf's *A Room of One's Own.*

Indeed, we would still be digging yam and cocoyam mounds in the torrid sun, after which we would be home, cook, and with genuflecting obeisance serve the Okonkwos and the Ezeulus (*Arrow of*

God) of this world. The African American pioneering female novelist, Zora Neale Hurston's Janie succinctly puts it to the dying Jody, characterizing male inordinate vanity as "All dis bowin' down, all dis obedience under yo' voice[...]" (*Their Eyes Were Watching God* 82). In past eras, the male sphere of activities covered wrestling, masquerading, warring or engaging in village council affairs; for leisure, men would regale their sons with tales of violence and warfare while the lazy Unokas would be lulling under shades of trees, watching the flight of birds, or making music with their flutes drinking "ahey and breathing the flattering air of the shade" like Armah's indolent men in *Two Thousand Seasons* (10). Of course, Okonkwo (*Things Fall Apart*) would never have belonged to the last group. He possessed too much restless energy to while away time uselessly. Otherwise, if he had too much time on his hands, he would think of some mischief like knocking about one of his multiple wives on one pretext or the other. No, we women have come a long way.

For our emancipation or liberation from the "'muledom' uh the world" we have to thank men like my father, John Ogugua Okeke (1910-1975) of Umuediabali, Umueze, Ihitteafoukwu, Mbaise who were enamored with the principle of learning, and possessed an egalitarian spirit, characteristic of the really very strong who do not feel their manhood threatened because women develop their potentials. He sent all his children - one son and four daughters to school, at a time when other "*paterfamilias*" "sold" off their daughters for an excessive dowry, which they then used to train sons only (See Buchi Emecheta's *Second Class Citizen*, Millie Ola's novel *A Dream Come True*), thereby undermining the handiwork of the good Lord by making intelligence "gender dependent." I do remember all the pep-talks on the importance of education that our father used to give to me and my siblings before we were due back to our different boarding schools. He would wake us up at the pre-dawn ungodly hour of five in the morning and from then until dawn, he would instruct, moralize and sermonize, insisting that his children, boy or girl, should maximize their advantages in order to fulfill all the promises of their glowing destinies, becoming by our own efforts, lawyers, doctors, engineers, governors or presidents. All these would happen because we went to school and made something of ourselves. If we failed, disaster would be the result: second rate marriages to second rate artisans.

African women must acknowledge a depth of gratitude to women and men -- mothers, fathers, husbands, uncles and brothers -- who, disregarding patriarchy and traditionalism ensured for them education. It is only through such enlightenment that African women writers have been able to dismantle the myth of female irrelevance by challenging such archetypal roles as witches, faithless women, *femmes fatales*, viragos, and playthings of capricious gods. In achieving this, such women writers have been supported by some male writers, labeled gynandrists, such as Isidore Okpewho, Ousmane Sembène, Ngugi wa Thiong'o, Mongo Beti, Henri Lopes.

Given the intensely patriarchal nature of traditional African cultures, African feminism cannot be considered radical. For white European and American women, feminism has predicated itself solely on ending gender discrimination, procuring equal job opportunities, and getting voting and property rights. For African, African-American, and other women of color, feminist ideology reflects specificities of race, class, and culture. It is for its implied radicalism that feminism as an ideology has failed to make any lasting appeal to Africa and its Diaspora. Because African women do not wish to alienate men, because African women do not wish to alienate the bulk of their uneducated, tradition-based sisters, because many traditional African customs and mores are worth preserving, most African feminists espouse the alternative ideology of Womanism, which Alice Walker defines as a philosophy that celebrates black roots, the ideals of black life, while giving a balanced presentation of black womanhood [...] . [I]ts aim is the dynamism of wholeness and self-healing (xi).

It is for this very reason that this work is dedicated to Christie Achebe, the wife of the icon we know and cherish, who subsumed perhaps a personal career to be with the husband, the father of African literature, thereby illustrating that women education and liberation are not incompatible with African traditional family values of love and fidelity.

Ultimately, the iroko is there for women to climb, after all. Educated African women, and those women and men in exalted, decision-making bodies, must and do realize their duty to make society an equitable place for their less-privileged brothers and sisters.

Equipped with education, resilience, and the will to survive, female eagles can scale and even soar over irokos, placing no limitations on their capabilities. Real life African women are making meaningful contributions: as lawyers, doctors; professors, and presidents of universities; as commissioners and ministers, senators and governors, and chairpersons of political parties; as directors and others involved in literacy movements and campaigns against forced marriages, exploited dowry system, clitoridectomy, obsolete widowhood practices and the lopsided emphasis on female virginity / chastity (while men are free to frolic unhindered by societal sanctions).

In reality, African women can outstrip their fictive counterparts to become partners with men in national progress and development, and to gain individual self-realization, fulfillment and transcendence.

Works Cited

Achebe, Chinua. *Things Fall Apart*. London: Heinemann, 1958.

---. *No Longer At Ease*. London: Heinemann, 1963.

---. *Arrow of God*. New York: John Day, 1964.

---. *A Man of the People*. New York: John Day, 1966.

---. *Anthills of the Savannah*. London: Heinemann, 1987.

Aidoo, Ama Ata. *The Dilemma of a Ghost*. Accra: Longmans, 1965.

Armah, Ayi Kwei. *Two Thousand Seasons*. London: Heinemann, 1973.

Awoonor, Kofi. *The Breast of the Earth*. New York: Nok, 1975.

Emecheta, Buchi. *The Joys of Motherhood: A Novel*. London: Heinemann, 1980.

--- *Double Yoke*. London: Ogwugwu Afor Ltd, 1982.

Equiano, Olaudah. *The Interesting Narrative of the4 Life of Olaudah Equiano, or Gustavus Vassa Written by Himself* (1789). In The *Humanities in the Modern World*. Boston, MA: Pearson custom Publishing, 2001.

Evans, Jennifer. "Women and Resistance in Ngugi's *Devil on the Cross*." In *African Literature Today*. Trenton, New Jersey: African World Press, 1987.

Gardner, Judith Keegan. 'Gender, Values, and Lessing's Cats' In *Feminist in Issues in Literary Scholarship*. Ed. Benstock. Bloomington: Indiana University Press, 1987.

Hurston, Zora Neale. *Their Eyes Were Watching God*. 1939. NY: Harper & Row, 1990.

Laye, Camara. *The African Child*. Trans. James Kirkup. London: Fontana, 1972. *L'Enfant noir*. Paris: Plon, Presses Pocket edition.)

Mezu, Rose Ure. *Women in Chains: Abandonment in Love Relationships in the Fiction of Selected West African Writers*. Owerri, Nigeria: Black Academy Press, 1994.

Ngugi wa Thiong'o. *Petals of Blood*. London: Heinemann, 1977.

--- *Devil on the Cross*. London: Heinemann, 1982.

Nnolim, Charles E. "Form and Function of Folk Tradition." *Approaches to the African Novel: Essays in Analysis*. London: Saros International, 1992.

Nwapa, Flora. *Efuru*. London: Heinemann, 1966.

--- *Idu*. London: Heinemann, 1970.

Ogunyemi, Chikwenye Okonjo. "Women and Nigerian Literature." In *Perspectives on Nigerian Literature*. Vol. 1. Lagos, Nigeria: Guardian Books, 1988.

Okonkwo, Juliet. "The Talented Woman in African Literature." *African Quarterly*.15.1-2.

Ola, Millie. *A Dream Come True*. Baltimore: Black Academy Press, 1996

Rich, Adrienne. *Of Woman Born: Motherhood as Experience and Institution*. New York: Norton, 1976.

Walker, Alice. "In Search of Our Mothers' Gardens." *In Search of Our Mothers Gardens: Womanist Prose*. New York: Harcourt Brace, 1983. 231-243.

9

Conversations with Chinua Achebe

(A telephone interview with Chinua Achebe conducted by Dr. Rose Ure Mezu from Baltimore, Maryland on March 11, 1996, 6 p.m.)

> [...] *there is no absolute anything. They [Igbos] are against excess - their world is a world of dualities. It is good to be brave, they say, but also remember that the coward survives.*
> (Chinua Achebe, *"Interview with Bill Moyers"* 333*)*

> *Some feminist critics of African literature are so fixated on issues in feminism, particularly the separatism of radical feminism, that they "see" what is not in the texts and refuse to see what the texts present to them.*
> (Obioma Nnaemeka, *"The Blind Women and No Elephant"* 91)

P reliminary telephone conversations had taken place weeks earlier, and the renowned writer generally warmed up to the idea of an interview, albeit *via* the telephone. His wife, Christie, was always there to mediate and explain certain things concerning his schedule, welfare, travel, *et cetera*. The novelist gave me an appointment for Sunday, March 11th, 1996. Promptly at 6 p.m., I called his home in Annadale-on-Hudson in Upstate New York. Christie told me he was just then emerging from his rest. It was the ideal time to call. I had waited until then to give them time to eat and rest. He promptly came on the line and the interview was under way. It was a scintillating conversation. He was cooperative, eloquent, alert to the nuances of any question and unmistakably put his views across.

He corrected misconceptions on certain issues. On the question of radical feminists' critiques of his works, especially the treatment of women in the seminal work, *Things Fall Apart*, he was very persuasive, and ended up winning me over to his way of thinking. People, he insisted, misread fiction, seeing it as representing "what ought to be" rather than "what is", or as Obioma Nnaemeka complainingly chimes in with respect to *Things Fall Apart*, "they 'see' what is not in the texts and refuse to see what the texts present to them."

Okonkwo, Achebe pointed out, is violent in his relations with both men and women, does finally in death receive a merited banishment to the evil forest in punishment for his predilection to excesses; so does Umuofia suffer foreign domination for its many moral flaws. Thus, Achebe restates his and the Igbos' preference for balance, the need to make choices in their world of dualism, his support and sympathy rather than denigration of the lot of African women. His vision of women, he insisted, had been progressive in keeping with society's pace, that Beatrice Okoh (*Anthills of the Savannah*) receives more of him than is generally known - "it is my knowledge which I translate into fiction." Certainly, Beatrice is the only character who grasps more of what is going on than the male characters. Achebe's interest in politics and concern about responsible governance are profound and abiding.

He expatiated on what in his view is the *raison d'être* for the existence of the story, "to make people think[...]" Another intellectual writer, Paule Marshall expresses identical sentiments to the Los Angeles Times, "My works ask that you become involved, *that you think*[...]On the other hand, I'm first trying to tell a story, because I'm always about telling a good story."

In Achebe's view, we must not let History be our master; rather, the lessons of History should be used to negotiate the present. He reiterated the urgent need for expanding the genre of Children's literature. Ultimately, African children, properly taught, represent the future hope of the Continent and hence the need for serious development of the genre of Children's literature. When I asked him if he would eventually go home despite the material comforts of a foreign land, his rejoinder was: "Home is Home." Asked what it was he missed about home, he answered simply - "an atmosphere that belongs to you!"

The full text of the Interview is as follows:

On Politics and the Writer

Mezu: Good evening, Professor Achebe, I hope you are feeling fine. Thanks for granting me this interview. We can now proceed.

In the past, you have taken a keen interest in the effect of the political process on the African/Nigerian society and literature. You have even participated in the formation of political parties during Nigeria's 2nd Republic (1979-83), written about politics, etc. What is your present stance? Is the interest still there?

Achebe: Yes, I have always been interested in Politics, not to run for office but sufficiently to want things to change. I even supported the party of Aminu Kano, not because it was the ideal one, but because *it was the least bad*, the best available for it had the advantage of cutting across ethnic lines. Amino Kano made me his Vice-Presidential candidate. And when he died, the weaknesses inherent in the Nigerian system started showing up even in that party [...] My interest in politics is profound.

Mezu: But what ideology do you think will cure the Nigerian political malaise? In your novel - *Anthills of the Savannah* if I remember rightly, you seem opposed to any radicalism, rather espousing a sort of *reformed orthodoxy*

Achebe: I could not have said "reformed Orthodoxy." I did use the word "reform." Belief in either radicalism or orthodoxy is too simplified a way of viewing things. I can understand one being attracted to these things - but *one must grow out of them* for real life is more complex. Evil is never all evil; goodness on the other hand is often tainted with selfishness.

Mezu: In the novel, one can see you under the different personae - Ikem, Chris, Beatrice, though she is a woman. Which of the characters do you believe reflects your views the most? If I am not wrong, I believe that Ikem does.

Achebe: You're right. I tried to put myself in the characters you mentioned and in fact, all my characters must reflect aspects of me. It is my knowledge that I translate into fiction. Ikem more than most, Chris also, and a lot of Beatrice. In fact, that is what amuses me about some feminists in their critiques. They say to themselves - ah! we have caught this patriarch!

You see Beatrice has been coming in stages through all my work. In *A Man of the People*, she is called Eunice. All along my vision of a woman's role has been developing, growing in intensity as the role of the Igbo woman has been growing in the Igbo society.

Mezu: In the *Anthills of the Savannah,* you tried to redress matters with the character of Beatrice. Do you believe that Beatrice who has a first class degree at a top English university received equal billings with Chris, Ikem, Sam and his 12-man-only cabinet, etc. as a subject rather than as object, since in spite of her education (she is not part of the 12-man cabinet). It is believed that she still functions as the comforter, the sounding board that helps the male characters clarify their different ideological positions; she holds things together?

Achebe: And who is to blame? You see, many people do not read fiction the way it should be read - as representing what is. They think it should show what *ought to be*. Fiction is not a political argument. The book showed what there is. If I was Sam, I would have made Beatrice a member of the cabinet. I was not Sam. I am telling a story that illustrates that society had a huge flaw. Tell me, how do you think I viewed women in *Things Fall Apart*?

Mezu: Idealistically. You viewed the concept of the mother idealistically. Women were treated sympathetically. In fact, Okonkwo received indictment for being violent with his wives.

Achebe: But Okonkwo was always violent with everyone. Both he and his society had weaknesses which included the female species, and the adoration of power. They paid terrible prices for these. Okonkwo paid a terrible price by being banished for ever in the evil forest, and so did the Igbo society by suffering defeat at the hands of an alien civilization.

Mezu: If foreign ideologies such as Socialism, Capitalism, Marxism, can not go down well with African political structure, what, in your thinking, is the ideal form of government for Nigeria, especially? But where really do you stand on the question of finding a workable ideology for Nigeria/Africa? Is there a solution to our problems?

Achebe: A writer is not a theorist. None of the "isms" - Capitalism, Marxism, etc. can solve our problems. Yet, solutions can be found -

in Negotiation, in History - knowing where we came from. We must not allow History to be our masters. We must not become slaves to memory. We must use History and knowledge, and experience to negotiate the present.

Igbos, for example, have a very important role to play in Nigeria - role of the conscience, because of the suffering they endured. Oppression is wrong. Because we tried to rebel against oppression, whenever and wherever we see it, we must say 'no'. We must not say foolishly, it is not our business. We all in Nigeria lost the opportunity to correct what was wrong. An election was held. Someone won that election. It does not matter who he is. Everyone should have supported him. If Abiola does not rule well, we say so and then choose another. It may not even be possible in this century to stage another political election. We lost the opportunity. Unless we go back to democracy, we nullify the political process. There was no reason for Shonekon or Abacha to have happened except for the opportunism of the intellectual and the political class who want political appointments. And now, this is my prescription - not to hope to solve the problem with the wave of the hand! That is superstition.

Mezu: Can you foresee a future when a woman will emerge as the chief executive of an African state?

Achebe: Why not? More so in Africa than in the West, especially in America. In fact, the Third World countries - Pakistan, Turkey, India, The Philippines - have produced more [women] presidents than America, the most advanced country in the world. The highest post any woman has aspired to in America was as a vice-presidential candidate.

Mezu: If a woman were to emerge as a presidential candidate in Nigeria, would you vote for her?

Achebe: Yes, I would. But then that is not the problem right now. Do you think a woman can be a president in Nigeria?

Mezu: Yes, I think so. If she has the ambition, the gumption, because it needs a lot of gumption since politics is a dirty process really. But if any woman has the wherewithal to run, I believe she should be allowed to exercise that right to run.

On Children's Literature

Mezu: let's turn to Children's Literature. What motivated you to turn to this tradition and are you happy with its growth and success so far?

Achebe: Having children myself and finding that there was nothing for them, to read. Our first child was growing up and reading really dangerous literature - colorful, expensive books bought from Kingsway stores, etc. - for those who could afford to buy them then ...they were very poisonous, and gave her the wrong image of herself. Once I discovered what was happening, it was clear that we had to produce our own writings. There is no where near enough good writing for our children. I went to a conference in Zimbabwe, and I spoke about the crisis in children's literature and I challenged every writer present to go home and write one children's book. They clapped, but they went home and did not do so.

Mezu: I have never believed I could write children's stories, although I have many children and do tell them stories. But I promise you, after this interview, I will try writing some.

On immortality and the artist

Mezu: I believe that writers achieve immortality through their art. You have occupied a unique position as a world-renowned, trail-blazing novelist and skilful writer. Most writers do not live long enough to enjoy their renown. Do you consider your contribution to the growth of African literature sufficiently acclaimed, at least, to the degree that you do feel appreciated?

Achebe: The happiness a writer gets is to be read by people who recognize what he is trying to do and they are happy and you see it on their faces. I see this countless times in all places. In the late 1980s, I had the biggest book-signing in Nairobi. The waiting line filled the street and spilled over. The line of people waiting for my autograph was endless. I had to be smuggled out because the line was interminable and I had other engagements. No, I can not complain.

Mezu: The African American students in my African Literature Course want me to ask you, having lived here now for some years, what you think of the problems of Black people in America. One asked me if it was true that Africans do not like African Americans. Can you comment on this?

Achebe: Some Africans are not knowledgeable and some African Americans are not knowledgeable. And then again, some are. We need to define the areas in which we can work together, as I tried to work with Baldwin. I was invited to the South where Baldwin and I opened the African Literature Conference together. We traveled together for a while. And we were to teach jointly at UMASS. And then he died, and I went to the burial. That is the trend now, working together for the good of the Black race.

Mezu: On Art and Artist …The Artist and the medium of language - your position on this is again, well-known.

Achebe: What is my position?

Mezu: If I read you correctly, you believe that though the Colonial languages are foreign, we have a stake in them because of the exploitation we have suffered, and because of our enrichment of the language. Therefore, English for instance, also belongs to us, and can be bent to translate our peculiar experiences. That it is not possible to replace English.

Achebe: This is only half the story. The other half is that I believe we should write in the African languages if we can. I do. Some of my best poems are written in Igbo.

Mezu: Can you see a day when an indigenous language can effectively replace the language of the erstwhile colonial masters as the official reading/writing language?

Achebe: One can not say that it is impossible to write in native languages? Whatever arguments we make, we make today. Situations change. What if tomorrow there is an Igbo nation and the government wants to use Igbo as the official language? Theoretically anything is possible. For now, however, I believe it is impossible to dispense with the English language. But those who have the ability to write in indigenous languages should do so. I do.

Mezu: On writing and its relevance, what do you consider as the core message in your works?

Achebe: To make people think. Just as a good story keeps revealing itself in different ways, in different connotations. The meaning is not finished. To make you see yourself in a different light.

Mezu: *That is the meaning of the word you used in the* Anthills – "Nkolika" - *the Story is Greatest?*

Achebe: Yes!

Mezu: On life and its surprises… this is a personal question and you do not have to answer it, if you do not want. But I would like to get an answer. Is there any good arising from this accident that has left you physically disabled, though intellectually as alert as ever? Do you see any advantages to you because of it?

Achebe: Whatever happens to us should make us better. That's what life is all about. If there is any destiny, any mind controlling our lives, what you learn from living should make us better. I have learnt that things can also happen to me not just to other people. It is one thing to hear about them and something else to experience them. What other people do for you becomes very clear; it also becomes clear to you how much you depend on others, your family, your friends. *Experiencing* is a very rich lesson. One hopes one is wiser.

Mezu: Do you miss home? Will you ever go home? What really do you miss about home?

Achebe: Yes, I will go home. And yes, I do miss home. What do I miss about home? An atmosphere that belongs to you. It is different no matter how welcoming a foreign land is. Home is home. You see, the Igbos have a name for a child born in a foreign soil - say, Lagos for instance - they call him *Nwaofia* - child of the forest. Yes, I really do miss home!

10

The Mezus Visit with the Achebes

(A Second Interview and a Visit with Chinua Achebe, June 15, 1999)

V ery early on Tuesday, June 15, 1999, my husband, Sebastian Okechukwu Mezu, and I set out from Baltimore, Maryland on a visit to see a fellow Igbo, Africa's premier novelist Chinua Achebe, now at Bard College in Upstate New York where he is the Charles P. Stevenson Professor of Literature. He is there at the invitation of Professor Leon Botstein, president of Bard College, following a car accident on 22 March, 1990 that confined Achebe to a wheelchair. I had called him the week before to inform him of our proposed visit. He promised to check his calendar and give us a likely date. When he called back and announced his name, my daughter Ngozi who took the call rushed to tell me that Mrs. Chinua Achebe was on the line. But it was the veteran writer himself. She had mistaken his soft, gentle voice for that of his wife Christie.

The visit was long overdue. I had been planning it since 1996 when I had proposed to take the students in my African Literature class and some of my colleagues at Morgan State University to visit with him. For several reasons, the planned visit did not come off; instead, we had a telephone interview on March 11, 1996. So, I was relieved that at last we would see him. I had actually been having nightmares imagining the worst - that I would be unable to see the living man in person. Here I was in Baltimore, Maryland and there he was in Upstate New York and yet the strains and stresses of life at end-of-the-century America might make it impossible to realize this dream. As Alice Walker said in her seminal essay collection, *In Search of Our Mothers' Gardens*, with regard to celebrated African American poet and novelist Langston Hughes, "we must not be known as people who throw away their geniuses." Walker's great comfort was that she had the opportunity to visit with, and care for Langston Hughes in the remaining years of his life. It is her decided opinion that the duty of Black artists is both to create and to preserve what was already created before them. Therefore, she would say that one of the best acts of her entire life was "to take a sack of oranges to Langston Hughes when he had the flu, about two weeks before he died"(135). Reading this account frightened me, for, here living not an ocean away, belonging to my own Igbo ethnic group, is a living Equiano, one of the acclaimed definers of twentieth century world civilization, easily the one who by modifying the traditions of fiction - an alien narrative form - had created an authentic African Literature today.

Indeed, Chinua Achebe with the seminal *Things Fall Apart* (1958) had picked up the baton of race-building where Olaudah Equiano had left it with his literary, groundbreaking, tradition-inaugurating *The Interesting Narrative of the Life of Olaudah Equiano or Gustavus Vassa the African Written by Himself* (1789). I would never forgive myself if we both live out our lives, a few hundred miles apart, and pass on to the Here-after without our paths crossing. So, I woke up one morning and knew I just had to call him. Once Achebe confirmed the date, I knew a feeling of lighthearted exuberance worthy of a Summer morning. I prepared!

By Igbo tradition, one does not visit a respected elder, or a family member who lives faraway without bringing gifts. In Igboland, it would be customary to go on such a visit with either prepared dishes or unprepared food items. Here in America, traditions undergo modifications mainly because food items one would need are not plentiful, being mostly imported. Here my own intuition and Walker's coincided for she again observed that we must send "small tokens of affection to our old and ancient poets whom renown has ignored" (*Ibid*). Well, renown has not ignored this literary Igbo colossus. In fact, *R*enown with a capital *R* sits comfortably on him, and God willing, he will yet live many a day longer. And so, I bought what I could the evening before and the following day at dawn, my husband and I set off.

It was a smooth journey. The lighthearted feeling of anticipation stayed with us. Intuitively, I knew it was going to be a historic visit. Mostly, we followed the Internet directions until we got closer to our

236

destination when we switched to the directions that Chinua Achebe had earlier given over the telephone. Having previously lived in Buffalo, New York, we should have been prepared for the rural and almost lonely nature of the long stretches of road, sparsely inhabited, with vast distances separating the towns. At last, we were there at Bard College - small, isolated, really rural.

At Bard College, my husband insisted we seek out the College cafeteria for lunch. He did not want us to impose on the author's hospitality. We called the Achebe home after lunch. Christie answered and gave further directions. Ten minutes later, we were there. We drove to the writer's woodland house nestling among tall trees, thick shrubs and a beautiful selection of plants and flowers - indeed, wonderful gardening which as we learnt later was a passionate hobby of his wife, Christie. We had the feeling that here was a haven of peace and tranquility, frankly almost too peaceful for me, but perhaps peace was what the novelist needed in order to heal and carry on with his writing. I kept thinking of the isolation of University of Nigeria, Nsukka - that Igbo University town where he used to teach or even of Thoreau's Walden Pond. But clearly, we had been expected.

We walked into the house, handicapped-friendly, custom-designed for a physically disabled person, and there was Christie whose face I was now able to match with that familiar voice over the telephone. For us, it was an emotional meeting with Chinua Achebe. I would have known the writer anywhere. Unchanged was the face familiar to millions of people the world over, the face - dear to us who own him as our racial treasure. I expected it to be ravaged by suffering and illness, but no! It was a peaceful face, a little aged but smooth and serene and alive with humor and greetings. We all embraced. We offered our gifts to them and that offering they both said was not expected; we were touched! It was my homage to the novelist who had granted me a telephone interview back in 1996. Clearly, we had been expected for lunch!

The table was set for four. He and his wife had been true to traditional Igbo mode of according warm hospitality. Truly, we did not expect them to cook for us; maybe, a light refreshment normally offered to visitors but not the full course dinner of soup, baked whole fish, well-garnished rice, side dishes with a choice of wines, dessert and coffee -- that was served. It was a royally Achebean feast! Again, we were touched by their graciousness! Apparently living in America had not pulverized nor diluted too much the Igbo cultural tradition of hospitality. It was an emotional encounter for me, especially to see the writer face to face, for the first time, but a reunion for my husband who had previously known the writer. At the time of his car accident, all over the world, most people who knew the man, the writer, his ideas and his works had prayed for his recovery. Although saddened by his ensuing confinement to a wheelchair, people had been relieved that at least his towering intellectual faculty, the part of him most useful to the world, had been preserved. However tragic, it was the best out of a bad situation.

Today, 9 a.m, Saturday, July 1999, at this juncture in my write-up of the account of our visit to Chinua Achebe, crippled as a result of a car accident on March 22, 1990, my daughter Kelechi rushed in after a phone call from my eldest daughter, Chinyere (living in Los Angeles with her husband), that J.F.K., Jr.'s airplane had disappeared. It was carrying him, his wife Jacqueline Bissette Kennedy, her sister Lauren, flying from Caldwell Airport in Fairfield, New Jersey to Martha's Vineyard, Massachusetts to attend his cousin, slain Robert F. Kennedy, Sr.'s youngest daughter's wedding (she was born after her father's assassination).

The airplane had been missing since the night before, with all the attendant anxiety. The local breaking news confirmed the ongoing search for the missing plane. The poem ("*As the Storm Clouds Gather Again over Camelot: A Prayer for JFK, Jr.*" included in my second poetry collection *Homage to My People*) captures the feelings uppermost in my mind at that moment (this write-up on our visit with Chinua Achebe was interrupted practically all day as we all waited anxiously for the news of JFK Jr. and his traveling companions). My heart was sad, sorely distressed like millions of people the world over at the tragic and incomprehensible loss - cut down while in the bloom of youth by the cruel gods - of healthy, beautiful young people with their promising intimations of greatness unfulfilled, never to be realized. It made me again think of Chinua Achebe's accident. Much later, I resumed writing because if I delayed too much, I would within days be unable to recapture the aura, spirit and details of that visit to Achebe[...].

Indoors, we all embraced. About 3 p.m., we sat down with Chinua and Christie around the dining table to eat and we did not get up to leave until around 7 p.m. It was an incredible, and memorable visit. Because we sat around the dining table, his wheelchair was barely visible and so it was easy to forget he was disabled. It was a relief to find him healthy, eating normal food, happy and full of good humor. His jokes sounded familiar because their tenor - rich and always with a funny twist - was akin to jokes that abound in his works. There was so much to discuss and we talked about everything. I looked at him in wonder. Here he was at last! This man whose mind had created the fictional worlds in which so many people the globe over have lived for so long, this man whose characters feel real like people we have known all our lives, this man whose intelligence, truth and invaluable human wisdom, extracted from his writings, have become of universal application. He is a writer who throws tough minded literary punches, yet whose style is gentle and kindly. We sat down to eat and talk. Our video camera was on recording the conversations.

My husband, Sebastian Okechukwu made jokes about the number of children we have and insisted that our number **ten** was only a beginning. I protested when he disclaimed any responsibility, laying the blame, if any, for my fecundity, at my door [...] the writer chimed in with a rib-cracking anecdote about a friend of his whose wife was always having babies; the friend became the butt of many jokes at which the man would say, *"Obum neme?"* meaning "Am I the one doing it?" at which his friend would assure him *"Mba, Oburo gi, obum neme - No, not you, I m the one doing it!"* A local Igbo joker would label Achebe's friend, "Innocent *Odinkemmere"* - an Igbo word that says the same thing as the English word "Innocent - *one who has done nothing wrong* - innocent." More Igbo jokes along that vein followed. Sebastian, tracing his ancestry way back in time became the Mezu of Naze who was a forbear to Jezu of Nazareth. Nazareth being a Hebrew diminutive of our own neighboring Naze near Emekuku, Owerri Nigeria.

Sebastian narrated the tale of those ancient, wandering Igbos who migrated and corrupted their name "Ibo" and in time, they would become known as "Hebrew" [Ibru]. Achebe made a rejoinder that indeed, the Igbo word - *Je nisisi* meaning "Begin at the beginning" is synonymous with the first book of the Bible - **Genesis,** the extrapolated meaning being that we Igbos were there at the first dawn of creation. The presumed affinity between the Ibos and the Hebrews in ethnic character traits, cultural practices, and sharp business proclivities, sometimes even to similarity in the names, has always been a standing joke among our Igbo people. Members of both cultural groups are uniformly hardworking, acquisitive and sharp in business; the two cultural groups are nomadic - being found in every part of the globe; and both groups are generally considered clannish when the need arises. The Ibos and Hebrews both practice circumcision as a religious and cultural feature of their traditional life, and practice innumerable rituals of cleansing and purification where applicable.[1]

Achebe's Health

We asked about the circumstances surrounding the accident that left him physically disabled, and the ensuing treatments. Achebe and his wife Christie were open about it. That on March 22, 1990, he was traveling with his son Ikechukwu to Lagos on their way to America where he had a scheduled lecture at Stanford University, when their car crashed and somersaulted. His son and the driver mercifully escaped serious injuries, but in addition to his breaking a number of ribs, Achebe's spine was affected. He was taken to a nearby clinic for emergency first aid treatment. Later, he was flown to England for spinal injury treatment. Christie made it clear that she had asked Chinua, her husband to choose the family member he would prefer to have stay with him during the treatment and that Achebe had insisted she come along. With respect to the accident, I asked, "Did you feel, 'Why me?'"

The writer said, "No, it never crossed my mind," because, he said, people encounter so many other big problems that it would be useless to question God. His wife added that at the time, there was hardly time for any of them to indulge in self-pity, because "he was in pain all the time, and was undergoing so many operations." Sebastian and I told him how devastated we and other people in and outside of Nigeria were and how we all prayed fervently for his recovery. The couple confessed they were touched by the volume of goodwill from peoples all over the world. Letters and sympathy cards were pouring in. My husband, Sebastian, wondered whether these were preserved and the wife replied in the negative. Sebastian added that these messages would have been of important historical value. He asked

Christie if she wrote down her experiences, as the whole ordeal must have been quite traumatic, since writing is a reliable medium of getting rid of any angst. She said she neither kept a diary, nor wrote poetry, nor a prose account of their travails at the period. Life was so busy! And we wondered out loud how she managed to find relief if she did not write, paint or play music. Her reply was that every person has a unique method of dealing with problems. Then, began a question and answer session amid other important discussions:

Sebastian: "How does it feel - I know this question is stupid - being married to a legend?"

Christy: "I don't feel I'm married to a legend. I can't be married to a legend and I did not marry a legend." Smart answer, I thought.

Sebastian: "Don't you know he is of the class of Michelangelo?"

Christy: "He grew. You appreciate his greatness and things like that."

Sebastian: "How do you feel when you attend these lectures and see all the adulation lavished on your husband?"

Christy: "How would you feel if you were to go to school and your daughter is the one selected to read the valedictory speech? The thing about my family is that we are appreciative of things. We respect and we appreciate and support him, but we are not in awe. It is for others to be in awe of him. It [his success] doesn't get into his head."

The discussion next covered the subject of the Nobel Prize for Literature which many all over the world felt and still feel should have been given to Chinua Achebe for *Things Fall Apart* and what the book accomplished. The author said nothing, but his wife did not manifest any reaction except to say, "what gives us and him even greater joy is that practically all over the world, the work is loved and revered. The book itself - this baby - has traveled more than he has. If it comes [referring to the Nobel Prize] it comes, if not, it doesn't matter."

And the questioning continued:

Sebastian: "Do you feel that he is so great that he somehow tends to overshadow your personality?"

Christy: "Well, if you read the biographies of famous men, you know what happens to their wives; it can happen."

Sebastian: "Do you feel intimidated? Would that be responsible for your reluctance to write out some of your experiences?"

At this juncture, Christie, on the verge of leaving the room, changed her mind, sat down again and observed:

"I am not someone who is easily intimidated. I have worked very hard. Within the family, he [Achebe] is the one that has the least paper degree. We have all achieved. I've worked as much as I can, gotten to a full professorship at Nsukka in 1988 and at Bard College. I know who I am. People get excited about what they don't have [...] but if you've been used to a Mercedes, for example, it doesn't matter much to you. If you ask me some of the qualities for which I love him, it is that he is humble. He is not taken in by these things [...] People feel I should be making a lot of noise about the fact that I'm Mrs. Achebe."

She added that sometimes people react differently toward her when they learn she is actually Mrs Achebe.

I observed to Christie that I also came on this visit to see her, and express my admiration for her courage and devotion to her husband. Life since 1990 must not have been too easy for her. She, I believe, misunderstood what I meant by the word **"see"** and observed that when people come, they usually would mistake her for someone in the house rather than recognize her as Achebe's wife. She narrated an interesting encounter with a lady who she said was dressed to the hilt in lace (as if going for her daughter's wedding), and who when she came in failed to recognize her, as the wife. The visiting lady actually grew impatient when she continued sitting in the room and wondered aloud why she, Christy, was wasting time instead of going to inform her **'Madam'** of her presence.

The source of all the misunderstanding rests on the fact that Christie is a woman who dresses simply, with no particular pretensions. She chooses to do her own gardening, raises her own roses and trims her own flowers. At the core of the misunderstanding is the well-known Nigerian disdain for manual labor. The average Nigerian prefers to engage gardeners and house servants to do every chore. For such people who suddenly change their attitude towards her when they finally learn that she is the wife of Chinua Achebe, she has nothing, she says, but pity. We laughed and the conversation continued for a little while in this vein.

For this lady who has so selflessly stood by a husband in sore need of the support and love from those he loves, one has nothing but admiration and we said so. Thoughtfully, mulling over the questions asked, she observed:

> I pay a lot of price for being the wife of Chinua Achebe in many respects. If I had still been at Nsukka and if there hadn't been this trauma we've had for nine years, I would have been in a situation where you would have been hearing more about me. It is almost as if my career was sequestered in order to face this. But there were choices to make and it was my decision.

What a marvelous woman, I thought! Sebastian lauded her loving choice and added that like the Biblical Martha, she had chosen the better part. Later, he clarified the intention behind the tough questions he threw at Christy: that he wanted for once to push her into the limelight since it appeared that whenever visitors came, their main interest would usually be the celebrated writer, who is always the center of attraction. This way also, his wife would have opportunity to express her views on issues even before her husband in conversation with visitors. Throughout this hot encounter, the novelist kept his head lowered, and like a turtle literally retreated into himself, and never added a word to this exchange

The conversation also covered other issues:

On the Uses of Adversity

The author looked calm and at peace with his condition. We spoke about this new wonder age and the swift pace of technological and medical advances that can make such a change in health conditions. We talked about the American national character trait of optimism that refuses to accept adversity; every obstacle must be challenged and overcome; remedy must be found for every ailment; every disability must be overcome. A prime example, the American actor Christopher Reeves (Superman), now late, who some years back had suffered a horseback fall and sustained spinal injury that left him paralyzed from the neck down, had vowed to walk again and was strongly encouraging an experiment using rats to discover a treatment for spinal injuries.

Achebe's response was that Reeve's resolve was admirable but their two cases were dissimilar. However, if a cure is discovered, that would be good; if not, no matter! Achebe had come to terms with his condition, accepting it as part of life's vagaries and inevitable experiences.

On Literary Creativity

Next, we talked about his writings. We said again what, no doubt, everyone tells him: how much we admired and enjoyed his writings especially the groundbreaking *Things Fall Apart* (1958). We discussed the fictional characters and what they signified. Achebe insisted that Okonkwo did not represent in entirety Umuofia nor the Igbo character. Maybe he did somewhat in his willingness to work hard and ability to excel but not in the way and manner in which he went about achieving these, or handling his family affairs.

Okonkwo, Achebe pointed out, did not pay attention to the softer side of life, represented by his son and his father. Then, Sebastian wanted to know if the early manuscript of *Things Fall Apart* was still available. Achebe replied in the affirmative, mentioning that initially the work was a trilogy - Okonkwo, his son's, and grandson's stories - three novels in one, written in long hand.

Sebastian: "In that 1958 when *Things Fall Apart* was published, did you know what you were getting into? Did the manuscript mean that much to you?"

Rose: [I added a question and urged him to take them all together] "It has been reported that you wrote *Things Fall Apart* to counter the image of Africa as portrayed in such novels as Joyce Cary's *Mr. Johnson* and *The African Witch*? Did Joyce Carey's stereotypes of Africans truly affect you so much that you had to restate your conception of Africa?"

Achebe: "I never really make statements that are so categorical, even when I'm quoted to have done so. If the manuscript had got lost, I doubt if I would have had the courage to go on. You know, it was handwritten. You had to be trusting to the point of foolishness to be able to do what I did. But if what you are doing is important to you, you have to go on. I was in Lagos and working in Broadcasting and writing it at night in Surulere where I lived."

Sebastian: "How did you get to know Heinemann to the extent of getting it to them?"

Achebe: "I took the manuscript to London in 1957 while I was there studying broadcasting."

Sebastian: "How did you move from the manuscript to Heinemann? Did you contact them? Or did they contact you? Was there an intermediary?"

Achebe: "Yes, there was an intermediary. In the BBC Staff School, there was a novelist there - Mr. Phelps."

Sebastian: "Well, now you are better known than he is!" (Laugh!).

Achebe: " . . I was doing the same course with Bisi Onabanjo [who would later become one of the Western Nigerian governors during the second Civilian Regime in Nigeria] who kept on saying to me, "Why don't you show your manuscript to Phelps? So, one day, I told Phelps and he was interested, but not enthusiastic, which is understandable for somebody who just walked up to you and said he had a manuscript. He [Phelps] said he would like to see it. So, I gave it to him. We came back from a weekend in the Midlands to hear that someone had called me from London and said I should call him back as soon as possible, which I read to be that he must have liked the book or why else would he call! A couple of days later, I went up to London and called him. He invited me to dinner and said he was very pleased, and was talking about showing it to his own publisher, Heinemann. And so that's how it happened. I took it home and rewrote it. [Phelps had advised Achebe to revise and separate the stories]. The first part was okay, I just developed that story. What eventually emerged were the stories about Okonkwo (*Things Fall Apart*) and his grandson, Obi Okonkwo (*No Longer at Ease*), the third one.

Sebastian: "So, there was really no third one, for the story of Isaac never was written?"

Achebe: [continuing] " [...] I came back home and did something foolish. I sent it away to be typed so it would look better; it was

still in longhand. And the people to whom I sent it (who I believe wanted to steal it) stopped communicating with me. When I wrote to them, they wrote back asking for Thirty-two pounds as the price of doing two typed copies. I immediately sent it to them in money order and then silence for about six months. At that point, I wrote to complain to Mr. Phelps who said he would get in touch with them once he came back from his vacation. And then a stroke of good fortune happened. I complained to my boss at the B.B.C."

Sebastian: "Do you know her name?"

Achebe: "Yes, Mrs. Angela Beattie - who is a very tough, difficult kind of person."

Sebastian: "Like Margaret Thatcher!" [great laughter!]

Achebe: "She went straight to them and must have put the fear of God into them. The people said they had sent out the manuscript to me. She asked to see their despatch book, which, of course, they could not produce. And she said that if the manuscript did not get to him [Achebe] by such and such a date, they would hear about it. And then, they sent me one copy.

Sebastian: "Where is the manuscript now. Do you still have it?"

Achebe: "No, the original manuscript was lost, stolen by a Cameroonian, a professor of English in Yaounde, Paul Meloni who is really a scoundrel. On a visit, I loaned it to him because he said he was writing a book comparing me and W.B.Yeats and he wandered off. He did not reply to my letter. He is now dead."

Sebastian: "Have you made any effort to get it back?"

Achebe: "I sent somebody as recently as last year to try and locate it. His brother, who is a lawyer apparently said he searched through his brother's effects and did not find the manuscript."

Sebastian: "How did it then move from you to the publisher, Heinemann's?"

Achebe: "I think it was Gilbert Phelps who sent the second version to Heinemann. I think it also went to a couple of other publishers."

Rose: "That started the first African Writers' Series?"

Achebe: "No, the series came much later. At that time, there was no series. They took the manuscript and were at a loss what to do with it. So, they kept looking for someone with experience of Africa. And finally, they found a professor from London University, Don MacRae."

Sebastian: "What's his field? Probably an anthropologist because that's all they were at that time!"

Achebe: "He was very, very well-read. I was introduced to him later [...] MacRae read it and recommended it, apparently the shortest recommendation they've ever received. He said, 'the best first novel since the war' - the War meaning 1939 - a seven-word recommendation."

Sebastian: "You have the letter they sent to you?"

Achebe: "No."

Rose: "My husband is an archivist, you must know by now!"

Sebastian: "I keep papers. I still have letters from General de Gaulle, Houphouet Boigny [first president of Ivory Coast], letters written by Ojukwu to de Gaulle, Haile Selassie, *et cetera*." [Sebastian Okechukwu Mezu helped set up the Biafran Office in Paris and worked there with Ralph Uwechue. Dr. Mezu was later appointed Biafra's Ambassador to Côte d'Ivoire; He translated Biafra's war documents into French, and acted as translator to Ojukwu during his visit to President Houphouet-Boigny (Cote d'Ivoire) and during the various Nigeria / Biafra Peace conferences in Niamey and Addis Ababa.]

Achebe: "I remember the letter said this was like a Greek tragedy. It was very enthusiastic."

Sebastian: "You know in 1971, I published in *Black Academy Review*, a contributor's article entitled, 'Chinua Achebe and the Aristotelian concept of Tragedy.' But how did you feel when you got the letter?"

Achebe: "Excited!"

Sebastian: "That says nothing. Use some more words."

Achebe: "Very excited!" [every body laughs at once.]

Thereafter, we spoke about the impact of his novel, *Things Fall Apart* on the world. Achebe declared he was satisfied with the accolade garnered thus far by his work. Particularly, of interest to him was its impact on peoples of other cultures such as the reactions of other nationals like the South Korean students who identified with Okonkwo's historical situation. The British colonization of Nigeria struck familiar chords within Korean hearts because of the British and Japanese colonization of Korea. They could really identify with the fact that Okonkwo was defending the validity of his cultural traditions and was willing even to die in the defense of his culture. His suicide was akin to the ethos of their world-view. Achebe laughed at some other reactions and the number of people who literally would quarrel with him for killing off Okonkwo in the novel when the man was doing nothing other than resisting imperialism and its attendant oppressions.

They understand, he said, the impossible dilemmas that necessitated Okonkwo's suicide which to these different cultures seemed to be an honorable way out. It pleased him, this knowledge of the function of literature to interlock worlds and human experiences - literature's capacity to bring out the universal human element. Thus, Achebe celebrates humanity with this work. He said with satisfaction in his voice, "One of the things that give me joy is that with *Things Fall Apart,* I have placed the Igbo culture on the world map."

In saying that, he was very conscious of the fact that he was a continuator of the tradition of rehabilitating Africa's cultural heritage and reaffirming the position of Africa on the world map, a literary feat begun by Olaudah Equiano, the Igbo who said he was born in Essaka in the present Imo State of Nigeria, who was captured at an early age and sold into slavery. Equiano in 1789 wrote *The Interesting Narrative of the Life of Olaudah Equiano or Gustavus Vassa the African Written by Hinself,* becoming the first African captured and sold into slavery who freed himself and put down in indelible print where he came from, and who defended admirably the beauty, validity and justness of his cultural traditions: "We are almost a nation of musicians, dancers and poets and musicians[...] ." Chinua Achebe's 1958 *Things Fall Apart* would authenticate Equiano's assertions regarding the Igbo cultural heritage.

Leadership and the Nigerian Situation

Really, a major aspect of our discussions centered on the Nigerian political situation. Whenever and wherever any two or more Nigerians meet, the topic of conversation would invariably revolve around the *Nigerian Situation* - Nigerian politics, leadership, cultural and economic problems. We discussed exhaustively. As things usually go, every one has a particular opinion. Achebe believed and has maintained this stance in his novels and pamphlets that the trouble with Nigeria rests with its leadership class that is unpatriotic, lacks vision, lacks a sense of right direction as well as of equity and the principle of merit. For him, the democratic process is not negotiable. Military rule was and will always be an aberration. "What we Nigerians have lost," he opined, "is the habit of knowing how to govern ourselves." And we ought to get back to it quickly. Ethnic divisions and conflicting loyalties would always bedevil attempts at honest detribalized governance in Nigeria.

These discussions about Nigeria normally do not produce happy thoughts. To my wondering question whether we would ever realize that dream of a progressive, excellence-oriented and just government, Achebe maintained that *it would come, but it would be a gradual process*. His political orientation has never bordered on radicalism or absolutism. His is the voice of reasoned moderation trying to examine and understand the merits of different viewpoints.

We delved into *Anthills of the Savannah* (1987) and especially some of Achebe's short stories such as "The Voter," which he said the people of Zimbabwe found particularly relevant to their need to disseminate enlightenment regarding politics and the vote. The authorities in the country had the crucial messages of the story reproduced in posters and pamphlets which they used as a tool to educate the populace regarding an honest commitment to a political ideology or to issues. Achebe appeared pleased with the way his writings had impacted persons, institutions and whole cultures.

During this Luncheon visit that turned into a discourse forum [we still had not left the dining table], the new democratic government in Nigeria was of great interest to everyone - its programs, the different ethnic groups and party affiliations, the new Head of State and his chances of success in installing an equitable government. Achebe appeared shocked that my husband, Sebastian Okechukwu Mezu had actually praised aspects of the Abacha regime and when Sebastian prophesied that time would come when Nigerians would go on their knees and pray for Abacha to come back, and [of course, Abacha would refuse to come back]. Achebe commented, "*You are not serious!*" Sebastian justified his statement by listing some of the [positive aspects of Abacha's period: the stable currency, with the Naira remaining stable at 84 to one dollar, whereas at the time of speaking, the rate had climbed to the N110 mark. Social stability was another strong point in Abacha's favor since he successfully contained incidents of ethnic/religious persecution that had flared on and off during General Babangida's eight year rule; then, there was the trial and imprisonment of most of the *sacred cows* of Nigerian political and religious elite - Dasuki, the Sultan of Sokoto, who was imprisoned, business magnates who owed money to the banks, Abiola who personalized social and political unrest especially in the Western Yoruba states (because of the June 12, 1983 elections annulled by military President Ibrahim Badamosi Babangida), former head of state Olusegun Obasanjo and his Chief-of-staff Yar'Adua, *et cetera*; Abacha's success in stabilizing the state of tertiary institutions by his strong-arm banning of strikes, etc.; Abacha's strong foreign policy, his Nigerian-led leadership of the West African region, his successful military interventions in Sierra Leone, Liberia, *et cetera*; his economic aids to poorer black African and Caribbean nations. Throughout this political lecture, Achebe's wife Christie remained unimpressed and wondered why and how a leader would do all these external acts of largesse when he could not take care of the basic needs of his own people such as good roads, steady water, and energy supply, or even pay them their justly earned wages.

For me personally, I added, all of the above accomplishments of the late General Sanni Abacha remain valid, and I appreciated his strength, fearlessness and his effective handling of foreign policy, et cetera. My problem with Abacha was the same as Christie's - the fact that Abacha could have, with a mere fraction of the accumulated foreign reserve, made life bearable for the ordinary people by ensuring basic amenities - water, steady urban lighting and rural electrification, good roads. Had he done these, he would have ensured his self-succession easily because the populace would have been behind him. Achebe was not swayed by my husband's theory: "Oh, Okechukwu," he laughed, "You are still a young man, fiery and revolutionary!" We all laughed. Sebastian showed off his grey hairs. But Achebe had through the years remained true to his convictions. Time and time again, he had reiterated them: any radicalism was not the way to go; military rule was an aberration and must be eliminated from the Nigerian polity. He is convinced that because the military has been in office for so long, Nigerians had indeed forgotten how to govern themselves. He stated insistently, "we must learn to govern ourselves again."

Indeed, the visit with the Achebes had promised to be relaxing and memorable and it was proving to be so. In the words of Chinua Achebe to a friend who telephoned him at this juncture, we were having "a nice discussion about everything." We indeed talked about everything ranging from world politics, socio-political situations of other African countries, Nigeria and Igbo culture, to Black nationalists past and present, the ideology itself, and W.E.B. Du Bois, its lightning rod, who all agreed was vastly spectacular in his achievements. Recounting the impediments Du Bois had encountered, my husband pertinently added that Du Bois would not have achieved the global stature he now has if he were white because there would have been nothing of urgency impelling him to accomplish all that he did.

Achebe's voice is the voice of reasoned moderation that advocates a gradual return to normalcy, to democracy - the ideal in self-governance. His position had not changed. He recalled his brushes with the Nigerian governing authority and the fact that he nearly lost his life because of the fictionalized *coup d état* contained in his 1966 novel *A Man of the People*. The army, he added, were a group to be dealt with from a distance. He recalled an incident that happened when he was visiting the late Mamman Vatsa, the soldier-poet who was executed by General Ibrahim Babangida. While he was visiting Vatsa, Theophilus Danjuma came on a visit along with Shehu Musa Yar'Adua. It had been intended that Yar'Adua was to be chairman of a social event holding that evening. When Danjuma, more senior in rank, inquired who was to be the chairman of the event, the now nervous Vatsa suddenly switched in favor of Danjuma. Yar'adua was not pleased. The normally quiet and taciturn Danjuma, Achebe recalled, had not spoken much - the moral being that with the military personnel, you are never on safe ground; they themselves were never on sure ground, even with one another, it seemed for Mamman Vatsa was later executed for treason!

Later, Achebe inquired about my school, Morgan State University, its student population, etc., and the Black Creativity Pan-African Conferences I had coordinated for three years running. He apologized for not being there in 1997 as keynote speaker. He and his wife have had rough experiences with institutions who would reassure them about existing handicap facilities only for them to discover otherwise on getting there. Well, I figured, it must not be easy to be bound not only to a wheel chair but also to be literally at the mercy of other people, in strange places.

When at last we got up to go, daylight was dimming, though it was nearly Summer. We said our good byes, and prepared to go outside, leaving the renowned, wheelchair-bound author inside. Christie escorted us to our car and we stood with her talking for a while. Then we looked back and there was Chinua Achebe now sitting outside in front of his doorway. He was waving; he had wheeled himself out to wish us one last goodbye. He looked so wistful, so venerable, so gentle, so kind! He was a dear sight! Again, the words of Alice Walker flashed into my mind:

We must cherish our old men. We must revere their wisdom, appreciate their insight, love the humanity of their words [...] it takes but a single reading of their work to know that they were all men of sensitivity and soul (*In Search of Our Mothers' Gardens* 135).

We glanced back at Chinua Achebe with love and fondness; we looked back again at this man, so talented, so full of creativity and wisdom yet so humble and never dogmatic, who had celebrated in immortal prose his love for the Black race, who is witty, soft-spoken yet tough-minded. He has vision and a dogged persistence, much like W.E.B. DuBois, Marcus Garvey, his much admired James Baldwin, and later Toni Morrison, and others who have ensured that peoples of African descent would have a scripted monument of their oral history available to them.

Achebe had with passionate insistence declared that if he were God, the one sin He would not forgive would be the acceptance by Africans of the label of inferiority because Africans had always had a history, a structured holistic society by no means perfect but one which was in existence long, long before the Europeans discovered theirs.

Describing the hallmarks of his art, G.D.Killam employs terms such as *deceptive profundity, discriminating insight, mental and moral fastidiousness, elegance and lucidity.* I would add to Killam's list - *a deep conviction, personal integrity, rollicking humor, wisdom and gentleness.* Achebe has given us so much of ourselves back to us, we Igbos, we Africans, we peoples of African descent! He has given back to all Blacks in the Diaspora that **something** which slavery had taken away. Inevitably, he has brought to himself so much eminence and glory that true to that mysterious, immutable law which tacitly has ordained a crown of thorns for every crown of roses, through his car-accident, he has also suffered so much as if to make up for his creative uniqueness and terrestrial glory. Yet, he is not bitter, but rather philosophical, chucking this misfortune down to mere *Experience* in keeping with his often–expressed views:

> [...] experience is necessary for growth and survival. But experience is not simply what happened. A lot may happen to a piece of stone without making it any wiser. Experience is what we are able and prepared to make with what happens to us.

He is indeed our Eagle who had perched on top of the *Iroko* tree and had flown safely back, loaded with materials needed to construct on solid rock his literary house! -- this book of Africana history that is bound in flesh and blood!

Notes

1. Igbos and the Jews

The reputed link between the ancient Hebrews and the Igbos has always been the subject of serious scholarship among the educated elite of both groups. In the 1980s, I came across some Jewish scholars visiting an American-trained Jurist Doctor (JD) from my husband's village and their quest was the tracing of the ancestral links between ancient Hebrews and the Ibos. Establishing the African origin of the Jewish people, Dr. Frances Cress Welsing of *The Isis Papers: The Keys to the Colors* (1991) traces the etymology of the prefix *Semi* - (Latin, akin to Greek *Hemi*) to mean *half* as in "semidiameter." *Hamite* therefore comes from the Greek *Hemite* which could refer to peoples who were Black. Thus both words – *Semi* and *Hemi*, she posits, merged to become

Semite referring to a mulatto-type mixture of Black and white and the combinations thereof, hence *Semi-* and *Hemi* would mean *half Black and half white* much like today's mixed Black or colored populations in the U.S. (223). Dr. Welsing continues:

> [...] Semites of the Jewish religion left Africa and went to Europe. With continuing genetic admixture with the European (white) population, operating under the definition that a Jew is "anyone whose mother is a Jew," it was possible, if enough white males had sexual intercourse with a sufficient number of Semitic or colored women, for the once Black population of Semites to become progressively lighter and lighter. All offspring from these white males and Semitic women of the Jewish religion then would become Jews (224).

Much of the confusion regarding the racial origin of the Jews, Dr. Welsing insists in her theory, stems from the "conscious and / or unconscious insistence on mixing a discussion of religion with a discussion of race, specifically as it concerns the Semitic population that practices the Judaic religion." She reiterates her assertion that the Jews, as a collective, emigrated from Africa and have resided in Europe for the past thousands of years. It is no wonder, she points out, that the "holocaust in Europe was the end result of the long-standing dynamic of anti-Semitism because *Semite* refers to a racial group [...] with a distinct racial (genetic) background, which incidentally practiced a particular religion (222).

In her opinion, Karl Marx (1818-1883) who had so dark a skin color that his children called him "The Moor," meaning "the Black," was as Semitic or mulatto as was Frederick Douglas, the offspring of a white slave master / father and a Black woman. Equally identified as "Black" was Albert Einstein (1879-1955) whose complexion was described as *"swarthy,"* a word that *Webster's New World Dictionary* defines as "having a dark skin, dusky; dark." Again, Dr. Welsing credits Frank Sulloway's "Did Freud Build His Own Legend" (July 23, 1979), a book review of *Freud: Biologia of the Mind* with the revelation that Sigmund Freud so idolized Hannibal, the Black general, that for years Freud was psychologically unable to enter Rome because "Hannibal had never set foot in the city" (*The Isis Papers: The Keys to the Colors* 225).

Frances Cress Welsing's point is that the Jews are but a religious collective who migrated from Africa thousands of years of ago and through miscegenation with the white people now possess a white color. Without delving into Dr. Welsing's main thesis in *The Isis Papers: The Keys to the Colors* which is the Cress Theory of Color–Confrontation and Racism (White Supremacy), it posits that white numerical inadequacy and genetic color deficiency / inferiority necessitated a defense mechanism / projection by which non-white peoples are inferiorized in complex psycho-sexual, socio-economic, political and other structures. The point she makes is very well taken: that there is only one human race (human should be read as *hu (e) man* - colored man, which had its origin in Africa.

In "The Cress Theory of the Holocaust," Dr. Welsing calls on the Jews who regard themselves as "God's chosen people" to show that they were really the chosen, and that they suffered so much so as to teach a very important moral which is, "never disrespect or be ashamed of the *Black genetic heritage of Africa*, and speak up for, own up to, protect and defend that heritage with your very life should conditions and events ever call upon you to do so. Be proud to be Black and be proud to be non-white. This is a profound lesson in self-respect for all of the people in the world" (229). Thus, it would not be too much of a stretch to consider the possibility that the ancient Hebrews, before their migratory movements beyond the Nile River to the Mediterranean region, and then to the East and to Europe, might be descended from the ancient Ibos who settled in Igboland in light of the common traits discussed earlier in this travel narrative - the subject of so much hilarity between us, the visiting guests, and Achebe the writer / researcher, and his wife, Christie.

BIBLIOGRAPHY

Select Works of Chinua Achebe

Things Fall Apart London: William Heinemann, 1958; New York. Astor Honor, 1959; New York: Fawcett Crest. 1991; New York: Doubleday, 1994. London: Heinemann Educational Books (AWS 1), 1962.

No Longer at Ease. London: William Heinemann. 1960: New York: Qbolensky, 1961; London: Heinemann Educational Books (AWS 3), 1963; New York: Double Day, 1994

The Sacrificial Egg and Other Short Stones Onitsha: Etudo, 1962.

Arrow of God. London: William Heinemann, 1964; New York: John Day, 1967. London: Heinemann Educational Books (AWS 16), 1965; revised edition, London: Heinemann Educational Books, 1974; New York: Random House, 1974.

Chike and the River. Cambridge: Cambridge University Press, 1986.

A Man of the People London: William Heinemann, 1966; New York: New York: John Day, 1966. London: Heinemann Educational Books (AWS 31). 1966,

Beware, Soul Brother and Other Poems Enugu: Nwankwo-lfejika, 1971. Revised and enlarged edition, London: Heinemann Educational Books. 1972, Reprinted as *Christmas in Biafra and Other Poems,* Garden City, NY: Anchor/Doubleday, 1973

Don't Let Him Die: An Anthology of Memorial Poems for Christopher Okigbo. Ed. with Dubem Okafor Enugu; Fourth Dimension Publishers, 1978.

Girls at War and Other Stories. London; Heinemann Educational Books (AWS 100), 1972. Garden City NY: Anchor/Doubleday,

1973, Includes in revised versions *The Sacrificial Egg and Other Stories*.

How time Leopard Got His Claws with John Iroaganachi, Enugu: Nwamife, 1972. New York:: The Third Press, 1973.

Morning Yet on Creation Day: Essays. London: Heinemann Educational Books, 1975; Nigeria: Heinemann, 1977. Garden City NY: Anchor/Doubleday 1975

"The African Writer and the English Language." In *Morning Yet On Creation Day*. London: Heinemann, 1975. 55-62.

"Chi in Igbo Cosmology." In *Morning Yet On Creation Day*. Heinemann, 1975.

"The African Writer and the Biafran Cause." In *Morning Yet On Creation Day*. London: Heinemann, 1975. 78-84.

"Named for Victoria, Queen of England." In *Morning Yet On Creation Day*. London: Heinemann, 1975. 65-70.

"The Novelist as a Teacher." In *Morning Yet On Creation Day*.London: Heinemann, 1975. 42-45.

The Drum. Enugu: Fourth Dimension, 1977 *The Plate*. Enugu: Fourth Dimension, 1977.

The Umuahian: A Golden Jubilee Publication Umuahia, Nigeria: Government College Old Boys Association, 1979.

Egwu Aguluogu, Egwmi edeluede Edited with Obiora Udechukwu. Okike Magazine, 1982.

The Trouble With Nigeria. Enugu: Fourth Dimension Publishers. 1983; London Heinemann Educational Books, 1983.

African Short Stories Edited with C. L. Innes. London: Heinemann Educational Books (AWS 270), 1985).

Anthills of the Savannah. London: William Heinemann, 1987: Nigeria: Heinemann, 1988; New York: Doubleday, 1988)

Select Bibliography

Acholonu, Catherine. *The Igbo Roots of Olaudah Equiano*. Owerri, Nigeria: Afa Publications, 1989.

Aidoo, Ama Ata. *The Dilemma of a Ghost*. Accra: Longmans, 1965.

Andrews, William L. *African American Autobiography: A Collection of Critical Essays*. New Jersey: Prentice Hall, 1993.

Aristotle. "Poetics." In *The Norton's World Masterpieces*. N. Y.: Norton, 1995.

Awoonor, Kofi. *The Breast of the Earth*. New York: Nok, 1975.

Carroll, David. *Chinua Achebe*. N.Y.: Twayne Publishers, Inc., 1970.; 2nd ed. New York: St. Martin's Press, 1980.

Clavreul, Jean. "Perverse Couple." In *Returning to Freud*. Ed. Stuart. New Haven: Yale University Press, 1980.

Collins Liturgical Publications. *The Holy Bible*. London. 1971.

Deleuze, Gilles and Felix Guattari. *Anti-Oedipus: Capitalism and Schizophrenia*. U.S.A.: University of Minnesota Press. 1968.

Douglass, Frederick. *Narrative of the Life of Frederick Douglass, an American slave, Written by Himself*. Ed. David W. Blight. N.y.: Bedford Books, 1993.

Du Bois, W.E.B. "What is Civilization? Africa's Answer." In *W.E.B. Du Bois: A Reader*. Ed. Meyer Weinberg. New York: Harper and Row, 1970. 374-382.

Edwards, Paul, ed. *Equiano's Travels*. London: Heinemann, 1967.

Emecheta, Buchi. *The Joys of Motherhood: A Novel*. London: Heinemann, 1980.

--- *Double Yoke*. London: Ogwugwo Afor Ltd, 1982.

Emenyeonu, N. Ernest. *Studies on the Nigerian Novel*. Ibadan: Heinemann, 1991.

Equiano, Olaudah. *The Interesting Narrative of the Life of Olaudah Equiano, or Gustavus Vassa Written by Himself (1789)*. In *The*

Humanities in the Modern World. Boston, MA: Pearson custom Publishing, 2001.

Evans, Jennifer. "Women and Resistance in *Ngugi's Devil on the Cross*." *African Literature Today*. Trenton, New Jersey: African World Press, 1987.

Ezenwa-Ohaeto. *Chinua Achebe: A Biography*. Indianapolis: Indiana University Press, 1997.

Ezewudo, Gabriel. "Christianity, African Traditional Religion and Colonialism: Were Africans pawns or players in the Cultural Encounter?" In *Religion and Society*. Ed. Rose Ure Mezu. MD: Black Academy Press, 1998. 43-61.

Farah, Nurrudin. "A Tale of Tyranny" in *West Africa*, 21 September 1987. 1828-31.

Felman, Shoshan. *Jacques Lacan and the Adventure of Insight: psychoanalysis in Contemporary Culture*. Cambridge, Mass: Harvard University Press, 1987.

Gardner, Judith Keegan. "Gender, Values, and Lessing's Cats" in *Feminist Issues in Literary Scholarship*. Ed. Benstock. Bloomington: Indiana University Press, 1987.

Gates, Henry Louis, Jr. Zora Neale Hurston. *A Negro Way of Saying Their Eyes Were Watching God*. New York: Harper and Row, 1990.

--- "James Gronniosaw and the Trope of the Talking Book." In *African American Autobiography: A Collection of Critical Essays*. New Jersey: Prentice Hall, Ltd. 1993. 8-25.

Gikandi, Simon. "The Language of the Dancing Mask: Arrow of God." In *Reading Achebe: Language and Ideology in Fiction*. London: Heinemann, 1991. 51-77-100.

Gikandi, Simon. "Writing in the Marginal Space." In *Reading Chinua Achebe: Language and Ideology in Fiction*. London: Heinemann, 1991. 78-100.

Girard, René. *Mensonge romantique, Vérité romanesque*. Paris, France: Edition Gallimard, 1961. (Translated into English as *Deceit, Desire and the Novel: Self and Other in Literary Structure*).

Gordimer, Nadine. "A Tyranny of Clowns." In *The New York Times Book Review* (Feb.21, 1988).

Hurston, Zora Neale. *Their Eyes Were Watching God*. 1939. NY: Harper & Row, 1990.

--- *Dust Tracks on a Road*. Second Edition.Urbana: University of Illinois Press, 1984.

Laye, Camara. *The African Child*. Trans. James Kirkup. London: Fontana, 1972. *L'Enfant noir*. Paris: Plon, Presses Pocket edition.

Laurence, Margaret. *Long Drums and Canons*. London: Macmillan, 1968.

Lillios, Anna. "Zora Neale Hurston's Eatonville." *MAWA* Vol.7, No.2, 102-106.

Lindfors, Bernth and Bala Kothan Daram (eds). *South Asian Responses to Chinua Achebe*. New Delhi: Prestige Books, 1993. pp. i-ii.

Machiavelli, Noccolò. *The Prince*. In *The Norton's World Masterpieces*. N. Y.: Norton, 1995. 2433-2448.

Mbiti, John. *Bible and Theology in African Christianity*. Nairobi: O.U.P., 1986.

Mezu, Okechukwu S. *Communalist Manifesto*. Washington, DC: Nigerian Students Voice, 1966.

--- *Léopold Sédar Senghor et la défense et illustration de la civilization noire*. Paris. Editions Marcel Didier, 1968.

--- *Tropical Dawn (poems)*. Buffalo: Black Academy Press, 1970.

Mezu, Rose Ure,. ed. *Africa and the Diaspora: the Black Scholar and Society*. Black Academy Press: MD, 2000.

--- "The Omnipresent Papacy: Pope John Paul II on Feminism, the Youth, and Africa." In *African Renaissance*. (May/June) 2005. 111-125.

--- *Women in Chains: Abandonment in Love Relationships in the Fiction of Selected West African Writers*. Owerri, Nigeria: Black Academy Press, 1994.

--- "*Things Fall Apart* and The Violence of Fear." The Leader. Owerri, Nigeria: Assumpta Press, 1974.

Mezu, Ure L. "The Odyssey and Legend of Olaudah Equiano." In *Leadership, Culture and Racism*. Eds. Mezu, Rose Ure and Burney, J. Hollis. Black Academy Press: MD, 1998.

Miller, Christopher L. *Blank Darkness: Africanist Discourse in French*. Chicago: University of Chicago, 1985.

--- *Devil on the Cross*. London: Heinemann, 1982.

Decolonizing the Mind: *The Politics of Language in African Literature*. London: James Currey Ltd., 1986

Niane, D.T. *Sundiata: an epic of Mali*. transl. G.D. Pickett. London: Heinemann, 1993.

Nnolim, Charles E. "Form and Function of Folk Tradition." *Approaches to the African Novel: Essays in Analysis*. London: Saros International, 1992.

Nwoga, Donatus Ibe. "The Igbo World of Achebe's *Arrow of God*. In *Research in African Literature 12* (Spring 1981).

Nwapa, Flora. *Efuru*. London: Heinemann, 1966.

--- *Idu*. London: Heinemann, 1970.

Ogunyemi, Chikwenye Okonjo. "Women and Nigerian Literature." In *Perspectives on Nigerian Literature*. Vol. 1. Lagos, Nigeria: Guardian Books, 1988.

Ojinmah, Umelo. *Chinua Achebe: New Perspectives*. Nigeria: Spectrum Books Ltd., 1991.

Okonkwo, Juliet. "The Talented Woman in African Literature." *African Quarterly*.15.1-2.

Ola, Millie. *A Dream Come True*. Baltimore, Black Academy Press, 1996.

Peterson, Kirsten Holst and Anna Rutherford, eds. *Chinua Achebe: A Celebration*. Oxford: Heinemann, 1990.

Rich, Adrienne. *Of Woman Born: Motherhood as Experience and Institution*. New York: Norton, 1976.

Rutherford, Anna. "Interview with Achebe." In *Kunapipi*, IX, 2 1987.

Sanneh, Lamin. *West African Christianity: The Religious Impact*. London: Christopher Hurst Publishers, 1983.

Soyinka, Wole. "The Writer in a Modern African State" in *The Writer in Modern Africa*. ed. Per Watsberg. N.Y.: Africana Publishing, 1969.

Searle, Chris. "Achebe and the Bruised Heart of Africa." In *Wasafiri*, 14. 199. 12-16. Wastberg. N.Y.: Africana Publishing. 1969.

Taiwo, Oladele. *Culture and the Nigerian Novel*. New York: St. Martin's Press, 1976.

The Humanities. vol.1. eds. Witt, Brown, Dunbar et al. 2 vols. Lexington, MA : D.C. Heath& Co. 1993.

Thiong'o, Ngugi wa. *Petals of Blood*. London: Heinemann, 1977.

--- *Devil on the Cross*. London: Heinemann, 1982.

Turner, Victor W. *The Ritual Process: Structure and Anti-Structure*. Chicago: Aldine, 1969.

Walker, Alice. "In Search of Our Mothers' Gardens." In *Search of Our Mothers Gardens: Womanist Prose*. New York: Harcourt Brace,1983. 231-243.

Walker, Wyatt Tee. "Roots – Musically Speaking;" In *Religion and Society*. Ed. Rose Ure Mezu. Baltimore, MD: Black Academy Press, 1998.

Additional Resources on Achebe and African Literature

Amuta, Chidi. *The Theory of African Literature: Implications for Practical Criticism*. London: Zed, 1989.

Begam, Richard. "Achebe's Sense of an Ending: History and Tragedy in *Things Fall Apart*." *Studies in the Novel* 29.3 (Fall 1997): 396.

Chinweizu, Onwuchekwa Jamie, and Ihechukwu Madubuike. *Towards the Decolonization of African Literature*. Enugu: Fourth Dimension, 1980.

Coeyman, Marjorie. "Africa's Great Storyteller, Chinua Achebe, on Language." *Christian Science Monitor* [92.249] 16 Nov. 2000: 16.

Davies, Carole Boyce. "Motherhood in the Works of Male and Female Igbo Writers: Achebe, Emecheta, Nwapa and Nzekwu." *Ngambika: Studies of Women in African Literature*. Eds. Carole Boyce Davies and Anne Adams Graves. Trenton, NJ: Africa World Press, 1986. 241-56.

Ebeogu, Afam. "Igbo Sense of Tragedy: A Thematic Feature of the Achebe School." The Literary Half-Yearly 24.1 (1983): 69-86.

Egejuru, Phanuel Akubueze. *Towards African Literacy Independence: A Dialogue with Contemporary African Writers*. Westport, CT: Greenwood Press, 1980.

Egudu, R. N. "Achebe and the Igbo Narrative Tradition." *Research in African Literatures* 12.1 (1981): 43-54.

Ekechi, Felix N. *Missionary Enterprise and Rivalry in Igboland 1857-1914*. London: Frank Cass, 1971.

Fleming, Bruce. "Brothers Under the Skin: Achebe on *Heart of Darkness*." *College Literature* 19.3 (Oct-Feb 1992): 90 (10 pp).

Gallagher, Susan VanZanten. "Linguistic Power: Encounter with Chinua Achebe". *The Christian Century* 12 March 1997, 260.

Gerard, Albert. *African Language Literatures: An Introduction to the Literary History of Sub-Saharan Africa*. Washington, D.C.: Three Continents Press, 1981.

Gikandi, Simon. *Reading Chinua Achebe: Language and Ideology in Fiction*. London: James Currey, 1991.

Henricksen, Bruce. "Chinua Achebe: The Bicultural Novel and the Ethics of Reading." *Global Perspectives on Teaching Literature*. Eds.

Sandra Ward Lott, Maureen S.G. Hawkins, and Norman McMillan. Urbana, IL: National Council of Teachers of English, 1993. 295-310.

Innes, C. L. *Chinua Achebe: Cambridge Studies in African and Caribbean Literature*, No. 1. Cambridge: Cambridge Univ. Press, 1990.

Innes, C. L., and Bernth Lindfors, eds. *Critical Perspectives on Chinua Achebe*. Washington DC: Three Continents Press, 1978.

Irele, Abiola. "The Tragic Conflict in Achebe's Novels." *Introduction to African Literature: An Anthology of Critical Writing from Black Orpheus*. Ed. Ulli Beier. Evanston, IL: Northwestern University Press, 1970.

Isichei, Elizabeth. *A History of the Igbo People*. London: Macmillan, 1976.

Iyasere, Solomon O. "Okonkwo's Participation in the Killing of His Son in Chinua Achebe's *Things Fall Apart*: A Study of Ignoble Decisiveness." *CLA Journal* 35.3 (March 1992): 303 (13 pp).

JanMohamed, Abdul. "Sophisticated Primitivism: Syncretism of Oral and Literate Modes in Achebe's *Things Fall Apart*." *ARIEL* 15.4 (1984): 19-39.

Jeyifo, Biodun. "Okonkwo and His Mother: *Things Fall Apart* and Issues of Gender in the Constitution of African Postcolonial Discourse." (Special Issue: Post-Colonial Discourse) *Callaloo* 16.4 (Fall 1993): 847 (12 pp).

Joseph, Michael Scott. "A Pre-Modernist Reading of *The Drum*: Chinua Achebe and the Theme of Eternal Return." *ARIEL* 28.1 (Jan. 1997): 149 (18 pp).

Killam, G. D. *The Writings of Chinua Achebe*. London: Heinemann, 1969. [Rev. ed. 1977.]

Kortenaar, Neil ten. "Only connect: *Anthills of the Savannah* and Achebe's *Trouble with Nigeria*." *Research in African Literatures* 24.3 (Fall 1993): 59 (14pp).

Landrum, Roger L. "Chinua Achebe and the Aristotelian Concept of Tragedy." *Black Academy Review* 1.1 (1970): 22-30.

Lindfors, Bernth, ed. *Approaches to Teaching Achebe's Things Fall Apart*. New York: Modern Language Association, 1991.

--- "Chinua Achebe: Novelist of Cultural Conflict." *America*, 20 July 1996: 23 (3pp).

Mezu, S. Okechukwu. Ed. *Modern Black Literature*. Buffalo: Black Academy Press, 1970.

McCarthy, Eugene B. "Rhythm and Narrative Method in Achebe's *Things Fall Apart*." *Novel* 18.3 (1985): 243-356.

Macdonald, Bruce F. "Chinua Achebe and the Structure of Colonial Tragedy." In *The Literary Half-Yearly* 21.1 (1980): 50-63.

MacKenzie, Clayton G. "The Metamorphosis of Piety in Chinua Achebe's *Things Fall Apart*." In *Research in African Literatures* 27.2 (Summer 1996): 128 (11pp.)

Mbiti, John S. *Introduction to African Religion*. London: Heinemann, 1975.

Niven, Alastair. "Chinua Achebe and the Possibility of Modern Tragedy." *Kunapipi* 12.2 (1990): 41-50.

Nnoromele, Patrick C. "The Plight of a Hero in Achebe's *Things Fall Apart*." In *College Literature* 27.2 (Spring 2000): 146 (11pp).

Nwahuananya, Chinyere. "Social Tragedy in Achebe's Rural Novels: A Contrary View." In *Commonwealth Novel in English* 4.1 (1991): 1-13.

Ogbaa, Kalu. "A Cultural Note on Okonkwo's Suicide." *Kunapipi* 2.3 (1981): 126-134.

Obiechina, Emmanuel. *Language and Theme: Essays on African Literature*. Washington, D.C.: Howard UP, 1990.

Okafor, Clement A. "A Sense of History in the Novels of Chinua Achebe." *Journal of African Studies* 8.2 (1981): 50-63.

Olney, James. "The African Novel in Transition: Chinua Achebe." *South Atlantic Quarterly* 70 (1970): 299-316.

Opata, Damian. "The Sudden End of Alienation: A Reconsideration of Okonkwo's Suicide in Chinua Achebe's *Things Fall Apart.*" *African Marburgensia* 22.2 (1989): 24-32.

Osei-Nyame, Kwadwo. "Chinua Achebe Writing Culture: Representations of Gender and Tradition in *Things Fall Apart.*" *Research in African Literatures* 30.2 (Summer 1999): 148 (17pp).

Owusu, Kofi. "The Politics of Interpretation: The Novels of Chinua Achebe." (Special Issue: Postcolonial African Fiction*) Modern Fiction Studies* 37.3 (Autumn 1991): 459 (12pp).

Palmer, Eustace. *The Growth of the African Novel*. London: Heinemann, 1979.

--- *An Introduction to the African Novel*. London: Heinemann, 1972.

Petersen, Kirsten Holst, and Anna Rutherford, eds. *Chinua Achebe: A Celebration*. Oxford [England] & Portsmouth, NH: Heinemann; Sydney: Dangeroo Press, 1991.

Rhoads, Diana Akers. "Culture in Chinua Achebe's *Things Fall Apart.*" *African Studies Review* 36.2 (Sept 1993): 61(12pp).

Sengova, Joko. "Native Identity and Alienation in Richard Wright's *Native Son* and Chinua Achebe's *Things Fall Apart*: A Cross-Cultural Analysis." *Mississippi Quarterly* 50.2 (Spring 1997): 327 (25 pp).

Sharma, Govind Narain. "The Christian Dynamic in the Fictional World of Chinua Achebe." *ARIEL* 24.2 (April 1993): 5 (15 pp).

Shelton, Austin J. "The 'Palm-oil' of Language: Proverbs in Chinua Achebe's Novels." In *Modern Language Quarterly* 30.1 (1969): 89-111.

Schmidt, Nancy. "Nigerian Fiction and the African Oral Tradition." *Journal of the New African Literature and the Arts* 5/6 (1968): 10-19.

Sugnet, Charlie. "Chinua Achebe: The First Truly 'African' Novelist." In *Utne Reader*, March-April 1990: 36.

Turner, Margaret E. "Achebe, Hegel, and the New Colonialism." In *Kunapipi* 12.2 (1990): 31-40.

Uchendu, Victor C. *The Igbo of Southeast Nigeria*. New York: Holt, Rinehard and Winston, 1965.

Wren, Robert M. *Achebe's World: The Historical and Cultural Context of the Novels*. Washington, DC: Three Continents Press, 1980.

Index

D

E

Ordering this book and other books by Adonis & Abbey Publishers

Wholesale inquiries (UK and Europe):

Gardners Books Ltd
+44 1323 521777: email: custcare@gardners.com

Wholesale inquiries (US and Canada):

Ingram Book Company (ordering)
+1 800 937 8000 website: www.ingrambookgroup.com

Online Retail Distribution: All leading online retail outlets including www.amazon.co.uk , www.amazon.com www.barnesandnoble.com, www.blackwell.com

Shop Retail: Ask any good bookshop or contact our office: www.adonis-abbey.com

+44 (0) 20 7793 8893

Printed in the United Kingdom
by Lightning Source UK Ltd.
129809UK00001B/36/A